He's dead now . . .

and everyone is taking a closer look at the dropout rabbi-turned-"evangelist": J.I. Rodale, the one-man movement who may be most responsible for today's increasing awareness of food facts and fallacies, from farm to table and all stops in between.

This book is an unprecedented evaluation of the life and work of J.I. Rodale, from ghetto to guruhood, including details of his most famous and bitter fights with the Establishment. Here are the facts: transcripts of court battles with the Federal Trade Commission over the issues of false and misleading advertising (and the far more serious war being waged beneath the measured legal jargon); his disagreements with the American Medical Association, which caused dissent among AMA members themselves; his losing tussle with New York drama critics . . .

Contradictions, one after another; fascinating, ironic and filled with implicit, often disturbing insights about an original man whose dream has just begun!

J. I. RODALE

Apostle of Nonconformity

CARLTON JACKSON

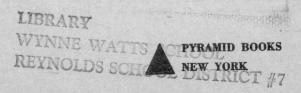

PYRAMID BOOKS
NEW YORK

J.I. RODALE: Apostle of Nonconformity

A PYRAMID BOOK

Second printing, November, 1974

ISBN 0-515-03403-7

Copyright © 1974 by Carlton Jackson
All Rights Reserved

Library of Congress Catalog Card Number: 74-1411

Printed in the United States of America

Pyramid Books are published by Pyramid Communications, Inc. Its trademarks, consisting of the word "Pyramid" and the portrayal of a pyramid, are registered in the United States Patent Office.

PYRAMID COMMUNICATIONS, INC.
919 Third Avenue
New York, New York 10022, U.S.A.

Contents

Chapter	Page
CHRONOLOGY	vii
1. "But Who Are You?"	19
2. The Early Years	37
3. The House of Rodale	60
4. "Natural Farming"—A Brief History	83
5. J.I. Rodale and Organiculture	101
6. The Health Front	123
7. The FTC Takes a Look	148
8. Short of the First Amendment	170
9. Rodale: Playwright and Patron of the Arts	191
10. The End of a Dream	217
11. Rodale: Renaissance Man?	235
SOURCES	249
INDEX	261

1898   Jerome Irving Cohen born in New York City, August 16; parents, Michael and Bertha (Rouda) Cohen.

1903   Public schooling began at PS 137. Continued at PS 75 and PS 62, his favorite.

1903–1914   Impressed and influenced during his childhood by the antagonistic forces of orthodox and reformed Jewry. Sang at local synagogue.

1914   Death of father, Michael.

1916–1919   Student at New York and Columbia Universities; accountant for several firms and government organizations.

1919–1920   Auditor for Internal Revenue Service.

1920–1923   Employee and later partner in the Pittsburgh office of the accounting firm of Robertson, Furman, and Murphy.

1921   Changed name to J. I. Rodale.

1923   Went into electrical manufacturing business with brother, Joe.

1924   Met Anna Andrews, his future wife.

1927   Married Anna in both a civil and a religious ceremony.

1928   Bought farm in Ridgefield, Connecticut.

1930   Moved electrical business from New York City to Emmaus, Pennsylvania; took up residence in Allentown.

1931   Published first magazine, *The Humorous Scrapbook.*

1934   Published second magazine, *The Clown,* later called *The American Humorist.*

1935–1940   Published numerous magazines, many of which folded very quickly.

1940   Bought farm at Emmaus, Pennsylvania; became acquainted with, and excited about, Sir Albert Howard's ideas on natural farming.

1942   First edition of *Organic Farming and Gardening*.

1942–1950   Concentration on *Organic Gardening and Farming* and creation of Soil and Health Foundation.

1950   First edition of *Prevention*.

1952   First "run-in" with Federal Trade Commission.

1952–1960   Several trips abroad: South America, Germany, Holland, England (start of English edition of *Prevention*).

1960   Playwriting career began with production of *The Goose* in New York.

1959–1963   Investigated by the FTC.

1964–1968   FTC hearings and trial against *The Health Finder*, et al.

1969   Plays produced widely throughout the country; visited Kentucky for performances of his plays at the Pioneer Playhouse in Danville.

1970   August 16, his seventy-second birthday. Noted trends in direction of acceptance of organic living; had become the "hero" of numerous communal farms throughout the country.

1971   Articles about him in newspapers and magazines; guest appearances on radio and television; June 7, while guest on Dick Cavett Show, suffered heart attack and died minutes later at Roosevelt Hospital.

To my children, Beverly, Daniel, Matthew

Acknowledgments to:

The Dick Cavett Show, Daphne Productions, Inc., for transcripts of the Dick Cavett Show, June 7 and 8, 1971.

Grossman Publishers for excerpts from James Turner, *The Chemical Feast; The Report on The Food and Drug Administration.*

Houghton Mifflin Company for excerpts from Rachel Carson, *Silent Spring.*

Institute of International Education for excerpts from Henry Steele Commager, *Meet The U.S.A.*

Oxford University Press for excerpts from Arnold J. Toynbee, *A Study of History.*

Rodale Press, Inc., excerpts from J.I. Rodale's writings.

Over and over it has been asserted in the history of this country that the United States has been, and is, the land of opportunity. Regardless of the conditions of birth or national origin, one can be whatever one wishes to be. The concept of the "American hero" is based largely on this idealistic premise.

Reality, however, all too frequently tells a different story. Patterns of conformity in America seem to be as set as in any other country in the world. Too often we hear the dean of a university or a supervisor in a factory tell a novice: "You'll go far if you just keep your nose clean." Keeping the nose clean, of course, means that the up-and-coming young apprentice must operate in a system, the value judgments for which were set long ago by someone else. To be sure, there is comfort of sorts in conforming; one obviously does not have to worry as much about job tenure and salary increments as peers who challenge the "straight and narrow."

Important in our thinking has always been the "team effort." While we idealize and romanticize the individual, woe betide the "loner" who expects equal advancement in the form of promotion and salary. We are at first amused, then angered, then frightened by someone who forcefully and publicly tries to break the "team" pattern.

This is where J. I. Rodale comes into the picture. He was born of Jewish parents in 1898, and if he had done what he was supposed to—what was expected of him— he would have opened a nice little clothing store somewhere in New York City, would have gone to synagogue each Saturday, would have made much profit, would have supported Zionist movements . . . But from the time of his childhood he had other things in mind (ambitions seem to be neutral in terms of national derivation), and in a very real way it is a pity that in this country he felt impelled to change his name before he could reasonably hope to accomplish them. (This point is not to be construed to mean that J. I. did what he did because he felt he was a member of a "suppressed minority." Except in a few instances, he never even noticed the fact.)

He wanted to be a farmer, an author, and a publisher. Before he was finished, he was all three—and then some. And he amused, angered, and frightened a good many American people by the things he said and did.

By the time it all ended on the Dick Cavett Show on that sultry evening of June 7, 1971, things were beginning to reverse. After thirty years of ridicule, J. I. Rodale was finally coming into his own in the areas of organiculture and preventive health measures. His detractors were not exactly beating a retreat, but many of them were indeed having second thoughts about their previous postulates.

This book is as reportorial as it is analytical. I have tried to show J. I. Rodale's faults as well as his strengths, and, hopefully, I have put together as accurate a portrait of his life and career as is possible at the present time. I am, of course, aware of the historical premise that only time will make possible true objectivity. I am equally aware, however, of the thought that as time passes, the legends multiply. As the eminent historian Carl Becker once said in effect, the aim of the historian is to tell the truth as he sees it. This I have sincerely tried to do.

Nevertheless, there will no doubt be those who, when seeing this book, will say that it is an "official biography" (as indeed some individuals even in the research stage concluded). I can only say that my degrees in the field and my experience in teaching history dictate against my writing an "official biography" of anyone. It is quite true that, at my invitation, J. I.'s son, Robert Rodale, read the book while it was in manuscript, primarily to seek out errors of fact. I have made several judgments of J. I. with which Robert disagrees, but at no time during the course of this research has Robert or any other member of the Rodale family suggested how I write the book. Unfortunately, I cannot say the same for several of J. I. Rodale's detractors.

Someone once truthfully stated that no one ever writes a book by himself. A book is really "community property." Its author will seek the advice, counsel, and comfort of family, friends, and sometimes even total strangers in his quest for material. This book is no exception.

I have deliberately left out footnotes for ease of reading, but I have identified my sources both in the text and at the end of the book. The book's title comes from a phrase used by newsman James J. Kilpatrick, who wrote about J. I.'s travails with the Federal Trade Commission. I am grateful to Kilpatrick for the use of his phrase.

So many people helped in the preparation of this book that I am loath to mention any, lest I forget some. Nevertheless, I must express my gratitude to J. I. Rodale's family: Anna, his widow; Robert, his son; Ruth and Nina, his daughters, for their time and cooperation. J. I.'s old friend Louis Ludwig graciously granted an interview. To him and all the other people in New York who knew J. I. and told me about him, I am grateful.

My thanks must go, too, to the American Medical Association for allowing me to use their records on J. I. Rodale, as well as to the membership of the Lehigh Valley Committee Against Health Fraud, Inc. Other people who were helpful include Albert Schaatz, Kathleen Daniels, Weldon Schock, Robert Drean, Gerald Honaker, Elaine Sobel, and Eric White. I am sure I have omitted others equally deserving of my thinks.

My friends and colleagues at Western Kentucky University, Lowell Harrison, Mary Clarke, and Donald Neat, read all or portions of the manuscript and saved me from numerous errors. For whatever are left, I am totally responsible. My friend and professor, Horace Montgomery of the History Department at the University of Georgia, gave valuable advice and counsel while the manuscript was in preparation. My student assistant, Frank Riley, performed yeoman service in tracing all the bibliographical information about Rodale. WKU history chairman, Richard L. Troutman, helped by putting typing services at my disposal. I wish to thank him and Mrs. Gayle Brandt for their efficiency. The WKU Research Committee, with its stipend, freed me from classes for a semester so I could complete the manuscript. To all these people: thank you.

Finally, I am pleased once again to express my gratitude to my family: Pat, Beverly, Daniel, and Matthew for their patience and understanding.

CARLTON JACKSON

Western Kentucky University
Bowling Green

J. I. RODALE:

Apostle of Nonconformity

CHAPTER 1

"But Who Are YOU?"

One day in 1945 J. I. Rodale visited the library of a well-known university and saw a man in the reading room going over a copy of *Organic Gardening*. Introducing himself, J.I. learned that the reader was a Louisiana agriculturalist who had been invited to the university to confer with one of its eminent professors. The two went together to see the professor, and for a while they talked about bagasse, the residue of crushed sugar cane. When the conference was over, the Louisiana man departed, leaving J.I. and the professor alone.

Suddenly the professor reached into his desk and brought out a book entitled *Pay Dirt*. "You see," he said, "I have read your book." Then he hooked his eyeglasses over his ears and nose, looked J.I. square in the face, and exclaimed, "But who are you?" He was, of course, referring to J.I.'s lack of academic credentials in the field of agriculture, taking the view of many professionals toward amateurs. It was like a professional historian wondering about the prowess of an amateur in the field who, though successful in terms of money and readership, has not earned his degrees.

The eminent professor was not quite omniscient. If he had been, he would have known that J. I. Rodale:

• Took, on a daily basis, or would soon begin taking, large quantities of natural food supplements, the amounts of which varied from time to time. The most consistent listing of J.I.'s natural food intake was 6 rose hips, 9 tablets of desiccated liver, 9 wheat germ capsules, 12 vitamin E perles, 9 dolomite and 6 bone meal tablets, 3 rutin and 3 lecithin capsules, 6 kelp tablets, and 4 perles of halibut liver oil, for a daily total of 67 natural food supplements. Later, in the 1960s, the total rose to over 100.

- Chewed a handful of sunflower seeds each day for good eyesight, along with a goodly quantity of pumpkin seeds to avoid prostate trouble.
- Was a wealthy businessman who got his start in accounting and electrical parts manufacturing but dreamed from childhood of owning a farm and operating it "scientifically."
- Was a dabbler in, and popularizer of, the English language, having produced such vocabulary-building volumes as *The Word-At-A-Time-System*, *The Word Finder*, and *The Synonym Finder*, as well as substitutes for the word "very."
- Was a patron of the arts, trying his hand periodically at writing plays and starting his own theater in New York for their performance.
- Was already in 1945 the owner of a large publishing house, Rodale Press, with branches in the United States and England.
- Was the self-acclaimed founder of the organic system of gardening and farming in the United States, after taking his cue from the eminent English agriculturalist Sir Albert Howard.
- Was the publisher and editor of several magazines, the most popular being *Organic Gardening*, with a readership of 30,000.

Even with these answers, the professor legitimately could still have asked, "But who are you?" The answer lay much deeper than a mere recitation of J.I.'s personal activities and accomplishments. It lay in the context of many undercurrents of American life.

One such undercurrent is versatility. In the colonial period Americans first learned to generalize their thoughts and actions, with much stock placed in such phrases as "everyman his own thinker," the "naturalness of knowledge," and "self-evident truths." The need to survive harsh experiences produced by environment and Indian attacks led to a pragmatism in which a foundation of systematic thought was rendered unnecessary and unwanted. How could a class of "thinkers" show a better way of surviving than the unsophisticated ones? This mood became the pattern in America; it was one that judged things on a "workability" basis. If it worked, it was good and true; if it did not, it was bad and false. Thus, there was a constant appeal to the undifferentiated man who was not just one thing but many. A colonist could be a farmer, a blacksmith, a doctor, a lawyer, a preacher, a soldier, and a host of other things—all at the same time. Long after this age of generalization and versatility passed—indeed, well into the "specialist" era—Americans, primarily through a collective, psychological memory, still emphasized "common sense." Even today they say they do, but frequently they disbelieve the person who says he is openly practicing it.

J.I. blended well into this mood of generalization and versatility. As a young man he studied accounting, first at New York University and then at Columbia University, but attended neither school for more than a year. In later life he credited most of his success in accounting not to the academic training he received but to the "school of hard knocks" that he experienced in working for the U.S. Government's Internal Revenue Service and later for the accounting firm of Robertson, Furman, and Murphy. Practical rather than theoretical knowledge was what he valued. In his young life, too, his hero was Andrew Carnegie, and his favorite author was Horatio Alger. Surely J.I. thought consciously or unconsciously as he worked his way up (he came from a poor family with eight children) that he embodied the trials and virtues of "Ragged Dick," or "Tattered Tom," or "The Young Salesman."

But what did he want out of life? Was his relation first to one business and then to another (accounting, stockholding, investing, electrical parts, proposed ice-cream cone manufacturing, publishing, agriculture, health and nutrition, writing, drama) merely a reflection of his wish to make a fortune? In part, yes. His goal was success, for he knew from childhood the importance that America puts on that word. This drive was especially intense because he was Jewish and suffered, as he said many times, from an inferiority complex. "Making good" became a passion with him.

It is quite incorrect, however, to say that he only wanted a fortune. In correspondence with his boyhood friend Louis Ludwig, he made many references, some as early as 1918, to the two boys' plans of making enough money through accounting or whatever to buy a farm and run it scientifically. "I don't know why the hell I ever picked accounting as a profession but if I stay in the accounting game until I am 40, if I live so long, I will be blind as a dormouse (whatever that is). My intentions at present are, to stick to accounting until a favorable opportunity presents itself for going into business . . . and then as soon as I or we can accumulate enough money, say at about the age of 30 or even sooner, to get out as quick as we can to God's land. I know you feel the way I do about it." Their youthful ambitions soon led them toward the garden state of New Jersey, but a trip to the area in the autumn of 1918 cooled J.I.'s ardor: "The farms in this section of New Jersey are PUNK. I rode from the Pennsylvania Station . . . thru, first, the manufacturing section of New Jersey with a few dirty farms in between. About 30 miles out you see farms which are not as bad as the first ones but which are not run scientifically. I do not know how the farms are above New Brunswick as I didn't have time to see them." At the time J.I. made these observations, he was twenty years old, and he and Ludwig had obviously been making such agricultural plans for years. Therefore, when J.I. bought his sixty-acre farm in Ridgefield, Connecticut, in 1928 and a dozen years later another farm in Emmaus, Pennsylvania, he was not acting on a spur-of-the-moment impulse to get back to nature but was consummating a lifelong dream.

One area of American life as a context in which to discuss and hopefully explain J. I. Rodale is science. Though Americans have always professed commitment to "science," our attachment to pragmatic and workability factors has made its definition difficult. Again, practical or applied, rather than theoretical, science has been America's chief direction. We have always been fascinated by gadgets such as David Rittenhouse's "orrerry" and Benjamin Franklin's lightning rods. Though they denied it several times, both of these citizens of the colonial period were frequently referred to as "scientists."

In our own time the confusion of what is science has, if anything, worsened. In the literature of a government agency such as the U.S. Department of Agriculture, the works of J. I. Rodale and Rachel Carson are branded as "unscientific." In much of Rodale's writing, the activities of the USDA are "unscientific." Likewise, Carson frequently notes the "unscientific" activities of government workers, and her followers at least impute "unscientific" motives and deeds to Rodale. Unfortunately, for the general public, not much explanation beyond the word "unscientific" is ever given, making it difficult for people of good will to decide whose side they support.

If science has the inductive "observation and classification of facts with the establishment of verifiable general laws" as its goals, how much is needed for verification? Who does the verifying? Can anybody do it, or should only those trained and educated for many years be given the responsibility? Would it be possible for a single person, such as J. I. Rodale, literally to turn his entire body into a laboratory, to observe and classify facts about his own physical being, and then to pronounce what he thought were verifiable general laws? As far as he alone was concerned, most people would probably answer in the affirmative. But did he legitimately have the right to project these things to other people? J.I.'s critics faulted him on these grounds. Throughout his more than 100 books, however, he makes and remakes the point that this is not the case because each individual is different and must observe and classify his own verifiable facts. True, in many instances he came close to asserting that "whatever is good for J. I. Rodale must be good for everyone else," but he did not make a fetish of it. Therefore, with his own body, he adopted the same procedures of observing, classifying, and verifying data that other people who called themselves scientists did. Perhaps his "sin" was that he described his experiments in a popular vein and believed that a person does not necessarily have to be a "scientist" to be "scientific." In the latter respect, he is not alone. An eminent American scientist said recently, "I would sooner trust a competent self-educated high school graduate on certain ecological subjects than many Ph.Ds I have known."

When J.I. made judgments about things other than his own body, he relied largely on the literature in the field. His magazines, especially *Prevention*, contained quotations from medical journals like *Lancet* and the various publications of the American Medical Association. In a sense his magazines were more reportorial than suggestive. He did not attempt cures for illnesses, with the exception of a therapeutic lamp, claimed to be "efficacious" in treating colds, headaches, and various other ailments, which was distributed in 1940 by the Rodale Manufacturing Company but subsequently taken off the market by an order of the Federal Drug Commission. Never once did he advise people to avoid doctors. Rather, he saw a connection between the health of the soil and the health of the individual who ate the things it produced. Doctors, he claimed, were too busy with curing people, not with preventing that which demanded a cure. The area of prevention, he felt, lent itself more to scientific possibilities than did the area of cure.

Useful, too, in pursuing the question of "But who are you?" is the relationship that business has played to farming in this country. The Frenchman Alexis de Tocqueville said in his book *Democracy in America* (1835) that the American farmer was really more of a businessman than a farmer. Every agriculturalist injected some kind of trade or speculation into his operations. Few farmers acquired land for permanent settlement; rather, they bought it, improved it for a few years, and turned it over for a profit. In America, as Richard Hofstadter stated in *The Age of Reform*, there is an "agrarian myth," one that makes a Jeffersonian connection between human goodness and closeness to the soil. This agrarian myth, however, is mostly the work, says Hofstadter, of the intellectual and literary classes—stamping it with a strong Romantic character—and does not denote the thinking of the agricultural class itself. The trading syndrome, the constant speculation, and the invariable tendency to "make something pay" in terms of hard, cold cash in reality put the farmer at the center of the American business ethic. He is, in effect, and always has been, the most business-minded of all Americans.

Thus, a business background was logical for one who intended to go into agriculture. Apparently, however, J.I.'s thought of farming was not merely an ambition for profit for, throughout his letters, he referred to his desire to run a farm "scientifically," though he did not explain, at least in the early years, what he meant by "scientific." In later books and articles he applauded his business background as helping him both in writing and in farming; such experiences taught him, he said, to be practical.

Though J.I.'s business abilities can be related to his ultimate intention to farm, his love of urban life did not comport with his yearning for rural experiences. J.I. was not one who suffered from urbanism; on the contrary, he thrived in it. His early letters to Ludwig praised and glorified the cultural and business opportu-

nities of big cities, especially his love for New York.
Perhaps homesickness while he resided in Washington
and Pittsburgh caused the overdramatized accounts of
his home town, but leaving New York for the rural
areas was most assuredly not a case of the "heartless
city-humble land" syndrome. Even when he was well
situated on his farms, he was in commuting distance of
the metropolis. Many, perhaps a majority, of notable
people in this country's history started with a rural
background and wound up in an urban setting. For
J.I., however, it was just the opposite.

One could assert that J.I.'s early life was instrumental in ultimately putting him on a farm. "My father,"
he said in his autobiography (called in its early versions
The Promised Land), "kept me in the little back room
... where I had to study in Hebrew after school. I
could hear the happy voices of the boys out in the
street playing . . . while I was a prisoner in that back
room, sitting hunched up, getting very little sun or exercise, without a chance to develop my lungs." Since
his father operated a small grocery store, J.I. sated
his appetite on all sorts of cookies, cakes, and other del-
icacies. In later life, he was to attribute his various
childhood ailments to a high-carbohydrate diet and too
much sitting.

Actually, the fortunes of business and of the times
led J.I. to the farm. In 1923 he and his brother Joe
started an electrical manufacturing company, with offices in New York first on West Broadway, then on
Broome Street, and still later in the Green Terminal
Building at Hudson and Canal. Their business, as well
as most others, was adversely affected by the onset of
the Great Depression in 1929. They suffered one year
in New York during the Depression; then in 1930, because of lower operating costs, they moved their entire
holdings to Emmaus, a small town in the valley of
Pennsylvania's Lehigh River. J.I. and his family took
up residence in Allentown, and it was here that his
farming interests were revived, for he gardened at every

opportunity. He could not keep his mind on electrical manufacturing, apparently, because in 1931 he entered into his first publishing venture with a small tabloid called *The Humorous Scrapbook*. From this point on, the pursuit of publishing in combination with his fascination with what goes on in the soil formed the guidelines of his life.

His publishing interests in the late 1930s centered primarily around his efforts to learn how to write. He read several books on the techniques of style and composition but, as he said, nothing helped. Then, being the innovative and audacious person that he was, he began to collect words and phrases from the books of well-known authors and hired high school and college students to search out still others. This collection became the basis for his publication *The Verb Finder* (1937). Shortly afterward he published such enticing titles as *The King's English on Horseback* (later changed to *The Sophisticated Synonym Book*), *Strengthening Your Memory*, and *Cross-Word Puzzle Word-Finder*. Again, self-training had triumphed over formal education, at least for J.I. Rodale. In his publications of the 1930s, he was a dabbler, a technician who was more fascinated in the production of the written word than in original thinking. In a way, his publishing during the period represented little else than a transferral of business procedures in electrical manufacturing to publishing.

The majority of his books, both in the 1930s and afterward, came out under his own imprint. He did try to find a publisher for *The Verb Finder*, but being unsuccessful, he published it himself. His writings were in a direct, simple style, full of folksy anecdotes, and were aimed at the great masses of the middle and upper-middle class in the United States. From the beginning he chose the mail-order system rather than placing his product in bookstores. This approach often prevented reviews of his books and caused reviews, when they were written, to take a generally negative stance.

J.I.'s early publishing ventures put him into another undercurrent of American life. There are, and have always been, hundreds of writers in the United States who, through their own belief in themselves and through their zeal and enthusiasm, manage to gain readers and influence but are at the same time considered to be "subliterary" by sophisticated reviewers. They are not unlike exuberant fan-club editors, and in a real sense, J.I. was always the avid promoter of a "super fan club."

This "fan-club" image did not go unnoticed by readers and critics throughout the country and the world. J.I.'s reputation ranged all the way from the consideration of him as an amiable, misguided "nut" to suggestions that he be given the Congressional Medal of Honor for standing alone so long on issues of vital importance. Many critics argued that Rodale and the things he developed in relation to organic gardening and disease prevention invited extremities of reaction—that is, either one accepted the tenets completely or one rejected them completely, there being no middle position. Indeed, one reason why he started *Prevention* in 1950 was that many readers of *Organic Gardening* objected to his frequent insertion of health articles on the grounds that if they wanted to read about health, they would subscribe to an appropriate magazine. But to those outside the Emmaus circle, to those who had only heard about the various activities without really inquiring into them, the image definitely was fixed that one either totally believed or totally disbelieved.

It was predictable that J.I. would be compared with several notable people—some famous, some infamous. A natural was the Reverend Sylvester Graham, who had traveled throughout the country in the early nineteenth century pronouncing maledictions on alcohol, tobacco, and white bread. The specialized shops that sold only "Graham-approved food" were early versions of the health food stores so much favored by J.I. and so much in evidence today. The most immediate comparison was with Bernarr MacFadden, who was, to some extent, J.I.'s hero. His and MacFadden's birthdays fell on the same date, August 16, and their careers were not dissimilar. By the time MacFadden was fifteen years old, he was an accomplished gymnast, specializing in weightlifting and wrestling. He started *Physical Culture Magazine* in 1899 and twenty years later had produced thirteen magazines and six daily newspapers with a readership of over 200 million. Calling himself a "kinestherapist" and a "physcultopathist," he wrote more than fifty books and carried out a lifetime campaign, as Graham before him and Rodale after him, against white bread. Throughout J.I.'s books and articles were references to his admiration for MacFadden, especially for his physical agility during old age. J.I. took delight in announcing to his readers and hearers that he was, after MacFadden, America's "number-one faddist."

All sorts of nostrum distributors, some said, furnished the background and the inspiration for J.I.'s work. There was Dr. Samuel Thompson, an early herbal doctor in this country who used heat treatments and a plant called lobelia to keep his clients healthy. Others were William Swaim, Benjamin Brandeth, David Hostetter, and Samuel Kier. These people mixed concoctions that they peddled through the mails and at various gatherings, and they claimed that their formulas could cure any number of diseases. Because J.I. was interested in preventing diseases, not in curing them, after 1940 he did not put any item on the market with curative claims. This did not protect him, however, from comparison with patent medicine vendors and with medical quacks.

Probably J.I.'s favorite comparison was with Andrew Carnegie, who, like J.I., started at the bottom of the economic and social ladder and worked his way to the top. J.I. read Carnegie's books and followed his career with much interest. He did not connect godliness and wealth to the extent Carnegie did, but he believed that the wealthy were obligated to less fortunate people. Part of this belief was indicated by the various scholarship programs begun and administered by the organic and health institutions at Emmaus.

Predictable also was J.I.'s doing something with his farm at Emmaus other than merely enjoying its produce. His compulsion to dabble probably caused him, in 1942, to come out with the first issue of *Organic Gardening*. Three years later he put many of his thoughts together in a single book, *Pay Dirt*, published first by the Devin-Adair Company in Old Greenwich, Connecticut, and kept in print by his own firm. (By the early 1960s it had gone through fourteen printings.)

The famous British agriculturalist Sir Albert Howard wrote the introduction to the first edition. Howard's book *An Agricultural Testament* was an old stand-by in the field of natural farming; in it he had spoken of compost fertilizer as being superior to chemicals and had given much space to his experiments in natural farming while he was the imperial botanist to the government of India. J.I. wrote to Howard, and for several years the two regularly corresponded. For a time, Howard was an associate editor of *Organic Gardening*.

Pay Dirt set the pattern for much of the future direction that organic farming took in this country. It was a transitional book, marking a transference from the "organic gardening" of Howard to the "Organic Gardening" of J. I. Rodale. Howard wrote glowingly in that introduction:

"Many things impressed me as this book [*Pay Dirt*] developed. What gave me most pleasure was to discover that Mr. Rodale possesses that priceless quality—audacity—without which progress is never made. With no previous experience of the land and its ways, nevertheless he courageously acquired a farm, learned how to get it into a fertile condition, and then observed the results of compost on his crops, his livestock, and afterwards on himself and the members of his family. He thus took his own advice before offering it to his

countrymen in the pages of this book and his new journal—*Organic Gardening*—which, as the years and
months pass, goes from strength to strength. All this is
very refreshing in a world which tends to become more
and more superficial, due in large measure to that disease of civilization—fragmentation—by which such in-
timately related subjects as agriculture, food, nutrition,
and health have become split up into innumerable rigid
and self-contained little units, each in the hands of
some group of specialists." Since *Pay Dirt* is a foundation work, one that set the tenor for much of the subsequent activities of "organiculture" in the United States,
it is important to know what J.I. said in it.

He began by discussing the dangers of chemical fertilizers to the fertility of the soil and the risks created
by chemical preservatives put into processed food.
Then he expounded the value of the earthworm to the
health of the soil, using Charles Darwin's *Vegetable
Mold and Earthworms* as his basic text. Chemical fertilizers were especially baneful to these little creatures,
called by Aristotle "the intestines of the soil." J.I.
wrote: "Many . . . chemical fertilizers are slowly but
definitely killing off the earthworm population . . .
strong insect sprays containing lead, arsenic, or copper;
lime-sulphurs and tar-oil, etc., destroy earthworms.
Where any one item in Nature's cycle is disturbed it
will be found that others are automatically affected.
Nature consists of a chain of interrelated and inter-
locked life cycles. Remove any one factor and you will
find that she cannot do her work effectively. Remove
the earthworm, and the bacteria fail to thrive."

"We cannot go on forever," said J.I. in *Pay Dirt*,
"treating the soil as a chemical laboratory and expect to
turn out *natural* food. What we are getting is more and
more *chemical* food. Instead of eating live matter which
can readily be absorbed by the body we are consuming
food which is rapidly becoming more and more artificial." This artificiality had its perils for the bird life in

communities: "Many birds like to scratch in the earth and snare insect larvae. One peck in sour soil that has just been dressed with ammonium sulphate should be sufficient to tell them they are in the wrong place and to fly to greener pastures. The farmer then loses valuable allies in his war against destructive insects."

Two recent uses of chemicals came in for J.I.'s special attention. One was the growth of "chemurgy," that is, the practice of raising plants for use by specific industries, such as "vegetable factories," and the production of soybeans by Henry Ford for use, as J.I. later claimed, in making automobile fenders. This procedure, he feared, might cause a return to the one-crop system that would ultimately, through chemicals and overuse, exhaust and erode the soil's productive capabilities. The other recently used chemical that disturbed J.I. was DDT, introduced in the early 1940s. He felt much evil would come from this "wonder product" that people wantonly used as an instant, magic "cure-all" for their pest problems. Breeding resistance-type plants, placing certain insect-attracting flowers and plants next to vegetables, and rotating crops to build a healthy soil were superior methods to DDT and most of the other insecticides on the market. Nevertheless, J.I. subsequently stated in other books that, in emergencies, sprays like derris, pyrethrum, nicotine mixture, and onassia and soap solution could be used without too much harmful effect.

After stating some thirty-six advantages to organic farming and gardening—which ran all the way from improving the fertility level of the soil to counteracting poisons—J.I. made some recommendations. He wanted, for example, an alliance between medicine and agriculture, and he suggested that a special section be established in the Department of Agriculture to study the relation of the soil to nutrition with a view toward linking soil conditions and human health. Another recommendation was the encouragement of the "back-to-the-land" movement that he detected in the United States in the mid-1940s: "People are going on farms who know absolutely nothing about agriculture. How simple it would be if they farmed by the organic method." He closed his book on an idealistic note: "I believe a whole new era of agricultural research is in the making—one that will benefit the country at large far more than all the research of the past has done, one that will more nearly help to create a healthy society and keep it in close touch with the land from which it gets its strength and sweetness—a country without city or rural slums, a country of homes and gardens, parks and forests, a country of prosperous farms and a healthy, vigorous people creating a fine, new community life 'in the pursuit of happiness.' "

This book started the process that ultimately caused J.I. to be called a prophet and a man ahead of his time but also a crank, a manure-pile worshiper, a humus huckster, and an apostle of dung. By now, perhaps, some readers may be comparing *Pay Dirt*, consciously or unconsciously, with one book they know: Rachel Carson's *Silent Spring* (1962). No evidence can be found to indicate that J.I. and Carson ever met, but J.I. accepted and admired her work. In part at least, she reciprocated; apparently she was a regular reader of Rodale's *Health Bulletin*. In answer to a questionnaire of April 3, 1963, Carson said: "I am of course most interested in your items on pesticides, and general atmospheric pollution. These have given me several useful tips on situations I have then followed up with interest." Nevertheless, Carson was quite averse to being associated with any type of "organic" venture. Once when a brief biography of her was being written for the Book-of-the-Month Club *News*, she refused to allow eminent philosopher Alfred North Whitehead's phrase "the organic view of life" to be used because it contained the word "organic." Some of Carson's friends relate that J.I. booked her one time—sometime in

1963—on a double lecture program, with J.I. sitting on the right of the podium and Carson on the left. This was done, apparently, without her approval and even without her knowledge. Before the announcement sheet was publicized to any extent, Carson had her name removed from the program.

Regardless of whether or not Rachel Carson accepted the tenets of Emmaus, her book *Silent Spring* does not strongly disagree with what *Pay Dirt* had said some seventeen years earlier. For example, she wrote: "The chemical weed killers are a bright new toy. They work in a spectacular way; they give a giddy sense of power over nature to those who wield them, and as for the long-range and less obvious effects—these are easily brushed aside as the baseless imaginings of pessimists" (pp. 68-69). Or "There is a strong tendency to brand as fanatics or cultists all who are so perverse as to demand that their food be free of insect poisons" (p. 178). And "As we pour our millions into research and invest all our hopes in vast programs to find cures for established cases of cancer, we are neglecting the golden opportunity to prevent, even while we seek to cure" (p. 242). These and many similar statements show that there is more to compare—even to the point of frequently quoting the same sources—than to contrast between the two books.

It makes little difference who said these things first. The important thing is that they were said and were finally, in some measure, listened to. But how can one explain the relative obscurity of *Pay Dirt* and the full attention that *Silent Spring* received? One possible explanation is style. Carson's technique is livelier and more learned than J.I.'s; also, the public was more receptive in 1962, due possibly in part to television, to a book of this type than in 1945. Too, she apparently won the favor and support of scientists throughout the country who quickly brought attention to her book. On the other hand, J.I. was fairly well known as a man who was overenthusiastic about the benefits of natural food supplements, giving him the stance of a mystic. Perhaps if he had stayed only in "organiculture" and had not begun to promote natural food, he never would have attracted as much controversy as he did—or attention. He propounded such strong ideas about the efficacy of food substances we take into our bodies that his agricultural views were pushed aside by many people and he was treated as one who indulged in a mishmash of more or less acceptable thought but came up with unacceptable conclusions. The ends he sought, in some minds, may have been right, but the means he employed were wrong.

Thus, the university professor who asked J.I., "But who are you?" unwittingly conjured up the ghosts of more than 200 years of social and cultural history in the United States. Innovation, inventiveness, ingenuity, pugnacity, audacity, and dabbling were the instincts that propelled J.I. Rodale—the qualities that in all periods have dubbed their holders with reputations of unorthodoxy and nonconformity.

J.I. was a kind, mild-mannered man who rarely got ruffled even when the criticisms and condemnations of him were at their worst. He attributed his sweetness of temper to eating organically produced food and to his massive daily dosage of natural food supplements. Physically he was five feet, six and a half inches tall, and he weighed 155 pounds (at least in later years after he had gone on a reducing diet). His silver-gray hair was brushed straight back from his forehead (he never used shampoo on his hair, believing that a daily wetting and a vigorous brushing were all that were needed for health and appearance), and he wore eyeglasses (not rimless ones, to be sure, for he believed they were instrumental in causing skin cancer) and, in later years, a mustache and a goatee. He had a high forehead, a distinctive nose, and piercing greenish-gray eyes. He often stated that he wanted to live to 102 years and 1 day, for that would mean that he had lived in three different centuries. Such was the man who, even if he did not quite know who he was in 1945, would give the answer several times in the years ahead.

CHAPTER 2

The Early Years

In the decades following the American Civil War, there was a vast immigration to the United States from eastern and southern Europe. Included in this throng were East European Jews, who by 1900 numbered around a half-million and who, unlike the earlier German Jews, tended to settle in big cities and become part of the rapidly developing industrialization. By 1880 the 60,000 Jews living in New York City made up approximately 25 percent of Jewry in the United States. The New York City Jews concentrated in Manhattan's Lower East Side, where they established schools and community projects to Americanize their children, a process that was noticeable in only a short time. As Henry Steele Commager said in *Meet the U.S.A.*, "It was the child of foreign born parents who had the upper hand, the child who set the pace, the child who was sophisticated, as his parents were not, the child who held the magic key to the mysteries of American life" (pp. 21-22).

A majority of the German Jews were peddlers, traders, and storekeepers; the East European Jews, however, were mostly skilled laborers, predominantly tailors. The distinguished British historian Arnold J. Toynbee, in *A Study of History*, talked about the genius that Jews developed for economics because of the penalties levied against them by overriding majorities: "The Jews . . . have overcome the social handicaps which their religious idiosyncrasy entails by holding their own successfully, as traders and financiers, in a great variety of human environments" (Vol. II, p. 236).

Trading and tailoring, therefore, became the hallmarks of New York and American Jewry.

Among the hosts of East European Jews was one Michael Cohen, who came to New York probably in the late 1870s (individual records of arriving "Hebrews" were not kept until after the turn of the century). He came from Poland originally but lived in England for a time before journeying to the United States. Some time after his arrival in this country, he met another Polish immigrant, Bertha Rouda, and soon married her. Michael typified the East European Jew and also fit Toynbee's classification, for he worked in a cloth manufacturing business making caps, and later he ran a grocery store at 47 Norfolk Street on the East Side. He and Bertha raised their family in a four-room cold-water flat in the rear of the store.

It was in this little flat that Bertha gave birth to Michael's fifth child and fourth son in August 1898. At first he was to be called Jacob Isaac, but an authoritative aunt disliked the combination and for some unknown reason chose "Jerome Irving," causing him later always to refer to himself as either Jerry or J.I. The smallest of eight children, he was the "runt of the family."

Jerry's earliest response to the world about him had much to do with his father, Michael. Though Jerry stated that he owed a debt to Michael for immigrating to the United States and keeping Jerry from being born in Poland, he still feared him: "My father was like the voice of God thundering. To me he was Jehovah, a wrathful God."

Michael had religious ambitions for young Jerry; he wanted him to become a rabbi. Thus, he forced the boy at an early age to study the Old Testament and the Talmud and to practice his singing. Even when Jerry was fifteen, he was still known locally as "the thirteen-year-old cantor" and was the "darling of pious old ladies all over the East Side," who affectionately called him Der Berimpter and Yeinkeleh, the choir singer. He sang on a regular basis at Beth Hemedresh Hagodol, with nonmembers frequently traveling several blocks and paying admission to hear him.

It could well be that Michael's strict orthodoxy in relation to Jerry (the only concession Michael ever made to a non-Jew was to attend some Caruso performances) was the thing that later triggered so much nonconformity in Jerry. He suffered silently through the religious training and relinquished it only after Michael died. But it was only the training he gave up, not the characteristics, for his later writings and his other activities had a distinctly religious fervor about them. He may openly have rebelled against the idea of becoming a rabbi: ("[strict childhood] gave me a demonlike urge to grow up so that I could be on my own; it made the fires of ambition burn savagely in my breast"), but the religious inclinations lingered on.

For years, Jerry's daily routine was to arise before dawn and deliver breakfast grocery orders. Afterward he would go to school, then to sessions of religious instruction from a rabbi called "Red-Donkey," and after that he spent time choir-rehearsing. His academic duties ended for the day, he would join his family at the dinner table, where stale crusts of bread and anemic-looking canned fish and meat were consumed. Michael had the practice of cutting slices of bread for his customers, and frequently they demanded that he start with a fresh loaf, leaving the remains of the old loaf to Michael's family. Also in this era before widespread refrigeration, customers purchased only portions of canned meat and fish, so after a day or two the remaining contents of the can could no longer be sold and accordingly found their way to Michael's table. Jerry later stated that his daily regimen of grocery delivery, of secular and religious instruction, and of eating food that was on the verge of contamination "made a man of him."

The Jewish ghetto of Jerry's early years was changing. It was a time of two cultures colliding with each other, subtly at first and then vigorously, producing what was frequently referred to as "America in the streets and Europe in the homes." In the old countries like Russia and Poland, the Laws of Leviticus forbidding activity on Saturday, the Sabbath, were strictly adhered to. Jews were prohibited even from building fires on that day and from performing any manual tasks. The more orthodox Jews—and Jerry's father, Michael, certainly was one—continued these practices after they were settled in the New World. But more and more of them slipped from the old ways: "It seems that the germ of the American spirit infected them, however insignificantly. In a city where there was a flat-iron building twenty stories high, and where Cossacks didn't paralyse them with fright every time they rode past, little innocuous subterfuges were resorted to to make life a little more liveable."

It became a practice in the Norfolk Street neighborhood to get "nonbelievers" to do "Saturday jobs." It was not proper to deliberately engage someone for these services; it had to be done obliquely. For example, there was a neighborhood derelict who did jobs in return for drinking money. The typical way of doing it was for someone to approach this man and say: "Now if this wasn't Saturday, I'd make myself a nice fire." The man would instantly get the hint and build the fire.

Young Jerry was thus exposed to the tenets of both orthodox and reformed Jewry. In his own home he was orthodox, taking special delight each year at observance of Passover (except for having to eat matzo, unleavened bread made of flour and water) when the practice of chumetz burning (of spoons used in Passover celebrations) occurred: "This was the gayest time of the year and we took off from school as well as from the toilsome grocery chores. If someone wanted a boy to do a special favor they would say 'do this and I'll give you my chumetz next Spring.'"

But other influences also worked on him. For instance, near the grocery was a jewelry shop run by a

Mr. Gold, a freethinker. Michael forbade Jerry to see him, but frequently it was impossible to avoid him. After Michael's death in 1914, Jerry regularly played checkers with Gold. Across the street from the Cohen grocery was an umbrella and suitcase store; three candy shops on Norfolk Street delighted Jerry and his young friends (Michael sold cakes and cookies, but no candy, in his store); and a family named Lefowich just down the street regaled all the children with the first phonograph brought into the neighborhood. Around the corner on Grand Street was Krug's Restaurant, and farther down Grand was Malbin's Movie House, where Jerry and his cohorts were entertained for three cents a showing. Two blocks from his home, on Essex Street, was Isaac Gillis' famous delicatessen, which became something of a gathering place for the young people of the area. Jerry and his best friend, Louis Ludwig, wandered each Sunday to Van Cortlandt Park on 240th Street to marvel at the acres of "raw, untamed" land. It is likely that these visits encouraged the two boys to formulate future plans for going into agriculture.

Secular schooling, which began for Jerry when he was five, produced other impressions. His first school was Public School 137, where most of his teachers were Gentile: "To have given us little Jewish boys Christian teachers ... had it been planned that way, would have been astute pedagogy. But I do not believe that is the way it was managed. Jews hadn't been in the country long enough and in sufficient quantities to have sent their children through the educational mill and to become teachers. These Gentile teachers left their impress on our youthful minds."

Apparently the relationship between Jewish students and Gentile teachers in these schools was cordial. Once at PS 137 at Christmastime, the teacher asked the students to bring some holly for decorating the classroom. Jerry's brother Joe must have misunderstood, for the next day he brought a handful of "cholly" (challah), a Jewish bread made every Friday for consumption on the Sabbath.

Each day after Jerry was dismissed from PS 137 he attended, until sundown, religious classes from "Red-Donkey" at a school located on the ground floor of a vest-making factory. Just outside was a small enclosure where the boys played until "Red-Donkey" (so called because of his beard) appeared. Some of the boys became adept at climbing a five-story pole in the enclosure, to which were strung tenement clotheslines. Other diversions included swapping cherry pits for marbles, campaign buttons, or cigarette picture cards and playing hopscotch, which they called potzy.

"Red-Donkey" was exceedingly severe in his ministrations of the Old Testament and the Talmud. He frequently punished the boy who did not do his lesson by physically beating him. Perhaps the strictures that Jerry suffered at the hands of "Red-Donkey" provided another reason for his later rebellion against becoming a rabbi. Though "Red-Donkey" strove very hard, he was unable to do very much with his charges: "Most of the boys," Jerry said later, "were beginning to take to the ways of America; to baseball, trips to the menagerie, shooting dice and smoking. The old Bible didn't stand a chance." Ultimately "Red-Donkey" admitted the futility of his work and returned to Russia.

For the fifth and sixth grades, Jerry went to Public School 75, and for the last two of his elementary years to PS 62 (his favorite, after which he later named his theater). PS 62 was noted for its athletes, partly because of the skills of Nat Holman, who later played for and then managed the Celtics basketball team. The Jewish students at PS 62 firmly believed that the school's athletic record was due to their loyalty and to the special cheer they used:

Aleveevo, alevivo,
Aleveevo, vivo, vo.

Ahlef, baiz, gimel, daled,
Sis, boom, bah!

The third line was composed of the first four letters of the Jewish alphabet and provided, they believed, an unbeatable combination.

Generally, Jerry was a quiet, unassuming, yet sensitive, lad. Rarely did he lose his temper or roughhouse. When he did either, however, it was usually to an extreme.

He was double-promoted from the second to the fourth grade at PS 137. On the first day of class, however, the principal, stating that Jerry was too young, put him back in the third grade. During his first day as a third-grader, then, he was angry and frustrated. To vent his hostilities, he flipped his inkwell cover up and down, much to the annoyance of his teacher, Miss Cousins, who gave him a good earpulling for his transgressions. In return Jerry gave Miss Cousins a solid sock in the jaw. Jerry did not report what subsequently happened, except that "I never was bad again."

At another time Jerry laid his hands on a Stevens .22 rifle that belonged to his older brother Archie. From Louis Ludwig's rooftop, Jerry practiced his "marksmanship," bad eyes and all, aiming at everything he could see except humans and animals. He kept shooting until a policeman started up to the roof; Jerry escaped by a back stairway.

Throughout his schooling, Jerry showed a marked proclivity for, and a love of, literature. When he was about twelve, he and his friend Louis sat on the stoop of the Norfolk Street State Bank and put a question to each other: "What will you be when you are twenty-one years old?" Jerry stated that by then he would have written at least one book and would be an editor. Though he was not an editor at twenty-one, he had written a book by that time—one on etiquette (which had a private printing of about 100 copies), which he presented to his pal Louis as a wedding present. Jerry always visualized himself as a famous writer—mostly of fiction.

As a youth, also, Jerry and his brothers were avid consumers of Horatio Alger novels, a practice that stayed with Jerry until late in his life. Each Friday morning a new Alger book was distributed by an agent on Grand Street, who loaned it out for a few pennies a week. Jerry waited until bedtime for Horatio Alger: "I slept next to the kitchen stove where I read Horatio Alger stories by gaslight turned to halfmast. The sulphurous fumes drifting out of the coals would furnish vivid colors to the scene where the heroine is tied to the railroad tracks and the Chicago Flyer is bearing down with fiendish relentlessness. I had to watch out for two villains, the one in the book, and my father's heavy forewarning footsteps. Thank God that my father was not given to pussyfooting. He always dramatically announced his coming by his quick, loud, heavy tread. Horatio Alger was poison to him. In fact, he figured that the reading of any English book was sinful and destroyed many a copy of these dearly beloved rags-to-riches opuscules."

Despite the multitude of school and family duties, Jerry still found enough time for part-time employment, at age fifteen, with a wholesale plumber named Horowitz. He began his plumbing work in the warehouse amid the pungent odors of oakum, where he learned the difference between an L-shaped pipe and a T. He was soon graduated to the office, where he became Horowitz's pet. Apparently, Mr. H. wanted not only to take Jerry into the business but to set aside one of his seven daughters as a wife for Jerry as well. Jerry did not stay in the plumbing business very long, "because that wasn't the way I wanted to choose a wife."

Two things happened to Jerry in 1914 that affected both his sense of ending and his sense of beginning. The first was the death of his father, and the second was his matriculation as a student at DeWitt Clinton High School on 10th Avenue at 59th Street.

Michael had had kidney and heart disease for as long as Jerry could remember. Before he became a grocer, Michael had participated in a strike at the cap factory where he worked. Long hours of picketing, it was said, damaged his kidneys and caused his legs to swell. A heart attack ended his life at the age of fifty-one— "same age as Napoleon," Jerry inserted into one of his writings. This death set the pattern for future family tragedies: Jerry's oldest brother, Archie, died at fifty-one; his brother Solomon died at sixty-two; his brother Joe at fifty-seven; his sister Tina at sixty-four; and his sister Sally at fifty-eight—all of heart attacks. Michael's condition and relatively early death were among the reasons why Jerry became so preoccupied with health.

Jerry's career at DeWitt Clinton was not as successful as his earlier academic ventures. By now his eyesight gave him considerable trouble, and this indeed was a contributing factor to his relatively poor showing in much of his high school work. When his teachers discovered that he could not even see the blackboard, they immediately took corrective measures. Another reason for trouble in high school was the abrupt change from the Jewish ghetto to the Christian environment. He and friend Louis usually either walked or skated to school each day to save their tram fares. This "economy," however, caused them to get into trouble more than once with the Italian boys along the way. At the end of his third year at DeWitt Clinton his academic percentages were: English, 83; French, 91; history, 90; algebra, 70; and physical training, 70. During his fourth year, he suffered a decline: English, 73; history 88; physics 78; trigonometry, 65; and elocution, 75. He was fond of saying in later years that math was his worst subject, "yet I turned out to be an accountant."

With the family breadwinner gone, the sons had to provide a living and to settle the debts of Michael's grocery. Jerry intermittently had kept books for the little store, so with this experience he got a job in June 1916 with the Gussow accounting firm. Then in October 1917 he became a junior accountant for the New York City Finance Department in the daytime and a student in the College of Commerce at New York University at night. Here he studied principles of accounting, political economy, business English, private finance, and law of contracts and agencies. His major professors were Gustenberg and Todman, and his academic record was only mediocre, his highest grades being made in political economy. Later, at Columbia University, where he studied for about six months, he made a straight B average in his work. While a night student at Columbia he worked for the New York accounting firm of J. Kleinman and for a time at Wright-Martin Aircraft Corporation in New Brunswick, New Jersey.

He faced a problem during his university days that was common to thousands of boys of his generation: World War I and the draft. He took great interest in the progress of the war, hanging a huge map in his hallway and following the battles with different colored tacks. He attempted to join the Student Army Training Corps at New York University to become an officer. He took a week's vacation without pay from his employer to go through the various processes of applying and spent so much time standing in lines that he had a "line complex" for the rest of his days. Jerry faced questions not ordinarily put to the other candidates because his father had been an emigrant from Poland. What, for example, did he feel about the Bolsheviks, then making themselves heard all over the country, and would he have any objections to serving in Siberia? Apparently he got through these obstacles satisfactorily, for he reached the point of the physical examination.

Jerry turned out to be quite physically fit except for one thing: his eyes. Without his glasses he had to move within five feet of the optical board before he could see anything. His sight percentage was 5/200 for each eye. This physical gave Jerry a classification of D, making him unsuitable even for limited service on account of his eyesight. (In his fifties and sixties, J.I. often wrote that his eyesight was vastly improved from that of his youth—that many doctors marveled at his seeing strength. He attributed this improvement to his addiction to raw sunflower seeds).

Jerry soon discontinued his academic pursuits and put all his energies into becoming a professional accountant. He advertised his services in *The New York Times* and had several quick responses. He worked for the Stitzel accounting firm, as well as a few others, for short periods.

His closest friend, Louis Ludwig, had taken a job in Washington, D.C. Their correspondence during this period emphasized nostalgic moods of things uttered in the past, fondly remembered: "I started thinking again about the farm and my mind was never as made up as it was last night. I thought probably that your going to Washington might have lessened your enthusiasm for it and I am glad to hear that you feel the way I do about it." It was not long before Jerry, at Ludwig's initiative, began making plans to go to Washington himself. He did have some reservations, however, because of the influenza epidemics sweeping the country: "The epidemic is pretty bad in New York, although according to newspaper reports it is not as bad as conditions in the District of Columbia, with its congestion of war workers. One statement in the *Times* said that the Red Cross in Washington had distributed gauze masks to be worn over the mouth and nose . . ." In the midst of his anxieties about the war, influenza, and a possible uprooting from his beloved New York, he continued his training in accounting by enrolling in a correspondence course with the Pace Agency.

The armistice with the Central Powers in late 1918 caused J.I., as he was now called, to make final his plans to go to Washington, first because returning veterans got the choice jobs available in New York City, and second because the Internal Revenue Service needed accountants to help catch up on back income tax returns that had been neglected because of the war. In early March 1919 he began his new career in Washington as a resident auditor for the IRS.

For a time in Washington, J.I. roomed with Louis on S Street. Almost immediately the two friends found themselves in financial straits. At one point they had seventy-one cents between them, and payday was three days away. They got through the emergency by eating only peanuts for seventy-two hours, which produced a condition afterward that required several boxes of Ex-lax to correct. Also, the two boys pulled a prank on their next-door neighbor, an elderly man who complained that J.I. and Louis made too much noise. In retaliation, they sneaked quietly to the old man's door one night and blew some sneezing powder under it. Before the joke was over, however, they became concerned, for they thought the old gentleman was actually going to choke. Soon, Louis went back to his studies in New York, leaving J.I. alone in Washington.

J.I. approached his new job with enthusiasm. He was in the auditing division that took care of tax returns from Tennessee—mostly those of farmers. He chuckled over one return from a farmer who on one line deducted a fee paid to a veterinary surgeon for administering to his sick mule and on the next line deducted the cost of one dead mule. Another return came in from a German meteorologist who stated that his wife's parents and sister in Germany would soon need his financial assistance, so he needed an additional exemption.

The young New Yorker acquired several lifetime habits in Washington. One was dancing, for which he paid seventy-five cents for fifteen minutes of instruction—"highway robbery," he called it, though it did have the advantage of favorably widening his social circle, except for the time, as he put it, he "got hooked up with a super-dreadnought." Another habit that he already possessed but became ingrained into him even more in Washington was reading. Each day after his work at the IRS, he walked to the Library of Congress, where he pored over books on accounting, copyrighting, and corporate finance. He also took advantage of many lectures and professional conventions that occurred in the capital city. He was enthralled by a series of lectures on the various religions of the world and concluded that he was fortunate in being a Jew. He reveled in performances by Al Jolson, Barnum and Bailey circuses, and the famous actress Billie Burke and delighted in watching the "Washingtons" go down in defeat to his favorite baseball team, the New York Giants. He began to take long walks each Sunday along the Cabin John Canal, where he became interested in the people, animals, and things about him. He decided that it was the height of Romanticism to watch lantern-swinging young boys search through Washington parks at night for fishing worms.

One temptation that he more or less successfully resisted was smoking. In a letter to Louis, he described his early disdain: "Last Sunday Tom [Tom Hanley, his roommate in Washington] and I took a walk and he says 'how about a smoke, kid?' I says 'nothin doing. I ain't gonna smoke for nobody.' So he goes into a cigar store and buys three pretty good cigars. We went home and I sat down to read. Tom fishes out one of his ropes and starts puffing away like a veteran. It certainly was a nice sight, with him making pretty smoke clouds and looking important and everything that goes with it. Well, in a few minutes Tom says he isn't feeling as well as he did that morning. In a few minutes more he says 'I think I'm going into the bathroom . . .' and he did and threw up his entire breakfast. Well, no more smoking for Tom." A little over a month later, however, J.I. modified his position somewhat: "I have decided to start smoking a pipe; and a pipe only ... If you don't inhale, there is no danger. And also there is no nicotine as in cigarettes. Of late, at times, I have felt as if a little smoke would have done me good. Well, it's great. A pipe, like a dog, is man's silent companion." J.I. did not long continue his affiliation with a pipe, but in later years he did smoke and "chew" a few cigars. (During his writing years he wrote several books on the dangers of smoking. One used downright scare tactics: *Smoke and Die; Quit and Live,* and another recognized the difficulty of breaking the habit: *If You Must Smoke.*)

It did not take the precocious J.I. long to adjudge himself superior to his supervisors in administering the federal tax law. And he may well have been, for he seemed obsessed with mastering all the intricacies and complexities of the federal income tax, which had come into existence just six years earlier. He threw himself wholeheartedly into the lectures presented by various tax experts, and almost every evening he studied for several hours. Increasingly, specific questions from taxpayers were channeled to J.I. for answers.

Early in April 1919, J.I. asked for, and got, a transfer to the corporate auditing section, which would allow him to travel to various parts of the country and examine the tax records of large corporations. While he served in this capacity, he had numerous offers for employment elsewhere. For instance, his immediate supervisor wanted J.I. to go to San Francisco with him and become his partner in an accounting and income tax business. Apparently there was a great shortage of such people in the West, and opportunities were limitless. But J.I. demurred: ". . . I probably would not care to go as far west as Frisco. About Detroit, Michigan is far enough west for me." Too, he was offered a position with the *Merchant's Trade Journal* in Washington to help subscribers with their tax problems. He declined the invitation, as well as one from a western bank to act as a tax consultant to its clients. All of this was heady stuff to a young man barely in his twenties. It certainly gave him a sense of confidence and sometimes even of youthful arrogance, especially when he found his abilities to be greater than most of his college-trained colleagues in the IRS.

There was, however, at least one chastening experience. J.I. took the CPA examination for the State of

North Carolina and after several weeks of anxious waiting, he learned that the results were negative. Undaunted, he then took the CPA examination for Ohio and passed.

As a traveling auditor in the IRS corporate division, J.I. visited the Commonwealth of Kentucky to examine the records of a steel company. That visit to Kentucky marked an important point in J.I.'s life and helped further to solidify his future plans for an agrarian existence: "One day while walking along a country lane I stopped spellbound. There congregated before me was a chattery group of farmers passing the time of day away in the midst of a heterogeneous assortment of horses and mules. From what I could gather these farmers came together at this point one day a week to trade in spavined and decrepit plugs, but mostly to chew the rag, to whittle, and to catch up on the neighborhood gossip. Chins were moving in slow Southern measures activated by word-power and chew-tobaccer [sic.] Laughter and back-slapping was ever-present. I was there for an hour and saw not one move in the direction of horse-trading . . ."

Another Kentucky sight charmed J.I. and made his yearning for the land even more acute: "A family . . . came to town on a Sunday morning to go to Church in a farm-wagon. The streets were quiet and calm with a holy Sunday air. There must have been a dozen of them sitting perched up there and scrubbed as if their very salvation depended upon it. The burly, bearded father handled the team with a fierce pride, as they trotted briskly down the street. The mother sat beside him and glowed in her Sunday-go-to-meetin' clothes. The children squirmed and wriggled for they seemed to know that soon they would have to sit quietly while the minister dealt out his usual quota of sulphur, brimstone, and hellfire. . . . [Being] among farmers and in farm country I was more and more imbued with the ambition of some day having my own farm and riding to town with my children on a buck-board drawn by two trusty horses."

In early 1920, an exultant J.I. apparently believed that he had "arrived" in the world of IRS procedures. He jubilantly reported to Louis Ludwig that he had been detailed to go to New York and examine the accounts of the huge Standard Oil Company. He apparently completed the audit in record time, or did not finish it at all, for within less than a month after his assignment, he had left the IRS and was working in the Pittsburgh office of the New York accounting firm of Robertson, Furman, and Murphy.

J.I.'s year with the Internal Revenue Service, from March 1919 to March 1920, caused him to form some definite conclusions about life in general. One was that experience far outweighed academic training in producing efficiency. His letters to Louis Ludwig touched frequently on this point: "I cannot help repeating that the training I am getting with the government is greater than I could secure at New York University—far greater." And: "I would not give the best University course for the training one gets in the income tax service. ... Offers of jobs are as numerous now as Bolsheviki in Seward Park." He was chagrined when IRS employees with college degrees received considerably more money than he for the same amount of work. This awareness of what he considered to be an inequity probably set him on the course thereafter of treating academic people with suspicion—of always lamenting their lack of "common sense."

The sojourn in Washington, too, was J.I.'s first extended absence from New York City. His letters of this period reflected a romanticizing of his more youthful days in which he and his friends had sought as much nature as could be found in the asphalt-covered streets of New York. The urge both for the simplicity of existence on the land and for the conveniences of a large city remained uppermost in his mind. The Washington period proved to him that he could be successful not only in business but in any other endeavor to which he set his mind. He was confident, therefore, that the day would arrive when he could go full-time into agriculture.

J.I. retained his agrarian ambitions in Pittsburgh, but now he added another dimension—health. The "smoky city" caused him to wonder about the relationship between health and environment. Also, he became quite conscious of the tone of his voice—he had apparently not yet experienced the voice change fully, and this embarrassed him when he interviewed important business officials. He went, therefore, to a Pittsburgh osteopath who was known for his therapy on opera singers. Within a short time, according to J.I., he "aged" about ten years under the osteopath's hands. "My voice took on a more mellow calibre which gave an ease and confidence in my general intercourse with all and sundry." He also began to pay closer attention to the heart murmur that he had had for several years. (Indeed, this was a prime reason why he developed such an intense interest in all aspects of health. He frequently quoted the adage "If you want to live long, find yourself a good disease which requires you to take care of yourself.") For the heart murmur, he went both to a chiropractor and to a physician and was at that time unsure about the efficacy of treatment by either man. (In later life, however, he frequented chiropractors' offices.)

In Pittsburgh, as in Washington, J.I. studied business books, invested in the stock market, and attended as many public lectures as his schedule permitted. He was fascinated by the golden-tongue oratory of William Jennings Bryan, who gave a lecture in the Carnegie Music Hall on "Ingratitude." The lecture he remembered the longest, however, was given by an Englishman, Sir Robert McGarrison, before the Society for Biological Sciences, entitled "Faulty Food in Relation to Gastro-Intestinal Disorders." Here, McGarrison described the unusually healthy conditions of a tribe of people in North India (now a part of Pakistan) known as the

Hunzas. He attributed their longevity to their organic agricultural methods in which the "law of return" was practiced; that is, everything taken from the soil was returned to it. This lecture was the real beginning of J.I.'s inclination toward organic gardening and farming, though he did not put it into practice until some years later. So fascinated was he by McGarrison's descriptions of the Hunzas that he began reading all the books he could find on the subject and entered into a lengthy correspondence with the Mir of Hunza. In 1948, he brought all of his sources together and, though he had never visited the area, wrote a book, *The Healthy Hunzas*.

J.I. continued the habit of frequent walks, though he complained about the Pittsburgh hills: "Personally, I don't care for these hills as it makes it so hard to walk sometimes." (In his forties, fifties, and sixties, however, he was to extol the superiority of hill walking). On these walks, he apparently became pensive, for he made two important decisions.

One had to do with marriage. He mixed a few amorous thoughts with business as he asked Ludwig in May 1920 if he thought diamonds would be higher a year hence than at the present moment. His reason for asking was that he thought he would soon be engaged, but he did not yet know to whom. "I do not intend to marry, however, before I am 25 years old." (He was twenty-nine when he did marry). He thought it would be sensible to get the diamond now because he had read that the blue clay diamond deposits in South Africa were rapidly being exhausted. He intended to pay for it on the partial payment plan at $25 a month.

Another decision that he implemented in Pittsburgh was to change his name. He had been pondering this change while he was in Washington but did not act on it until he was living in Pittsburgh. It had been clear all during the time he worked as an auditor and accountant for both private and governmental enterprises that his ambition was to have a business of his own. He had been in a quandary about which type of business to enter. He thought once about an ice-cream cone factory, but publishing seems to have lured him at an early stage. He and his brother Joe started the District Publishing Company (presumably in New York) but kept it for only a short time. In the fall of 1922, they sold it for $250, losing $50 on the deal. This modest undertaking must have whetted his appetite for bigger things and caused him to balance up the inconveniences that the name "Cohen" might cause him.

Also, it seemed that a Jewish name was a handicap for one who wished to go into certain lines of trade. Publishing, utilities, and land were generally thought to be the exclusive province of the native-born and not open to foreigners or their children, or even to those with foreign-sounding names. It is also clear that in these early years, J.I. had writing ambitions—he visualized himself as becoming a famous novelist—and he must have concluded that a man named Cohen could not succeed in this endeavor.

Another possible factor in the name change was the attitude of many Americans in the wake of World War I. The early 1920s were notorious for their "Red scares," in which it was thought that a foreign element was working to do harm to this country. There was indeed a great deal of Bolshevik propaganda during this period, and U.S. Government agencies were established specifically to combat it. One such agency had an office in Pittsburgh next to the place where J.I. worked, and J.I. became friendly with its personnel. Possibly they helped him to make final his plans to change his name, an action identical to that of thousands of other Jews of this time.

A final possible motivation was something of a rebellion against his Jewish heritage. J.I.'s father had been quite strict with him, forcing him into long hours of religious study, preparatory to becoming a rabbi. This regimentation, plus the harsh treatments by "Red-Donkey" may have produced a latent, subconscious desire to repudiate the severity of his youth. Moreover, Cohen was not his ancestral name. While Michael had been living abroad prior to his immigration to the United States, he had changed his name to Cohen. Before the change, the name had been Lachofsky.

Having made the decision to change his name, the next step was to decide what his new name would be. He had hit upon a new name, with Louis' help, even while in Washington. His mother's maiden name was Rouda (meaning "red beard," and apparently streaks of red showed up in the beards of J.I.'s male relatives). So he began to repeat this name: "Rouda, Rouda, Rouda." At one point he must have allowed an "L" sound to enter into his pronunciations, making it "Roudal." In the course of time, he dropped the "U" and added an "E" and came up with "Rodale." He quickly informed his friends that the emphasis was on the first syllable and that the name was "Rodale," not "Rawdeal."

The change was legally made in the January 1921 term of the Court of Common Pleas for Allegheny County, Pennsylvania. The decree was handed down on January 19, 1921, and from that day forward he was known as J. I. Rodale.

After the name change, J.I. plunged even deeper into his work and became a partner in the firm of Robertson, Furman, and Murphy. He spent his time interviewing business executives and going over their records for tax purposes. Still paramount in his thinking, however, was the plan to have a business of his own. His chance occurred in 1923, and in September of that year he severed his connections with the accounting firm, selling all his interest in it. He then became a partner with his brother Joe in New York in the Rodale Manufacturing Company, a maker of electrical parts.

In 1924, J.I. met his future wife. One Sunday afternoon in June he visited a dance pavilion at 53rd Street and Broadway, and there he became acquainted with nineteen-year-old Anna Andrews, who had been born of Lithuanian parents in Mahanoy City, Pennsylvania. She was struck quickly with J.I.'s tendency toward health and self-analysis. Once when they were visiting friends, J.I. excused himself to go to the bathroom and urinate. When he came back he said, with a big grin on his face, "Say, did you know you could smell it, when you've been eating asparagus?" He remained fascinated with asparagus for the rest of his life; he was lauding its virtues on the day he died.

Although J.I. saw Anna regularly during the next several months, he took frequent trips in his Buick Twin into the Catskill Mountains, in part to look for a bride. One day he came to Anna and showed her a picture of a Polish girl he had met in the Catskills who, he said, wanted to marry him. Her chief flaw, in his opinion, was that she suffered from halitosis. J.I. asked Anna's advice on how to handle the problem of the Polish girl; that was the first indication that he was getting serious about Anna. Afterward, he courted Anna assiduously, on their nights out usually taking her to the Vincent Lopez Club, where he became fond of Lopez's song "Kitten on the Keys."

J.I. and Anna were married in a civil ceremony on December 21, 1927, and again in a religious ceremony on December 27. The reason for the two marriages was that J.I. was Jewish and Anna was Catholic. After some initial reservations, Anna was accepted into J.I.'s family. Anna's parents had died when she was quite young, so she had been raised by her maternal grandmother. J.I. passed muster with the grandmother because he "looked like a priest." When Anna told her that his nose was so long that they bumped noses when they kissed, the grandmother replied: "A long nose is good. It pokes about and learns things. He'll find out what life is about." At the very beginning, then, J.I.'s relationship with Anna's family was off to a good start. For a time they lived in the Bronx and visited Anna's grandmother as often as possible.

The trips to Pennsylvania took them through the east-central parts of the state, not far from the coalfields. J.I. was impressed with Allentown because its main street was lined with trees and stated that if his business ever moved from New York, this would be the place. The opportunity came in 1930.

Emmaus (generally pronounced E-may-us) is a little town about six miles from Allentown. Called "Macungie," or "feeding place of the bears," by Indians, it was first settled by whites in the 1730s. Moravians established a "gamein-ort," or congregational village, and in 1761 named it Emmaus, after the biblical town that had been the destination of Jesus' walk on the first Easter. Emmaus was one of several small Pennsylvania towns competing for New York business during the Depression. The town fathers offered free to the Rodales an empty silkmill in which to manufacture their sockets and plugs and other electrical equipment. Also some citizens offered to purchase stocks if the Rodale plant were in Emmaus. These lures, plus the already positive feelings toward the Allentown area, were sufficient reasons for leaving New York.

J.I.'s formative years show him to have had great energy and curiosity. For the most part, he was a quiet, serious person but one who still had the ability to indulge in frolics and jokes with his family and friends. He studied his work carefully and put in long hours so that he would become an expert in his profession. This compulsion toward expertise carried over into all his endeavors. He may have held several jobs during these years, and he may have thought about owning several different businesses, but there was one ambition that remained constant: that of having some affiliation with the land. Also in the early years he acquired a consciousness toward personal health that would lead him into a practice of self-experimentation and into numerous controversies with those who disagreed with him. Finally, he indicated that he was not content to remain within the limits that had been set for him—for example, becoming a rabbi or entering a business acceptable for Jews, such as clothing. Rather, he would set his own goals and work hard for their fulfillment. Already he was on the road to becoming an "apostle of nonconformity."

CHAPTER 3

The House of Rodale

When he was twenty-five years old and an employee of Robertson, Furman, and Murphy, J. I. Rodale wrote two treatises that hardly changed the world but did show that he had become competent in his field. One was entitled "Wartime Depreciation and Open Hearth Steelplates and Rolling Mills," published first in the magazine of the national Association of Cost Accountants and reprinted in the national *Income Tax Magazine*. The other was "Charging Depreciation on Cost Value or Replacement Value," again written for the Association of Cost Accountants.

Turning from these weighty questions, J.I.'s next major writing effort came in 1927 when he responded to an invitation from the Lower Manhattan Industrial Association to submit a proposed solution to New York's growing traffic congestion. As *The New York Times* of June 19, 1927, reported, he wanted to enlarge the scope of "one-way thoroughfares from the streets to certain avenues." The plan he described was in fact an early version of the entry and exit procedures used today on interstate highways:

"A car desiring to cross Fourth Avenue at Twentieth Street, for example, will have to turn in with the stream of northward moving traffic. In doing this it hugs the curb on the left side of Fourth Avenue, which is comparatively simple, as there would be no southbound traffic as is the case now. The mass of traffic moving northward can easily digest such side-street traffic, because the main stream will keep to the centre of the avenue, leaving a lane on each side of the street, which may be used by cars from the side streets in turning into the avenue.

"The car then gradually edges its way toward the right, so that by the time it reaches Twenty-second Street it is close to the curb, which makes it easy to turn eastward into Twenty-second Street. The same method would be followed in cars from the side streets in turning into the avenue. ... The main idea behind this system is that traffic will be moving in a steady stream." Gradually the New York authorities implemented variations of J.I.'s plan. In December 1946, J.I. made a similar proposal to the Allentown Police Department.

Thus, J.I. was innovative and multifaceted from an early period in his life. He frequently referred to himself as a congenital compiler: "In the cradle I was already compiling, arranging, digesting. This is something you can't learn; it must be inherited along with narrow arteries [and] a supercharged thyroid . . ." Little wonder then that J.I. broke away from the confines of electrical manufacturing and went into the more exciting field of publishing at the earliest opportunity. His earnings in the electrical business gave him the necessary capital for his publishing ventures.

The Allentown *Morning Call* on December 7, 1930, published a story about *The Humorous Scrapbook*, just about to hit the market on a nationwide basis. J.I. got the idea for this journal by reading Mark Twain's opinion that someone would have a publishing success by reprinting interesting items from the past. The first and only issue of *The Humorous Scrapbook* was dated January–March 1931. The word "humorous" was somewhat a misnomer, for the little journal was filled with material not exactly designed to provoke mirth. It reprinted several stories from *Century Magazine*, excerpts from Dickens' *Pickwick Papers*, a short essay by Isaac Disraeli, father of the Prime Minister, and some of the writings of Robert Ingersoll. It was a nice, tidy little magazine that sold for a quarter. J.I. quickly discovered that even Mark Twain could have an erroneous opinion, that readers were more interested in contemporary problems than in things that belonged to a previous period. He accordingly discontinued *The Humorous Scrapbook*, after losing approximately $1,500 on its single issue.

J.I.'s next publishing venture was *The Clown* in 1934. With a budget of around $12,000, *The Clown* was an effort to make people laugh in the dark days of the Depression. It had a somewhat more successful career than *The Humorous Scrapbook*, because it stayed in existence long enough to have its name changed to *The American Humorist*. It soon failed, however, for the mid-1930s was no time for humor: "I thought the people wanted to laugh but they wanted to be sad." (At least this seemed to be true for the printed word, though radio comedians of this time were highly popular.)

Undaunted by these failures, J.I. continued to sink his financial resources into yet another magazine. *Health Digest* made its appearance in August 1935. The first issue contained articles about birth control in Germany, life in Ethiopia, and excerpts from Huey Long's filibusters in the U.S. Senate. From this point forward, though he did not make much profit, he never again suffered the financial losses that he did with *The Humorous Scrapbook* and *The Clown*. Between 1935 and 1940 he always had several magazines going at one time or another. These were *Fact Digest, Everybody's Digest, Biography, Science and Discovery, Health Guide, You Can't Eat That, You're Wrong About That, True Health Stories,* and *Modern Tempo.* He edited all of these publications himself in his office in Allentown, with a staff of one assistant. He did a tremendous amount of magazine reading to find articles suitable for his digest journals, and he was convinced that this training in the field of editing served him better than would any number of journalism courses.

One day in the late 1930s, while reading an English

publication, *Health For All*, he came across an article written by Sir Albert Howard, the famous British agriculturalist who had spent much of his life in India in pursuit of natural farming techniques. So excited was J.I. about what Howard said that he wrote to him. From this correspondence there developed a friendship between the two that led J.I. closer to his long-time dream of working directly with the land.

In the early 1940s, therefore, J.I. began to sell or otherwise dispose of all his journals to concentrate on a new magazine in farming. He was encouraged to do so from his reading of Howard's articles, from correspondence with him, and from reading *An Agricultural Testament*. He relinquished the last of his magazines in May 1943, when he made preliminary agreements with Publishers Service Company for the sale of *Fact Digest*, *Science and Discovery*, and *Health Guide*. The deal included all back numbers and the entire morgue. Selling price for the three magazines was $30,000.

Even before the transaction with Publishers Service Company, J.I. had begun publication of his farming magazine, which he first called *Organic Farmer*. Prior to publication, he sent thousands of brochures and subscription blanks to farmers throughout Pennsylvania and the eastern United States. He got orders for less than two dozen. He attributed this disaster to two main factors: first, he had aimed at large-scale farmers who were geared to wartime production; second, he had failed to consider the seasonal aspects of farming—that farmers are generally interested in articles that will be of assistance to them at the time of reading. J.I. accordingly changed the intended format of his magazine and retitled it *Organic Farming and Gardening*. The first issue, in May 1942, contained a statement of purposes and aims written by J.I., articles against the uses of tobacco and chemical fertilizers, a description of Howard's "Indore" method of composting, an article by Ehrinfried Pfeiffer on "biodynamic technology," and extracts from Charles Darwin's work on vegetable mold

and earthworms. The masthead listed J. I. Rodale as
the editor and a few editions later Sir Albert Howard as
the associate editor, a position Howard held until his
death in the late 1940s.

Several years after this initial edition, the magazine
was divided into two parts. *Organic Farmer* continued
to be slanted toward moderately sized agricultural endeavors, while *Organic Gardening* turned its attention
to the ever-growing urban and suburban communities
with an appeal to city dwellers to grow at least some of
their own food. *Organic Farmer* was issued as an inde-
pendent publication from 1949 through 1953. In January 1954 it was merged with *Organic Gardening*. Since
that date, the main agricultural journal of the Rodale
Press has been *Organic Gardening and Farming*.
Though for the first ten or fifteen years of its existence
it operated at a loss, OGF circulation by the end of the
1960s was approaching one million.

In late 1971 a British edition of *Organic Gardening
and Farming* appeared. For some time J.I. had debated
whether to include organic gardening subjects in his
other English publications or to come out with a sepa-
rate magazine. He decided on the latter. It was unsuccessful, however, due partly to initial overinvestments.
The British edition of OGF was discontinued in September 1972.

Though OGF is the oldest current Rodale magazine,
it did not always remain J.I.'s favorite. He was especially partial to *Prevention*, the first edition of which
was issued in June 1950. He was more interested in the
health and nutritional aspects of gardening and farming
than in actually tilling the soil. A main reason for starting *Prevention* was to alert the big-city dweller to the
possibilities of obtaining wholesome food either through
selective buying or through finding a minute plot on
which to grow a few vegetables. The first issue of *Prevention* was devoted almost entirely to polio, with one
article on the benefits of bone meal. "What *Prevention*
soon became," said J.I. years later, "was a medical

journal for the people, over 90% of the material being excerpted from medical journals and other orthodox medical sources, always the name and date of the sources being given, but written so that the average person could understand it. . . . Yes, that was a day! The day we began publishing *Prevention!*" Today, the American circulation of *Prevention* is well over a million and *Prevention* book club sells health books to subscribers. In 1955, J.I. in a letter to H. Curtis Wood estimated that the number of medical doctors who read *Prevention* each month was between 2,000 and 5,000.

In 1956, a British version of *Prevention* appeared and is still being printed. Efforts were made in the mid-1960s to start a French *Prevention*, but French corporation laws made the effort economically unworkable because, as in England, J.I. wanted to sell food supplements as a part of his publishing venture. Today, English *Prevention* is selling in the French market and is attempting to open operations in Germany as the Common Market becomes more of a fixed idea in Europe.

Throughout the 1950s, Rodale Press concentrated on *Organic Gardening and Farming* and *Prevention*, to the exclusion of almost everything else in the magazine field. Sometime in the mid-1950s J.I. did publish a journal, first called the *Journal of Clinical Nutrition* and later the *American Journal of Clinical Nutrition*, under the imprint "Nutritional Press." According to J.I. in his book *An Organic Trip to England*, the various journals of the American Medical Association used a great quantity of the materials that were printed in this publication (p. 61).

In the spring of 1960 a new journal was brought out, called *Compost Science*, subtitled *Journal of Waste Recycling*. This magazine, still going today, is slanted toward city governments, offering suggestions on how to reclaim plant nutrients in municipal refuse. It abounds with articles by university scientists on how the cost of municipal composting can be made feasible, and it also advertises several machines to do the job. It is, apparently, a widely used and respected journal among directors of city governments.

In August 1964, J.I. began publishing yet another magazine, this one having little to do with farming and health. It was *Quinto Lingo*, an effort that complemented J.I.'s long affinity for dabbling with words. His first venture in devising methods of foreign-language instruction was in the late 1930s, when he created card games that required the use of French, German, and Spanish words. He sold his card game to the Wible Language Institute in Allentown and turned his attention to printing books in the three languages. Next he decided that jokes provided good and enjoyable ways of studying a foreign language, so he began to collect anecdotes in French, German, and Spanish, intending to use them in a new foreign-language magazine. The joke idea expanded into producing a new magazine each month on a special subject such as painting, safety, and prisons, which would include news items, essays, short stories, and a page or two of jokes.

Originally the magazine was intended for only four languages—German, French, Spanish, and English. The pages were to consist of four columns with the material duplicated in the four languages. Before publication date in August 1964, however, J.I. decided to add an additional language—Italian—to his format. Thus, the new journal was dubbed *Quinto Lingo*. Rodale Press published it from 1964 to September 1971, when it was sold to Learn-En-Joy, Inc., of Arlington, Virginia.

J.I.'s love for and long affiliation with New York caused him in 1966 to start *Rodale's New York*. This was mostly a forum for J.I.'s never-ending stream of articles, essays, and reviews. He wrote the bulk of the material himself for this journal, with pieces about health and gardening, play reviews, and excerpts from diaries kept while on trips abroad. It moved closer to being a theater journal when its name was changed nine months after its appearance to *Rodale's Revue*.

Even with its new title, it did not succeed; the last issue was in January 1967.

Perhaps *Rodale's Revue* folded, in part, because of J.I.'s interest in a journal to support the legitimate theater. The first edition of *Theatre Crafts* appeared in 1967. For years J.I. had been interested in the theater, even to keeping a file on those words that, for some reason or other, made audiences laugh. He found two words that did it, he said, every time: "cockroach" and "Lithuanian." For a while J.I. wrote a column, "In the Theatre," for *Backstage*, a New York journal. Ultimately, he became a co-publisher of *Backstage* because he thought it would become one of the most important "newspapers" in the industry, and he was "willing to back it until it did." *Theatre Crafts*, however, took precedence over *Backstage* because it was devoted more to the stage than to show business in general and because it complemented J.I.'s new career of the mid-1960s, that of writing plays. *Theatre Crafts* is still a Rodale publication.

In late 1967 Rodale Press started *Fitness for Living*, a magazine that combined much of what was found in *OGF* and *Prevention*, with an emphasis on physical exercise. In early 1970, still another magazine came from J.I.'s ubiquitous pen. This one, *Yiddish Lingo*, had the purpose of showing the beauty of Yiddish and making a contribution to keeping it alive as a language. It did not succeed, however, because possible subscribers wrote in to say that Israeli Hebrew was the modern language and that Yiddish was either dead or dying. The magazine lasted for only one year, with its final issue in January 1971.

In addition to these magazines, the Rodale Press has also published numerous newsletters designed primarily as public relations devices. The first of these was the *Health Bulletin*, which made its debut in March 1963. Its inception was in 1961, when J.I. began thinking about a weekly newsletter to be distributed free to newspapers, legislators, and executives of large corporations. Since it was the first of the Rodale newsletters, *Health Bulletin* caused something of a stir within the Rodale editorial staff. One staff assistant was opposed to the idea, believing that more could be learned about health in *Prevention* than in a newsletter. He did feel, however, that a new department in *Prevention* called "organic living" would be worthwhile in alerting readers to the problems of the modern world. Other employees were enthusiastic about the idea, some with the feeling that *Health Bulletin* should concentrate on activities of the Food and Drug Administration and the Federal Trade Commission.

Two other considerations arose in connection with *Health Bulletin*. Originally the newsletter was to be called *Health News*, but Clyde Irion of Belmont, California, was publishing *Health News Digest*, causing the Rodale title to be *Health Bulletin*. For several months J.I. held back on publication of *Health Bulletin* until he could find an adequate editorial staff. For a time he thought of offering Irion a position as Rodale western correspondent, but he finally settled on the idea of a Washington office with Wade H. Jones as the editor. With much of its editorial content written in Washington, *Health Bulletin* could be, and was intended to be, a resource journal for health- and environment-minded legislators. *Health Bulletin* ran from 1963 to April 1970, was discontinued for two months, started again in July 1970, and stopped for good in June 1972, because its ideas were being spread more effectively through the regular Rodale publications.

The majority of the other Rodale newsletters belong to the early 1970s. For example, these appeared in 1970: *Environment Action Bulletin*, to help guide government officials in pollution control; *Executive Fitness Newsletter*, describing exercises that desk-bound businessmen can do; and *Organic Food Marketing*, to aid producers of organic food in selling their produce. In 1972, after J.I.'s death, these were started: *Organic Family Farming, YMCA Fitness Finders Newsletter*,

The Soil and Health Foundation News, Organic Gardening Club Newsletter, and *Lehigh Valley Organic Shopper* (later changed to *Lehigh Valley's Better Foods Shopper*). All but the *Lehigh Valley's Better Foods Shopper* (discontinued in September 1972) are still being published.

Over a space of years, therefore, J.I. built up a sizable repertory of magazines and newsletters, the bulk of them dealing with health and related activities but still having enough diversity to cover other subjects such as the theater and language studies. J.I. personally read everything that went into the magazines and most of the material that was printed in the newsletters. As if this were not enough, J.I. constantly thought of new things to do. One of his friends referred to his propensity in this regard as "idearrhea," comparing it to "diarrhea," or a "continuous flow."

For example, in his diary for 1953 he talked at length about a new magazine he planned to publish, to be entitled *The Lighter Medical Side* or *The Literary Medical Side.* Also, he thought about a medical journal dealing exclusively with statistics: "I know that statistics are not being studied properly by physicians. . . . I believe that a very interesting magazine with light medical statistics and articles interpreting them should be read. None of these magazines would have a very high circulation, but are badly needed." He toyed with the idea of getting into Christmas tree light manufacturing; he wanted to start a clinic in Allentown and staff it with physicians who would examine people from a nutritional viewpoint; he thought of establishing an orphanage in the Allentown area, giving the children organic foods only and following their progress until they were twenty-three years old (this idea, as well as the nutritional clinic, has recently been revived by officials at Rodale Press); he planned to set up an extensive laboratory to study the effects of electricity and magnetism on growing plants. There apparently was no end to the ideas and innovations issuing from J.I.'s fertile brain. In the 1953 diary entry he described his methods: "I have a system by which if I want to be reminded of an idea later, I mark a P on the upper right hand corner of the sheet, write the idea down, and then my secretary, Vernice [Kemmerer], puts it in my pending file which consists of one folder for every day of the month. Then each day she puts a folder on my desk and I go through the 5 or 6 things that are in there, taking out those that require action, leaving those in that I want to see later on. Thus, an idea keeps on coming to me and is not lost."

J.I. extended the House of Rodale with an involvement in various foreign operations. In the early 1950s he became affiliated for a short time with the Madaus Company of Cologne, Germany, a manufacturer of drugs. After several initial reservations, he agreed to the German commitment because they made all of their drugs from plants that were organically grown. A 1953 diary entry showed his thoughts about the Madaus operation: "I don't believe in drugs but I figured people are getting sick every day anyhow, so if we cure them with better drugs, safer drugs, grown organically from plants, I would be doing some good."

Also he became involved in selling vitamins and natural food supplements in England and Europe in connection with *Prevention*. The Organic Vitamin Company was formed to supply vitamins to people of the British Isles who thought J.I.'s ideas were sound. In time this company outdistanced all others in selling natural vitamin supplements in England. Today, J.I. Rodale and Company, Ltd., in England sells "natrodale" products, which range all the way from acerola capsules to hand lotion.

Many of J.I.'s critics in the United States have long speculated about the nature of his American advertising. For example, advertised products such as bone meal and desiccated liver make no specific claim about their ability to deal with certain health problems. Articles in *Prevention*, however, and in other Rodale magazines praise these products and make claims for them that the advertisements cannot. The critics, therefore, wonder if J.I. ever owned any interest in the companies who advertised in his journals and did business in the United States. If this were so, unlike in England and certain European countries, he would quite possibly be creating legal difficulties.

There seems to be no evidence to support the theory that J.I. owned, in whole or in part, any of the companies that advertised in his American journals. On February 4, 1952, he did write in a letter to Joseph Frazer, president of an engineering company in New York: "Incidentally, I believe we could be of help to you in bringing business your way. Personally I do not want to benefit from this in any manner for I am vitally interested in the movement to improve our soil and our food. But we do have the Soil and Health Foundation [formed in the late 1940s, discussed in Chapter 5] which is giving grants to institutions. 99% of the money received goes to these institutions. No salaries are taken. I'm wondering if we can work out an arrangement so that if we can get you some business, would you earmark a certain percentage of this business to the Soil and Health Foundation? This offer of course is subject to your investigating on the foundation to see whether it is honestly run and the money used in a field that will eventually mean more business for your [compost] digestors."

By February 20, J.I. had had second thoughts about his letter of the fourth. He wrote to Frazer again that it would be unethical to ask for a commission for recommending Frazer digestors: "After thinking it over I found that that would be quite wrong, for that would influence us in making recommendations. I would rather that our service be based on a study of the situation and a recommendation for what we think is the best process for the work." Wherever legal, as in England and certain parts of Europe, it seems that J.I. did own companies in whole or in part that advertised in his or other magazines; wherever legal problems were highly predictable, as in the United States, it seems he did not. (Actually, there is no law in the United States forbidding a vitamin and food supplement company, or for that matter any other company, from publishing its own magazine. The Food and Drug Administration, however, can interpret articles in such magazines as labeling for products and can seize the products for false labeling if they do not agree with the editorial statements about them. The action in these cases was always taken against the products, not against the pieces of writing that explained them).

Though magazine and newsletter publishing was a prime effort of Rodale Press, books were a major concern as well. Most of J.I.'s own books came out under the Rodale imprint, but he also published volumes that had little to do with health, gardening, and farming. In the late 1930s and on into the 1940s, he conducted a lengthy correspondence with several well-known authors in an effort to publish or republish something they had written.

One was Upton Sinclair, who in 1906 had become famous for his muckraking novel about the Chicago meat industry, *The Jungle*. In 1938 arrangements were made for Rodale Press to bring out an edition of a Sinclair novel, *The Flivver King*. When he signed the reprint contracts, Sinclair gave an insight into the type of reader attracted by his books: "Answering your questions about advertising, the only places I have found who pay with my books are liberal magazines, *The Nation*, *The New Republic*, *Commonsense*, *The New Yorker*, and the *Christian Century* of Chicago. The readers of the Communist and Socialist papers are interested in my books, but apparently have not the money to buy cloth bound books. I've also found the *New York Times* and *Herald Tribune* reviews and *Saturday Review of Literature* worthwhile. Daily papers and the general magazines would hardly pay because only a small percentage of their readers are book-buyers."

As time passed the relationship grew between J.I. and Sinclair. In May 1939, J.I. suggested that Sinclair submit an "anonymous" novel to Rodale Press. This did not materialize because Sinclair had other commitments for his work. J.I. apparently had also approached Sinclair to write a novel about the fast-growing organic movement in the United States. Sinclair scotched both the idea of his own anonymous novel and the one about organic farming when he wrote to J.I. in May 1939: "As it happens, I have an anonymous novel, written by a friend of mine called *Dear Janie.* . . . My name is not to be mentioned in connection with it. You will understand my position when I tell you that I am about ⅓ of the way through what is going to be the longest novel I have ever written. The scenes are laid in Europe during the last 25 years. I have never been able to use other persons' ideas successfully. I have so many of my own that I cannot write them."

In January 1943, Rodale Press published another Sinclair novel, *Our Lady.* After this event, there was a lapse in the two men's correspondence with each other, but J.I. still did not give up the idea of having Sinclair do an organic novel. Sinclair again rejected the suggestion in June 1944 and said: "My dear Rodale. Bless your heart. Of course I remember you. And I'm never going to forget you or your oddly named town." Other matters of mutual interest between J.I. and Sinclair included some of the plays Sinclair wrote. In 1962 J.I. became interested in stage productions and wanted to put on a Sinclair play, probably *Cicero,* which they had talked about earlier. Sinclair wrote to J.I. on June 27, 1962: "Dear Rodale. Of course it's ok to try out my plays in your school [discussed in Chapter 9]. Report results. As ever, Upton Sinclair."

Another prominent author with whom J.I. had dealings was historical novelist Kenneth Roberts. In

August 1954, J.I. showed that he was still interested in publishing an organic novel. He asked Roberts to do one in much the same way that Sinclair had done *The Jungle*. It did not take long for Roberts to respond, negatively. In a letter of August 6, Roberts said the suggestion was out of the question because he had so much work on hand that it would be impossible to take on anything else. Roberts was, however, favorable to J.I.'s organic gardening program. "The greatest hurdle to surmount," he added, "is the impossibility of small home gardeners finding room, or being able to go to the trouble of making muck piles." Throughout his entire career, J.I. kept talking about the "great organic novel." For a time he thought about writing it himself, but he preferred to be its publisher. Such a novel is yet to be written.

One author from whom J.I. sought advice in connection with his "word" books and other matters was H. L. Mencken. First, J.I. wanted Mencken to do an introduction to a proposed biography of Upton Sinclair that J.I. presumably planned to publish. After this refusal, Mencken turned down J.I. again on a request to assess a manuscript: "I have ceased to do book reviews, and I have been under a long standing oath to avoid blurbs." In the early 1940s J.I. must have forwarded a stack of his "word" books to Mencken, for on September 21, 1942, Mencken wrote: "Unhappily I am only slightly interested in pedagogical enterprises, and so I fear I can't give you any effective help with your books. ... My private belief is that all attempts to reduce English to rules must fail inevitably in the long run. The people always break through such rules. I see no objection to that fact. Indeed, it is the main reason why English continues to be alive."

In 1939 the Rodale Press published a book by Cyril Clemens called *My Cousin, Mark Twain*. To do the introduction, J.I. engaged renowned author Booth Tarkington. Shortly after the appearance of Clemens' book, J.I. heard from the Limited Editions Club in New

York that Tarkington's introduction was a duplication of the one he had done for their edition of *Huckleberry Finn* and was thus a violation of the copyright laws.

Tarkington's secretary, Elizabeth Cotten, stated in a letter to J.I. in June 1939 that she and Tarkington had assumed that Clemens knew the introduction had been used before and would obtain the necessary permissions. Tarkington offered to assume the amount of any obligation that might be forthcoming to the Limited Editions Club. J.I., however, thought it best to wait until the club mentioned the matter again and to look on the experience as an object lesson. J.I. believed that the club would not "demand its pound of flesh. We are sincere when we state that we are interested in seeing the printed word go as far as possible and we are not exactly trying to get the last penny that it is possible to squeeze out of our books and magazines." Apparently, the matter was indeed dropped, but from then on J.I. was much more astute in checking out sources and reprint permissions.

Louis Bromfield was another famous author J.I. tried to interest in Rodale publications. He sent Bromfield a copy of *Organic Gardening* in 1943, which impressed Bromfield because "all the plans seem to agree very closely with a great many ideas I have held for a long time." A letter from Bromfield on May 24, 1945, indicated that he was favorable to becoming an honorary director of J.I.'s Soil and Health Foundation, then in its incipient stages.

For years J.I. tried to publish Bromfield's books, but could not because of Bromfield's contractual agreements with Harper's in New York. By the mid 1950s, however, J.I. and Bromfield had become disenchanted with each other. For some reason, Bromfield lost his earlier affinity with organic methods and began attacking the system. In a letter of April 5, 1954, to Mrs. F. D. Roosevelt, Jr., J.I. summed up his feelings about Bromfield: "You may be interested to know that Mr. Bromfield is far from an organic farmer. In his first book, *Pleasant Valley*, he spoke well of the organic farming people, but in his later books he attacked us actually. I believe it was when he got ideas of possibly becoming Secretary of Agriculture if Dewey had been elected that made him veer toward the orthodox chemical methods. I was amazed at reading his book, *Roots in the Earth* to hear him taking us to task as cultists."

J.I. continued his efforts to involve famous personalities in his publishing ventures when he asked feminist Carrie Chapman Catt to do an introduction to a book he was planning about elderly people. She refused, on January 25, 1938, by saying: "I am much behind in my work and would probably not be able to get to it. While I am not as old as some folks are, my capacity for turning out work, I regret to say, is much diminished." Other figures with whom J.I. dealt in some fashion or other included Pearl S. Buck, who told him in a letter of January 7, 1947: "I am interested in hearing of your ideas of compost fertilizing. I believe in this, very much." Another was the comedian Sam Levinson, who turned down an offer to write an introduction to a Rodale book. There was also Frederic Dannay, known to the world as Ellery Queen, who suggested a mystery and detective series in Rodale publications. Harold Ickes wrote to say that he had authored some columns in the past on organics, "and our reckless dealings with our natural resources generally." Movie actors were among those who supported the organic and antichemical fertilizer activities in Emmaus. These included Henry Fonda, Robert Young, Robert Cummings, who congratulated J.I. on his "enormous patience and courage in gathering all that material and setting it down in such a simple, understandable form," and Eddie Albert, who not only lauded the organic system but conversed with J.I. about some of J.I.'s plays, notably the last one J.I. ever wrote, *John Hancock: Portrait of an Empty Barrel.*

In striving to build his publishing enterprises, J.I.

probably got more than his share of turndowns from famous personalities. As time passed, he became less and less inclined to contact them in efforts to get them to write books for him or to "decorate" other Rodale books with their introductions. Increasingly, his interests veered toward the reprint market—especially of those books that could be designated as "classics."

Even as early as the mid-1930s J.I. had distributed copies of a volume he called the *Golden Book*, which printed short stories by famous authors and included excerpts from the world's classics. One day, long after the *Golden Book* was discontinued, J.I. came across some old copies, and this gave him the idea for a project he called Story Classics. These were reprints of some of the world's most famous literature. They included such selections as Longfellow's *Continental Tales*, Chekhov's *The Beggar* and *The Seagull*, selected stories of Alphonse Daudet, Pedro Antonio de Alarcón's *Tales From the Spanish*, and Prosper Mérimée's *Tales of Love and Death*, and Molière's *The Doctor in Spite of Himself.*

The Story Classics, which began in the late 1940s, generally operated at a loss, though complete lines of them were sold in England and the Commonwealth countries. When he went to Germany to open discussions with the Madaus Drug Company, he returned via England. There he came into contact with William Green, who at that time was working for the Golden Cockerel Press. J.I. arranged for Green to represent the Rodale interests in England, thus beginning the chain of events that led to British *Prevention* and to a complete line of Story Classics. J.I. showed in his 1953 diary that he came close to believing in fate: "If it hadn't been for the fact that I was interested in the organic methods, I wouldn't have made Madaus [and hence would not have met Green]. If it hadn't been for my father's inordinate ambition for me, I wouldn't have been health conscious, and I wouldn't have found out about the organic method." Thus, "chains of events" and "chance happenings" were always auspicious occasions for J.I. This proclivity did indeed help his foes to criticize him on the grounds that he took the coincidental as "scientific proof" and regarded "chains of events" as tantamount to "cause and effect."

In 1955 four British Rodale books were selected for display at the International Book design exhibition, the most noticeable of which was Peter Schlemill's *Counterblast to Tobacco*. Rodale Press in England came in fifth at the exhibition in terms of appearance of books and numbers chosen for display. The publishers in front of Rodale were Oxford University Press, Cambridge University Press, Fabers, and Penguin.

J.I. wanted to extend his book publications into yet other areas. He was incensed at the dearth in the United States of popular books in foreign languages. Therefore, he began to publish books in French for distribution not only in France but in this country as well. Also, he was always on the lookout for foreign books to be translated and published in English. Once while in Madrid he found copies of Molinas' *Les Tres Maridos* and discovered that there was no English version of it. Also, Flaubert's *Idée Reçu* had apparently never appeared in English. These "finds" caused J.I. to come out with a new series in the mid-1950s called Classic Firsts, which generally followed the format of the Modern Library. They were without illustrations, sold for around $2.50 each, and represented an English translation for the first time. The Classic Firsts project was not ultimately successful because of difficulty in finding appropriate books.

During all the promotional activities for his publishing ventures, J.I. kept up an enormous stream of his own personal writings. Each month in *Organic Gardening and Farming* and *Prevention*, he wrote editorials or series of articles on things that interested him. As already noted, he personally supplied most of the material for *Rodale's New York* and considerable quantities of material for his other journals. In addition to these, he sporadically kept a diary and began work on his autobiography. He never lost his desire to write fiction. A diary entry of August 4, 1953, showed his continued interest: "I am reworking my novel again [probably *Tarry at Jericho*], and I've become so excited about it in view of the new action that I decided that I will write the first ten chapters thoroughly and then work on the last part of the book, the next 17, Book II, writing it extremely fast to indicate it as an outline to the publisher." He thought of Doubleday-Doran as his publisher for this novel, but apparently nothing ever came of it. (Garden City Press, a division of Doubleday, once brought out a quite successful edition of J.I.'s *Word Finder*.) J.I. later retitled *Tarry at Jericho* as the *Three Ambassador Men*. He also finished a novel manuscript called *Babylon*, as well as one titled *King David and Mr. Zimmerman*. The only novel he ever published was under his own imprint. Titled *The Stones of Jehosaphat*, it dealt with the amorous adventures of King David's favorite servant. This novel was part of J.I.'s series called the 64s. These were short works of approximately 15,000 words that became 64-page books. J.I. described the 64s in his book *Are We Really Living Longer?*: "The 64s are our answer to those polls which tend to indicate that books are losing out in public favor, that fewer people are buying books today than they did formerly. . . . Many a 300-page book could be done—and done better—in 64 pages." The overwhelming majority of the 64s—some two dozen of them—dealt with health, gardening, and farming.

Despite the manifold activities of Rodale Press, it never even remotely approached the size or output of the giant publishing companies in the United States. However, J.I. did have some contacts with them. He thought once about Doubleday as a distributing agent for him. This did not materialize, but in June 1970 he made arrangements with the David McKay Company "to distribute Rodale books in the trade in accordance with standard sales and distribution."

An article in *Time* magazine, March 22, 1971, called "Catching Up To Rodale Press," quoted J.I. as saying, "The health magazines are growing fast and the cash register is ringing." A while later, before an audience at the Allentown Art Museum J.I. claimed he was misquoted by *Time*: "We don't use cash registers, we use wheelbarrows." He went on to aver that he, as the company's chairman of the board, owned only three suits of clothes, but he had a shipping agent who owned eight. Certainly there is no doubt that J.I. was a millionaire, at least in the last fifteen or twenty years of his life. But he was the kind of millionaire traditionally respected the most by Americans—one who worked his way to the top after having been born into conditions that approached poverty. His magazine and book publishing, in addition to his other activities in electrical manufacturing and selling food supplements and vitamins in England and Europe, put him well over the million mark. There had been times, however, in the early days, when he had not made expenses.

Examining motives, one must ask if J.I. was sincere in putting out all his magazines, newsletters, and books. Did he really believe that organic methods were superior and that natural food supplements would help one retain health? Or did he merely hit upon a good way to make money? In respect to his newsletters, all of them—including *Health Bulletin*—were, and are, money losers. Long after he had reached financial independence, he still ventured forth with new ideas on alerting the citizenry to the dangers of chemicals in the form of fertilizers and food additives. Indeed, one of the major reasons he went into playwriting in the mid-1960s was that he thought this medium would be a successful way to get his message across.

His opponents claim that the newsletters are deliberately unprofitable—that he distributed them as lures for his more affluent publications, *OGF* and *Prevention*. There seems to be little basis for these assertions. The critics have also faulted him for accepting paid advertisements in his magazines, as though this widely accepted practice were some kind of transgression. In view of J.I.'s very early references to health and farming—in his 1917-1923 letters to Ludwig, for example—he did not just suddenly realize that activities and publications in these fields would be profitable. Of course he made money—ultimately. Certainly he had a cocky nature—this is traditionally true of those millionaires who come from a poor background. And definitely he had debunking characteristics. Such characteristics, however, generally come from dedication to a cause that is not completely tied up with making money. He was wrong on numerous occasions, but then one can never know if he is right about something unless he is willing to take the chance of being wrong. J.I. was by no means a specialized man—he went wherever the facts led him. He often remarked that the bane of modern civilization is specialization into narrow fields that dictated against seeing the interrelationships of things as a whole. Even if it could be shown that he was insincere in the beginning, that all he wanted to do was make money, one would still have to cope with the seriousness of his beliefs in later years. In America, much stock has always been placed not on what a man *is* but on what he ultimately *becomes*. This is probably the most important reason today why J. I. Rodale's "message" is so much in demand.

Of the twenty magazines and nine newsletters that have been published in the history of Rodale Press, five of the magazines and seven of the newsletters still exist. Today the "House of Rodale" employs nearly a thousand people in its various activities of electrical manufacturing and book and magazine publishing. Its main publishing building is located at "Organic Park" in Emmaus. In raising his "house," J.I. came a long, long way from his days of grocery delivery on Norfolk Street.

CHAPTER 4

"Natural Farming"—A Brief History

J. I. Rodale, as the publisher of numerous digest magazines, scanned an unusually large number of journals and books each month to glean materials from them. His long-time interest in the land and his productions of *Organic Gardening and Farming* caused him to extol "natural" processes as opposed to artificial. This did not lead him into a condemnation of individual farmers who used chemical fertilizers, pesticides, insecticides, and so on; but it did produce a long-time controversy between him and the producers of such things, and it intensified his persuasive talents in trying to bring farmers back to the older, more traditional ways of treating the soil. He lamented organizational structures that made it well-nigh impossible to pinpoint any one individual or even a group responsible for the flood of chemical and artificial devices used in agriculture. The impersonal character of big industry as it affected farming techniques was, in J.I.'s opinion, one of the greatest dangers faced by modern man.

In a real sense, there is no such thing as "natural" farming. Any kind of deliberate cultivation, whether "organic" or "chemical," is essentially destructive of natural balances. In this context, man has not farmed "naturally" since Neolithic times. Before that period, man was a "food-gathering" instead of a "food-cultivating" animal. Of course, J.I. did not deny the demand on the land that any type of farming imposed upon it. He came to believe, however, that the straight organic method was more benign than the others, that it would replenish the soil most effectively for future farming endeavors. Keeping the soil in good condition—not necessarily producing a bigger and better crop—became the credo of the "natural" farmers in the twentieth century.

Throughout the history of the Western World, there have been those who wrote agricultural treatises. Because of their profound influence upon J.I. Rodale and others, it will be useful to examine a few of them. It is noteworthy that most of the agricultural essayists, especially those in the United States, were only informally trained in agrarian ways. By no means were they specialists, most having a multitude of jobs in other areas. Interesting, too, is the similarity of much of their advice to that which can be found today in organic literature. Let us begin with a brief description of some Roman writers.

The first essayist to be considered is Cato the Censor, a Roman citizen who lived from 234 to 149 B.C. Of course, the agricultural methods of his day were purely "organic," since the "chemical revolution" did not occur until the mid-1840s.

Cato continued the practice that all civilizations have had—that of lauding the virtues of the agricultural classes, sometimes to a point of disproportion. He stated in his book On Agriculture: "It is from the farming class that the bravest men and the sturdiest soldiers come, their calling is most highly respected, their livelihood is most assured and is looked on with the least hostility, and those who engage in that pursuit are least inclined to be disaffected." Cato's book is really more a manual of farm operations than a treatise on agriculture. He gave long descriptions, for example, of the duties of masters, overseers, and workers and of how to make compost out of straw, lupines, chaff, beanstalks, husks, and oak leaves. Practical advice abounded throughout his work—all the way from considerations a person should have when he buys a farm to divisions of labor on the farm itself.

The Roman poet Vergil (70-19 B.C.) noted that agriculture always comes at a price. As T. R. Glover, in his 1904 biography of Vergil said: "The forest had to come down; the land on which it stood had been idle for years, and man required it. But while the axes swung and the trees fell, the young poet ... saw the havoc made of the birds' immemorial homes; he saw the frightened birds hovering in the air over the spot where they were to build no more: and though he hailed the cultivated field that was to be, he never forgot the sorrow of the birds. ... In later days Vergil lingered in his story of the reclaiming of the land to pity the ruin of its most ancient inhabitants" (p. 15). Vergil often asserted in his writings, notably the *Georgics*, that life on a farm is hard but that man's life from the beginning of time had been so and that this hardness accounted for advances in civilization.

The ancient writer who came closest perhaps to describing what would later be the organic farmer's basic tenets was Pliny the Elder (A.D. 23-79). In his massive *Natural History*, he included an entire volume on agriculture.

Pliny's advice on land fertility was not unlike that given by J.I. and others in the organic movement: "The plan of improving one soil by means of another, ... throwing a rich earth on top of a poor one or a light porous soil on one that is moist, ... is an insane procedure . . ." He described the various manures that were used in Rome and its provinces: marl, ash, stable dung, dust, and lupines, among other things, and gave instructions on how to build a compost heap: "[Make] dung-heaps in the open-air in a hole in the ground made so as to collect moisture, and [cover] the heaps with straw to prevent their drying up in the sun." A hard oak stake should be driven into the ground next to the dung heap to keep serpents away. The dung, when under preparation, periodically should be passed through a sieve, with the "stench and look of it being transformed by the action of time into something actually attractive." When dung is being scattered on the ground, care should be taken that the sun is not too hot and the dung not too strong. The wind should be from the west during dung-distributing time, and the moon should be in its "dry phases."

Pliny got close to modern organicists and ecologists when he used portions of his book to complain about certain practices that had begun to creep into Roman agriculture. Saying that man imputed his own crimes and faults to Nature, he averred that ". . . we dye even the rivers and the elemental substances of Nature, and turn the very means of life into a bane. . . . Let us therefore confess our guilt, we who are not content even with Natural products . . ."

Pliny also lamented the passing of the old ways of Roman agriculture. He saw that the Romans' agrarian heritage as it had come to them from the Greeks was slipping away. In the old days, generals and even kings had been proud to be engaged in agricultural pursuits. To give instructions in agriculture had been of the highest dignity. "But nowadays," he regretted, "agricultural operations are performed by slaves with fettered ankles and by the hands of malefactors with branded faces!" He mourned the demise of the small farm: "If the truth be confessed, large estates have been the ruin of Italy, and are now proving the ruin of the provinces too . . ." Largeness and specialization of labor were two chief reasons for the decline of Roman agriculture and hence Roman power. Some contemporary historians, Arnold Toynbee among them, give the implication in their writings that the United States at present occupies much the same relationship to western Europe as Rome occupied to the Hellenic civilization of Pliny's day. Many observers feel that the amount of distortion of legitimate agriculture is directly proportional to the decline of a civilization. Therefore, organicists claim that their work is not really a matter of profits and losses but of survival itself.

After the decline of Rome, major agricultural activities shifted to western Europe, where, before the discovery of America, they found their highest calling in

Spain. There the Moors had many talents for farming and for commercial enterprises. As a group, they fit Toynbee's description of a minority becoming adept at developing special skills in one or two areas because of the majority barring them from other pursuits. The expulsion of the Moors along with the discovery of America by Columbus in late fifteenth century marked the points at which Spain's great powers began to decline.

With Spain's growing weakness, England became more and more important. Agriculturally, England developed grain growing and animal husbandry. As time passed, garden culture to supply the table with salads and greens became a leading practice. The first American colonists used only a modicum of the English agricultural experiences. The colonists developed agrarian practices in the context of English tradition and native American procedures.

There is much evidence to show that the earliest colonists were not primarily interested in agriculture. Only a third of the Jamestown Colony was assigned agricultural duties, and their crops for the first year or two were miserable failures. Lyman Carrier, in *The Beginnings of Agriculture in America* (1923), said that it was not until 1609 "that the conceit of the English was sufficiently humbled so they could take instruction in agriculture from the Natives" (p. 119). John Smith's "work or starve" decree also helped considerably in producing an American agriculture.

The chief money crop in early America, one that indeed saved the life of the Jamestown Colony, was tobacco. It is understandable, due to tobacco's economic significance, that the colonists sometimes made extravagant claims for the "Jamestown weed." It was argued in some circles, for example, that tobacco smoke was magnetic; thus, if it were inhaled into the lungs it would gather up all the impurities therein and expel them. Tobacco was just one of numerous plants in the colonies that were related in some way to preventive and curative medicine.

This relationship of agriculture to medicinal factors has always affected man's thinking. Pliny, for example, included long descriptions of plant concoctions for various ailments and conditions: turnips for chilblains, parsnip as an aphrodisiac, leeks for nosebleed, garlic for asthma, lettuce for toothache, cabbage juice for earache, asparagus for improved vision, poppies for sleep inducement, hemp seeds for making animals impotent.

In the American colonies the connection between health and botany was evident from the beginning. Colonial pharmacists roamed throughout the woods and fields in search of leaves, roots, and herbs that would have medical value. In their diaries and other writings the colonists gave detailed descriptions of plants, where they grew, and what their purposes were. This closeness between plants and health continued on into the federal period of our history as "herbal" doctors became a breed of their own. Even into our own time, we either put much stock in, or at least are fascinated by, "folk medicine." A book in 1958, *Folk Medicine*, by D. C. Jarvis, medical doctor and member of the American Medical Association, received a wide following. J. I. Rodale definitely continued the tradition with his suggestions for eating certain plants and berries, not as a cure but as a preventive. He included in this category items like sunflower seeds, pumpkin seeds, hawthorne berries, and rose hips. Whether one agrees or not that these practices are beneficial, one should at least recognize that they go back to the earliest times in this country. J. I. Rodale was most assuredly not the inventor of the tradition, but he became one of its foremost practitioners.

The art of agriculture in the United States was developed slowly in relation to trade and industry. As Milton Whitney pointed out in *Soil and Civilization* (1925), industries like transportation and clothing "have a start over agriculture of perhaps 150 years. This means literally that at the time of the signing of the Constitution of the United States the industries ... above named were no further advanced than agriculture is today." Whitney made the statement in 1925, and in a distinct way, agriculture is still in the process of evolution.

One important aspect of a developing American agriculture was the government's role in it. Efforts were made as early as 1796 to create an American Society of Agriculture with a secretary paid by the government. After the failure of this proposal, there were periodic attempts to create some kind of governmentally sponsored agricultural organization. For years the Patent Office contained an agricultural division, whose job was mostly the gathering of statistics on farms and farm personnel. Efforts were made, too, to establish ties between federal and state governments. In 1859, for example, a bill sponsored by Justin Morrill of Vermont and passed by Congress allowed federal lands in certain states to be used for agricultural experimentation. The bill fell, however, to President James Buchanan's veto. (Later, in Lincoln's presidency, the Morrill bill, laying the foundation for the land-grant colleges, was passed.) Finally, in May 1862 an agricultural department won the approval of Congress and President Lincoln. Its duties were to gather statistics, collect and distribute seeds and plants, answer inquiries from farmers, undertake chemical analysis of plants, soils, and fertilizers, establish professorships, and organize an agricultural library. The first Commissioner of Agriculture was Isaac Newton, who came from New Jersey. Many organicists of today feel that the department's power is too great and should be curtailed, that it has become too much the tool of the big agricultural chemical enterprises.

It was not until the 1740s that agricultural literature began in America. In 1748 Jared Eliot of New Haven, Connecticut, published his first essay in agriculture, an event, said Carrier, that "induced others to start farm journals or diaries in which they recorded their observations and experiences" (p. 229). Commercial farm journals, however, were a long time in gaining popularity, due primarily to the American farmer's propensity to distrust the written word and to pay attention only to those articles he could use at the time of reading.

Jared Eliot was a physician and clergyman as well as a farmer; he personified the versatility of the colonial period. In the preface of his first essay he showed the necessity for agricultural literature in America: "There are sundry Books on Husbandry wrote [sic] in England: Having read all on that Subject I could obtain; yet such is the difference of Climate and method of Management between them and us, arising from Causes that must make them always differ, so that those Books are not very Useful to us" (p. 2). As had most agricultural essayists before him, Eliot regretted the lack of attention given to farming literature: "It is acknowledged by our best Writers, That while other parts of Learning less useful, have been cultivated, Agriculture or Husbandry, has been strangely Neglected. Some suppose the Reason of this Neglect is, that the Subject is too low for polite writers." In his essays, Eliot gave practical advice on the drainage of lands and on the proper distribution of fertilizers. He felt that much of the colonial farming experience dealt with enriching the soil because the "unacquaintedness" of the country caused the first settlers to choose the worst lands. Worn-out lands, he said, could be restored by planting wild clover and spreading shell sand and dung over it.

Eliot spoke of some agricultural societies coming into existence in Scotland, one in Edinburgh and one in Ormistown, and suggested that "If something of this Nature were set on foot in this country, it might be of Advantage" (p. 13). It was not until after the Revolution, however, that such societies were born. The Society for Promoting and Improving Agriculture and Other Rural Concerns was organized in South Carolina in 1784; similar societies were formed in New York,

1791; Massachusetts, 1792; and Connecticut, 1794. These organizations held meetings from time to time at which papers on agricultural methods and experiments were presented. Some even published agricultural journals for their membership.

In addition to the various state societies, several individuals by the revolutionary period had become prominent for their work in agriculture. There were, for example, John Winthrop, Jr., whose experiments in brewing beer from corn were well known; John Bartram, who established a botanical garden on the Schuylkill River in Pennsylvania to grow native American plants; John Binns of Loudon, Connecticut, who experimented with gypsum as a fertilizer; George Washington, who used English essayist Jethro Tull's methods of farming in crop rotation and fertilizing; and Edmund Ruffin of Virginia, who became perhaps the most celebrated experimental farmer of his day. Since the revolutionary period in America, agriculture has always been under one form of experimentation or other.

The coming of the industrial revolution to the United States caused profound changes in agriculture. As people moved to the cities to take up factory jobs, farming gradually became more a specialized endeavor than a family concern. Efforts were made to grow more food on less land than ever before. This is why, in part, the work of a German chemist, Justus Liebig, ultimately became so important.

In his book *Organic Chemistry in Its Applications to Agriculture and Physiology* (1840?), Liebig said: "Perfect agriculture is the true foundation of all trade and industry, ... it is the foundation of the riches of states. But a rational system of agriculture cannot be formed without the application of scientific principles; for such a system must be based on an exact acquaintance with the means of nutrition of vegetables, and with the influence of soils and action of manure upon them." He seriously questioned the time-honored tradition of using manures for fertilization: "We discover ... that the excrements of men and animals are supposed to contain an incomprehensible something which assists in the nutrition of plants, and increases their size. This opinion is embraced without even an attempt being made to discover the component parts of manure, or to become acquainted with its nature. But what does the soil contain, and what are the components of the substances used as manure? Until these points are satisfactorily determined, a rational system of agriculture cannot exist" (pp. 188-189).

Liebig stated that crops were not always abundant in relation to the quantity of manure used on them. He believed that other, more convenient substances could be substituted for manure. Fermentation, decay, and putrefaction, he claimed, were chemical transformations that "could be effected by an agency which has hitherto escaped attention." He used a good portion of his book to attack those who were seemingly immune to being impressed by chemical experimentation. "The critical repetition of another's experiments must be viewed as a criticism of his opinions. It is too much forgotten by physiologists [those who study the characteristics of cells, nerves, and tissues of living organisms] that their duty really is not to refute the experiments of others, nor to show that they are erroneous, but to discover truth, and that alone. It is startling when we reflect that all the time and energy of a multitude of persons of genius, talent, and knowledge, are expended in endeavors to demonstrate each others' errors" (p. 88). Such passages in Liebig's book demonstrate a quest for "closing up the ranks" among scientific experimenters ("their duty really is not to refute the experiments of others, nor to show that they are erroneous, but to discover truth, and that alone"). The most obvious question about a point like this is what happens if the truth is in fact the refutation of some experiment?

In the 1840s Liebig patented a commercial fertilizer made of prepared salts to equal the chemical composition of guano. From this point forward, chemical fertilizers have been used. Liebig had many critics, even during his own day. Some latter-day opponents included Whitney, who was once the chief of the Bureau of Soils in the U.S. Department of Agriculture, who said of Liebig: "His views were dogmatic and were too narrow to meet the conditions of life and his opponents bitterly assailed him, hurling at him fact after fact that his theory did not cover" *(Soil and Civilization*, p. 113). Liebig's chemical fertilizer came at a time, said Whitney, when the soil was looked upon as a static and not an ever-changing entity. Few thoughts were given to the residual effects of chemical fertilizing on the land: "The idea that chemical fertilizers are a substitute for human endeavors cannot be considered for a moment to be logical" (p. 185).

Another modern critic of Liebig's system, one who was more severe than Whitney, was Sir Albert Howard, whose 1940 book *An Agricultural Testament* influenced J. I. Rodale's agricultural endeavors to such an extent. According to Howard, Liebig did not attach any importance to the active humus found in surface soil: "[Liebig] . . . did not perceive that critical field experiments, designed to find out if chemical manures were sufficient to supply all the needs of crops, should always be done on the sub-soil, after removing the top 9 inches or so. If this is not arranged for, the yield of any crop may be influenced by the humus already in the soil. Failure to perceive this obvious fact is the main reason why Liebig and his disciples went astray" (p. 182). Howard felt that Liebig was qualified only as a scientist, not as a farmer. Increasing the produce of the soil embraced a number of scientific disciplines, including not only chemistry but physics, bacteriology, and geology as well. Furthermore, said Howard, a judicious selection of artificial manures could be used to "prove or disprove anything or everything."

To be sure, Liebig's work was not universally attacked. In England in 1844 Sir John Lawes began the Rothamsted agricultural experiments, which were profoundly influenced by the Liebig tradition. They grew mostly wheat, using only chemical fertilization, and reported results far superior to any previous crops.

The Rothamsted experiments were faulted by several people, including Milton Whitney, Sir Albert Howard, and J. I. Rodale. Whitney said: "Rothamsted believed that rain would affect fertilized and unfertilized soils the same way. They did not then know that the rainfall affects not only the plant but the organisms of the soil ..." (p. 155). Sir Albert emphasized what chemical fertilizers might ultimately do, not necessarily to the nutritional value of the plant but to the growing capabilities of the soil. J.I., in his book *Organic Front* (1948), asked several questions about the Rothamsted experiments that, at least in his mind, had not been answered. Why experiment with wheat, for example? Why not with corn? What was the condition of the manure that the Rothamsted experimenters deemed unsatisfactory? Was it rotted or green? Was it used only by itself or in combination with plant material? J.I. claimed in this book that the Rothamsted people did not use their own wheat seeds but got them from other sources. Also, said J.I., there was a deficiency of gluten in the Rothamsted wheat that made it unsuitable for eating.

The controversies that began 130 years ago over the question of chemical versus organic fertilizers are still raging. On the one hand the chemicists argue that their method is the only way to stave off worldwide starvation. Nobel Prize winner Dr. Norman E. Borlaug was quoted in *The Journal of Nutrition Education* (Summer 1972) that "if agriculture is denied the use of ... chemicals because of unwise legislation that is now being promoted by a powerful group of hysterical lobbyists, ... then the world will be doomed not by chemical poisoning but from starvation." On the other hand, the organicists speak of the powerful chemical lobbyists and their influence on the U.S. Department of Agriculture and the Food and Drug Administration. Most organicists claim that the real danger in chemicals is what they do to the organisms in the soil. They destroy, for example, the mycorrhizal relationship between plants and the soil. (Mycorrhizae are funguslike threads that go from the plant to the soil.) Also, chemicals tend to destroy earthworms, which, say the organicists, are vital to continued land fertility. There is compelling evidence on both sides of the question, but in the bitter quarrels between the two groups—sometimes even down to character assassination—the general public is mostly at a loss as to whom or what to believe.

There will probably be no definite solution, or at least in the near future, to the controversies that rage between the chemicists and the organicists. A prominent scientist, Frank Egler of Aton Forest, Connecticut, labels the organic movement as the "far left," in contrast to the chemical fertilizer-pesticide people, who are the "far right." In the *American Scientist* (March 1964) Egler stated the impact of organicists: "The extremists and alarmists of the 'left' have made little impression on government, little impression on other social groups except for gardening and horticulture, but considerable impression on the general public" (p. 127). Egler's designation of the organic movement as the "far left" shows the problem of trying to label any kind of movement. From the point of view of our own times, it is to the "left"; from that of history in general it is the older and more conservative method and thus to the "right." In the United States, the Pennsylvania Dutch, who settled in the area where J.I. lived, have practiced organic farming methods for well over 200 years.

J.I. and Egler agreed with each other in respect to the age of organic methods. Before a congressional committee on chemicals in 1950, J.I. made statements about the history of the organic movement: "There is a tendency to say that the organic method is as old as history and was practiced by the oldest civilizations. This is not true as evidenced by the downfall of those civilizations. [Not taking into account at all other factors such as development of political hierarchies, foreign rivalries, and competition of elitist groups, among other things.] It is possible that with the practice of the extended organic method on a widespread scale in any civilization, that civilization will be able to persevere indefinitely and not go the way of Babylonia and Rome. These old civilizations countenanced the burning of manure as a fuel and stood idly by while the most rudimentary principles of basic agriculture were violated. The world has never seen, except in a few isolated cases, the practice of a thorough organic method, and with such a practice there is hope of building a civilization such as has never before been seen, for not only does physical health come from our food through the fertility of the soil in which it grows, but also our minds and characters are nourished and nurtured through that very soil."

J.I.'s mentor, Sir Albert Howard, apparently did not accept the thesis that it was primarily the use of manures as fuel that led to the decline of ancient civilizations. Rome, for example, started downhill, according to Howard in *An Agricultural Testament*, because of a constant drain of the countryside's manhood for service in the legions, the operations of Roman capitalist landlords, the failure to work out a balanced agriculture between crops and livestock for soil fertility, and the introduction of slave to replace free labor. He believed that the vast and "mysterious" East had much to teach the West about maintaining the capabilities of the soil. Eastern methods had been developed long before even the Roman Empire began. It is not the condition of the soil that produces periodic agricultural disasters in countries like India, for its soil is among the richest to be found in the world. Other factors such as lateness of the monsoon season, insect scourges, and population pressure are more explanatory in relation to poor crops than is the condition of the soil. Howard believed that one should view successful segments of the various parts of the Eastern populations, not the catastrophes of the whole. In this respect, he mentioned the work of Sir Robert McGarrison in northern India, with emphasis on the Hunzas.

Howard had a long and distinguished career, one that influenced J.I. to a great extent. Howard became a mycologist in the West Indies in 1899, primarily studying sugar cane production. Then, after teaching botany for a short period at Wye College in Kent, he became, in 1905, the imperial economic botanist to the Government of India, with headquarters in Bihar State at the Pusa Agricultural Research Institute. The descriptions of his experience here was well received by people of J.I.'s temperament: "My real training in agricultural research then began [at Pusa]—six years after leaving the University and obtaining all the paper qualifications and academic experience then needed by an investigator." The peasants and the peats became his professors in India: "By 1910 I had learnt how to grow healthy crops, practically free from disease, without the slightest help from mycologists, entomologists, bacteriologists, agricultural chemists, statisticians, clearing-houses of information, artificial manures, spraying machines, insecticides, germicides, and all the other expensive paraphernalia of the modern experiment station." After spending some time in Pusa, Howard went to Indore in the Indian state of Madhya Pradesh. There he experimented with crops on several acres and developed a method of making compost called the "Indore system." He described his experiments in a 1931 book, *The Waste Products of Agriculture*, and again in *An Agricultural Testament*.

Howard felt that the industrial revolution had encouraged monoculture in the Western countries, with the machine rapidly replacing the animal, and artificials replacing natural manure. Claiming that the specialist approach is bound to fail, he asserted that no effective system of agriculture had ever been devised that left out animals: "The replacement of live-stock by artificials is always followed by disease the moment the original store of soil fertility is exhausted." He believed that the insect problem came mostly from crops imperfectly grown and that the use of sprays, powders, and the like was unscientific and unsound. Even when such procedure was successful, it "merely preserves the unfit and obscures the real problems—how to grow healthy crops."

Despite his criticisms of modern farming practice, Howard did not wholly condemn the use of artificial fertilizers. He sanctioned a middle course with humus used for the most part, but supplemented occasionally with an artificial. On the quarrel between chemicists and organicists, Howard wrote: "Mother Earth, rather than the advocates of these various views, will in due course deliver her verdict . . ." He ended *An Agricultural Testament* with the prophecy that half the illnesses of mankind would disappear once the food supplies were raised from fertile soil and consumed in a fresh condition.

J.I. always referred to Sir Albert Howard as the founder of the organic method. More accurately, however, Howard reinstituted an art that had been in use for centuries. His methods, as J.I.'s later on, always worked better on relatively small plots of land rather than on huge tracts, which are common in the United States.

Many writers who basically support the organic method argue that it is nevertheless impractical from an economic viewpoint. Such an author is Dr. Wayne Davis, who writes an environmental column for the Louisville (Ky.) *Courier-Journal and Times*. In his article of June 25, 1972, he stated his concern toward the deterioration of soil, estimated to be about 1 percent a year, at least in the best farmlands in Iowa. This deterioration is due primarily to massive doses of chemical fertilizers and very little, if any, use of purely organic material. From a pragmatic standpoint, however, "the cost of gathering, transporting, and distributing this bulky material [organic material] in large quantities is prohibitive when compared with the cost of using commercial chemical fertilizers."

The organicists argue that it is possible to gather large quantities of organic material at relatively low prices. This would involve cooperative efforts among municipal governments, merchants, industries, and citizens. It would take a few years of strenuous labor to get the practice of municipal composting established, and after that, its price would drop to more workable levels. Even if the price remained inflated, organicists argue, this would still be superior to the gradual deterioration of farmlands. Many organicists, especially those among the young who have gone back to the farms, believe that farms should be limited in size—that the most any person should farm should not go above 200-300 acres. They argue in terms of Jeffersonian simplicity and urge the creation of "organic homesteads" throughout the country. They do not agree that organic farming is impractical; on the contrary, they see it as an imperative for survival. They admit that, at the moment, the movement attracts mostly the middle and the upper-middle classes; that the poor, at least those of the urban areas, cannot yet have a meaningful role in it, but as sentiment for the movement swells, it will eventually encompass all levels of society.

The benefits the organicists have to offer, they claim, are continued soil fertility, the creation of a life style that emphasizes health, a return to individualism in terms of selective buying, and a feeling of harmony between themselves and the environment. These benefits are worthwhile in their own right, quite apart from any nutritional differences there might be between the organic product and that raised by chemicals. (Though the point is sometimes rather hotly disputed between chemicists and organicists, there seems to be no scientific proof to show that there is any difference.)

In summary, it seems clear that:

- Most of mankind's farming has been done by the organic method.
- The "chemical revolution" did not occur until the middle of the nineteenth century.
- Continued overuse of chemical fertilizers does appear to cause soil deterioration in terms of fertility.
- There does not appear to be any appreciable nutritional difference between organic and chemical produce. (Although there is evidence that overuse of chemical fertilizers, particularly nitrogen, can cause soil problems that result in lower mineral values of the food grown on it.)
- Organic methods do seem to be superior to chemicals in maintaining soil capabilities.
- There are "blind followers" of both sides who close doors to any kind of compromise or quest for moderation in the use of fertilizers. In this respect, many prominent nutritionists and soil scientists throughout the country are just as "unscientific" as they proclaim J. I. Rodale and his followers to be.

J.I.'s critics charge that he took Sir Albert Howard's methods of farming and converted ("perverted" is often used) them into his own profit-making schemes. It is now appropriate to examine closely J.I.'s philosophy and ideas in relation to organic gardening and farming.

CHAPTER 5

J. I. Rodale and Organiculture

Admirers and critics alike seem to agree that J. I. Rodale was sounder in his views on agriculture than in the areas of health. There is not the same scientific aura surrounding land management as there is around health problems. In the minds of most people, one does not have to be a scientist, or even scientifically inclined, to be a farmer. The land is, and always has been, a permanent fixture in the American mind, whereas preventive and curative medicine has possessed a variable, shifting quality. We feel that since the land has always been here, it always will be, and that it is capable of making comebacks no matter how much and in what ways it might be abused. Also, the land is still an entity that produces images of Romanticism; hence, the constant use of such terms as "the good earth" and "Mother Earth" and the almost insatiable desire of city and suburban dwellers in recent years to acquire "rustic" surroundings. When an individual reminisces on his past life, the nostalgia is frequently associated with the land. It does not seem to matter whether such an individual ever owned land or not; it is the lure that counts.

J.I.'s shrewdness in the business world enabled him to know some of the emotional characteristics of this lure of the land. He possessed them himself and he inculcated them in others. Thus, his gardening and farming publications took many readers back in thought to a time in their lives they reckoned to be happier than the present. J.I. started with the small or moderately sized agricultural enterprises, but as time passed, he became increasingly convinced that organic methods were workable on a large scale as well. He coined the word "organiculture" as his chief farming method. Within this context he developed a step-by-step process of how best to grow and consume food.

Obviously, the first consideration was preparation of the soil, and here humus was the most significant ally. There were two ways of preparing humus: the first was called "biodynamic," and the second was the "Indore" method. "Biodynamic" humus, developed by Dr. Ehrenfried Pfeiffer, consisted of two kinds of compost heaps, one made exclusively from vegetable matter and one exclusively from manures. "The "Indore" method, Sir Albert Howard's creation, featured vegetables and other plant material in combination (3:1) with manure. J.I. favored the latter method because it provided a sounder "return to the land" of those things taken from it than the "biodynamic" system. Soil treated with humus, said J.I., became porous, with ample aeration, and gave the billions of microbial agencies a chance to do their work, in league with the indispensable earthworm. This kind of soil had moisture-retaining capabilities that reduced exessive rain runoff with its attendant erosion.

For smaller farms J.I. recommended that the compost be distributed just before plowing and planting time. For large enterprises, "sheet composting" was the logical procedure. This entailed broadcasting the compost in the fall and either plowing it under at that time or letting it remain on top of the soil until it was turned under in the spring.

J.I. frequently became eloquent when he talked about composting. Judging composting as man's "God-given right," he asserted in Organic Merry-Go-Round (1954) that the "greatest pleasure of all is when our composter stands close to his heap in the gathering twilight, when the day's work is done. His whole body is filled with a sense of creation. He is mysteriously moved by its radiations and emanations. He is stirred by the thought that some vital force is at work which could improve the face of the earth, and he feels a part of and enveloped by a mighty God-force of creation" (p. 16). The true composter, he declared, is the man who checks the progress of his compost heaps each day before he even kisses his wife. The compost heaps should ultimately yield great quantities of dark-colored humus. This was the major fertilization needed by fields along with, perhaps, certain kinds of ground-up rock.

The next step in preparing the soil for planting was determining whether or not to plow. In his various writings, J.I. frequently mentioned a book by Edward H. Faulkner called *Plowman's Folly*. Here, Faulkner argued against plowing in favor of discing, and at first J.I. agreed. He came to believe, however, that this method hampered the "digestive" capabilities of the soil, that the topsoil needed a periodic and thorough shifting for creating the necessary porous, aerated condition. Faulkner's method, said J.I., was destructive of the earthworm and encouraged the growth of excess weeds. Humus application, plus a good spring plowing, were the principal steps in soil preparation.

J.I. was opposed to the use of chemical fertilization in any step of the agricultural process. In this respect, he differed slightly from his hero, Sir Albert Howard, because, as noted in Chapter 4, Howard did not totally condemn artificials. J.I. believed that the whole organic movement resulted from an excessive use of agricultural chemicals. He stated that chemical fertilizers are to the plant as whips are to a horse. They speed up the growth process but hasten tiredness. Chemicals strain plants by imposing themselves regardless of whether or not plants need them. Other disadvantages of chemical fertilizers, according to J.I., are that they retard the formation of carbon dioxide, lower the soil's moisture level, create poor aeration, decrease the soil temperature, and kill earthworms.

He lashed out at the "gargantuan" chemical industries that apparently wanted the government to decree that all farming be done chemically. In *Organic Front* (1948), he saw the possibility of this development, since the "Government itself is in the chemical fertilizer business, manufacturing superphosphates as one of the by-activities of the TVA" (p. 25). In some instances, J.I. accused the chemical companies of being motivated only by profit in their activities, but generally he felt that "the agricultural chemical industry believes honestly that their product is needed and that therefore their business is justified. It is up to the organic group in a legitimate manner to teach them the error of their way" (*Organic Front*, p. 147). While he feared governmental dictates in favor of chemical fertilizers, J.I. apparently had no qualms about possible governmental intrusion in organiculture, believing that people, through the right of eminent domain, should have healthy foods: "By this principle the Government should force farmers to run their farms as rounded units, containing sufficient animals to furnish manure. Where health is concerned, surely the principle of eminent domain applies" (*Organic Front*, p. 91).

J.I. believed by the early 1970s that organicism was making some inroads against the chemicals, as evidenced by renewed public awareness, by more severe governmental tests on new chemicals, and by the large numbers in the "back-to-the-land" movement, especially among young people. He was fond of quoting John Stuart Mill's statement that ideas go through three distinct phases: ridicule, discussion, and adoption. J.I. labeled the 1940s as the first stage for the organicultural idea, the 1960s as the second stage, and the 1970s as the stage of adoption. In *Organic Merry-Go-Round*, he predicted: "Critics will come and go, but the organic method will progress steadily because it has a truly scientific basis—more so than our so-called present day scientific agricultural methods. Each year sees more farmers taking up our method and I have yet to see the first farmer who, having begun to practice it, has abandoned it" (p. 37).

After preparing the soil, attention should then be given to proper planting methods. In his *Organic Gardening and Farming* editorials and in several books, J.I. talked about the "compatibility" of certain plants to each other. J.I. believed that cultivated gardens and farms should, to the greatest extent possible, duplicate the arrangement of nature itself. This meant the planting of one vegetable in association with another or a group of others for purposes of preventing strains on the soil and for keeping down the insect menace. J.I. quoted Pfeiffer's book *Biodynamic Farming and Gardening* to show some examples: tomatoes growing close to asparagus will repel the asparagus beetle; mint, hemp, tomatoes, rosemary, or sage next to cabbage will discourage cabbage maggots; peas complement and protect carrots; bush beans are good for celery; beans and corn defend cucumbers; corn and potatoes are good partners; and parsley is deferential to tomatoes. Not only does planting in combination and association help to preserve the soil and battle insects, it is also instrumental, J.I. believed, in producing a healthier, better-tasting vegetable. There were numerous other combinations listed by J.I. and his editorial staff. They believed that "compatibility" factors were most important and that they had been largely overlooked by agricultural textbooks.

Protecting the plant from insects and disease is the farmer's next major occupation. If the soil has been prepared correctly and if proper planting procedures have been followed, especially in respect to companion and affinity factors, a healthy plant should result. The plant's health is its own best defense against insects. With few exceptions, J.I. noted time and again, a bug will not attack a plant "which is growing under the proper conditions and in the right place" (*Organic Gardening*, 1955, p. 122). The insect is nature's censor because it helps to destroy unwanted vegetation. Anyway, putting up with periodic insect attacks is far better, said J.I., than risking the long-term accumulative effects of poisonous sprays.

In large measure, J.I. blamed the consuming public for the proliferation of sprays. The consumer became interested in the beauty and the eye appeal of fruits and vegetables, causing farmers to become agricultural cosmeticians. This was the same kind of trend, argued J.I., that led Americans to automobiles with chromium fittings, to the belief that white eggs are "purer" than brown ones, and to artificially colored oranges: "Industry scandalously pandered to the consumer's taste—to all items of food regardless of how it damaged their nutritional value" (*Organic Gardening*, p. 176).

He blamed the overuse of poisonous sprays on the "NPK" (nitrogen, phosphorus, potash) mentality, and he was especially alarmed at the introduction of systemic sprays throughout the country. The systemics saturate every cell of a plant, making it completely impossible for a consumer who wishes to avoid poisons to do so. He spoke at several meetings against the use of all poisonous sprays, and he testified against them in congressional food and drug hearings. Generally, however, he was either laughed away or politely shunned at such gatherings. He conducted these excoriations over a long period—from as early as 1941 to the time of his death in 1971. If anyone in this country, therefore, should receive the credit for pioneering the message that all was not well in the use of agricultural sprays, that person must be J. I. Rodale.

J.I. was equally opposed to food additives, and in 1950 he was a prime witness before the House Select Committee to Investigate the Use of Chemicals in Foods and Cosmetics. Congressman James J. Delaney of New York was chairman of this committee, whose work led later to the Delaney Clause, an amendment to the Food and Drug Act, which prohibited cancer-causing additives to the food supply. (The action against cyclamates in soft drinks, for example, came under the auspices of the Delaney Clause).

At the committee's hearings, J.I. and Congressman Thomas G. Abernethy of Mississippi swapped verbal barbs with each other. J.I. stated that he had been rejected for service in World War I because of his bad eyesight. Abernethy wanted to know if J.I.'s poor eyes had been attributable to eating food grown with chemical fertilizers, whereupon J.I. appealed for a serious tone in the conversation. Abernethy pushed J.I. for a presentation of his agricultural credentials. J.I. replied that he sat in a place where all the results of agricultural experimentation came to his desk, even from the government. He mentioned some of his books: for example, *The Word Finder* had been selected by the Book-of-the-Month Club, and his *Sleep and Rheumatism* had been cited favorably in the *Journal of Nervous Disorders*. He then said to Abernethy: "You see, I am just a man of general intelligence. I want to demand a few minutes, because the purpose of what you are doing is to try to belittle me."

Abernethy finally asked J.I. if he advocated a complete withdrawal of chemical fertilizers, insecticides, and additives from the market. J.I. replied: "It cannot be done overnight. I do not advocate it. My purpose is merely to cause the government to investigate and not have these scientists say there is no evidence, and refuse to investigate. They are afraid. There is something hidden that makes them fear investigating this." This portion of the hearing ended with Chairman Delaney complimenting J.I. as a pioneer in the new field of organiculture. Delaney was responsible for adding three amendments to the Food, Drug, and Cosmetic Act: the Pesticides Amendment in 1950; Food Additives in 1958; and Color Additives in 1960. (Today, there are efforts to repeal or at least modify the Delaney Clause. A recent Associated Press news story by John Stowall stated that the food chemical industry expected to grow from a business of $485 million in 1970 to $750 million by 1980. Much of this growth is predicated on an emasculation of the Delaney Clause).

Long before Rachel Carson became famous for *Silent Spring* (1962), therefore, J. I. Rodale was spreading the word that there was no scientific way of predicting what the residual effects of additives would be. If just one additive were taken on a daily basis, probably nothing would ultimately happen; but J.I. stated that, on the average, an American took in twenty-two different chemicals a day in the form of food additives. Individually and in small quantity, the additives may not be dangerous, but collectively and in combination, there is no way of forecasting possible consequences. We take so many of these freshness, preservation, and appearance additives that J.I. expressed the opinion that "our society is coming more and more to resemble a pure culture of bacteria in a Petri dish" (*Our Poisoned Earth and Sky*, 1964, p. 8). It will be that same public, however, that ultimately dictates against the saturation of food produce by chemical sprays and additives. There was evidence that this antichemical feeling was in its genesis stage at J.I.'s death, and it has been pursued since by consumer groups, so that today the level of awareness of possible chemical dangers is higher than ever before.

Once the growth process was completed, the next stage in the system of organiculture was harvesting, storage, and consumption. Freezing units, on either an individual or a cooperative level, could be employed for preserving produce. J.I. believed that vegetables should be eaten raw if at all possible, that cooking them destroyed much of their vitamin content. He personally took great pleasure in going into his garden and eating corn direct from the stalk. The same "direct eating" was true with potatoes, carrots, sunflower seeds, tomatoes, and asparagus, and he thought it was a crime to cook peas; they should always be eaten in their raw state. He felt it was ironic to see people eat cooked peas and then take vitamins.

Organiculture offered the best opportunity for growing and consuming fruits and vegetables under optimum conditions and for knowing the true relationship between the soil and the health of the individuals who ate the things it grew. Of course, J.I. described his system in idealistic terms; it worked well wherever citizens could obtain small plots of land to grow gardens. He did maintain that the suburbs were excellent sites for organiculture and occasionally suggested that rooftops of tenement buildings, areas on fire escapes, or even pots situated in windows could be used in growing at least some organic produce. Frequently, he noted the large amounts of surplus land owned by factories and business establishments. Instead of water fountains and formal gardens, why not hire people to farm it organically and sell the produce to the employees?

J.I. did not completely come to grips, however, with the problems of distribution, of how to get these organically grown products to the urban consumer. He recommended the patronage of roadside fruit and vegetable stands whose produce was grown organically; even if the consumer got such products for only a portion of the year, that was better than none at all. J.I. lauded the trend that began in the late 1960s and continued into the 1970s of supermarkets setting aside certain areas for the display and sale of organically grown material, and he was pleased and excited about the proliferation of health-food stores throughout the country. Indeed, one reason why he became so favorable to natural food supplements is that he felt this was one way for the city-locked dweller to receive the benefits of organiculture. J.I.'s system was more expensive than the chemical methods. He argued, however, that if organiculture were widely adopted, its cost would fall. Even if it did not, and if organiculture was the best method for the health of a nation—indeed its survival—the price would be well worth the effort.

The most obvious question about J.I.'s system of organiculture is "Was he right?" Did he have an important message for Americans and the world in respect to growing and consuming food? Or did he, as his critics assert, merely cry panic and make his cash registers ring as a result?

In defense of his system, J.I. printed thousands of letters from readers of *Organic Gardening and Farming* and *Prevention* that gave glowing reports of success. Frequently, he apparently mistook these reports as showing the superiority of his system. But testimonials from eager readers cannot be taken as scientific proof that J.I. was right. The testimonials should probably be dismissed, therefore, as inconclusive evidence in support of organiculture and treated instead as remarks of enthusiastic fans.

Much of the scientific community, however, agreed with J.I. and his organiculture. Even those scientists who did not accept his teachings frequently asserted that science needed renegades to stir up trouble and controversy to keep scientists from becoming complacent or from pursuing their work in intellectual vacuums. Ironically, perhaps, many of these scientists agreed that the "stirring up" should come from one who is not formula-ridden or locked into research patterns—indeed, from one who was largely "self-educated" in various fields of endeavor.

From John J. Biesele, a professor of biology at the University of Texas: "I believe Rodale rendered a real service to us in reminding us again and again that mankind is highly dependent on the earth's surface, with all the interactions of matter and energy that occur there, and that maintaining the soil as a fertile, living interface between the sterile subterrane and the atmosphere is a highly important aspect of the continued existence of the biosphere . . ." From prominent scientist Barry Commoner, at St. Louis' Washington University: "There is no reason, I believe, a priori, to denigrate non-professional views about gardening—when they are clearly based on actual observations properly recorded. On these grounds, amateurs can contribute a great deal to the field. The general view that natural processes, such as the incorporation of organic matter, are essential to long term soil fertility is a sound one."

From Paul Erlich at Stanford University: "In the

case of Mr. Rodale, while I would not agree with all his opinions and conclusions, he performed a valuable service in developing an unorthodox approach to agriculture in a time when orthodox agriculture was pursuing what now appear to be dangerous trends. . . . Mr. Rodale felt that synthetic pesticides might be harmful if sprayed on food and then consumed. Opinion in biology and medicine [is] now beginning to share that view at least in part, although a few short years ago, the orthodoxy held that pesticides were entirely harmless to people. I feel that every scientific field should have its renegades, and since formal training tends to suppress such tendencies, renegades are more likely to come from the ranks of talented amateurs."

From Richard H. Goodwin at Connecticut College: ". . . I am convinced that there is much to be gained by an organic approach to agriculture, not only from the point-of-view of immediate productivity, but especially with respect to sound long-range ecosystem management. I believe a middle of the road position on the health significance of organic produce is in order. Extravagant claims are made both on behalf of the chemical and the organic approach." From an environmental scientist, Charles Wurster, in New York: "I do not believe that a person needs medical training to be competent in certain matters relating to health. Furthermore, I know a number of people who do have M.D. degrees who are quite incompetent in such matters. The pesticide industry, for example, hires some of them. I would much rather listen to Rodale regarding what goes into my stomach." From a biologist, R. G. Haines, in California: "Many of his [Rodale's] concepts (truly a combination of being a skilled 'green-thumber' and ardent surveyor of food production technology) were indeed useful to the small gardener or even highly specialized, well-placed commercial grower, e.g., one whose land became rapidly surrounded by urbanization and who turned to the lucrative roadside-stand business." And, finally, from Robert F. Mueller, a geophysicist in

Maryland: "Perhaps one of the most important insights of the 'organicist' is that so called modern agriculture has become totally and dangerously dependent on our vanishing fossil fuel energy. This point has been stressed particularly by Rodale."

The above statements were made by highly trained scientists who spend their time in the classroom and the laboratory. Their opinion of Rodale may be unique in the framework of the scientific community at large, but they do show that Rodale was by no means condemned by all men of science. They tend to treat him as a "naïve genius" who, without formal training, went wherever the facts and his curiosity led him. One may conclude, therefore, that J.I. finally amassed a sizable following, or at least a toleration, from scientists in the area of organiculture.

Some scientists and academicians, however, regard the organic movement as anti-intellectual. For example, Yale University Professor Arthur W. Galston once offered a course entitled "Biology and Human Affairs" and wrote an article about it in *Natural History* (May 1972) entitled "The Organic Gardener and Anti-Intellectualism." Galston accepted the general scientific belief that there is no nutritional difference between organic and inorganic foods, but apparently his students did not. He found the students to be "emotionally" committed to organic gardening, "partially because they are in revolt against 'the establishment' and the synthetic, plastic world it has created" (p. 28). The attitude of the Yale students does indeed seem to be widespread among young people, particularly those who have gone into agricultural communes. Herbert A. Otto, writing in the *Saturday Review of Literature* (April 1971), stated that "many of these communes cultivate crops as organically grown grain, vegetables, and other produce, which are then sold to health-food stores, health-food wholesalers, or supermarkets" (p. 17). Robert Houriet's book, *Getting Back Together* (1971), mentioned some 2,000 different communes throughout the United

States, and Cleveland Amory, in the *Saturday Review* (September 1971), described several communes he had visited and reported that the "magazines I saw most . . . were *Organic Gardening and Farming*." One Rodale correspondent, an English professor at the University of Pennsylvania, wrote to tell about one of his former students who had moved to a communal farm in North Carolina. The professor, who had just read *Pay Dirt*, offered to teach the former student how to make a compost heap. The young man exclaimed: "Rodale! He's our hero!" There does seem to be ample justification, therefore, to assert that J.I. became the leading force, and continues to be, behind the agricultural communes. There is, however, at least one major exception to this statement. One of the largest communes in the country, at Summertown, Tennessee, uses chemical fertilizers and regards J.I. as a faddist, "way out on the end of that continuum."

Besides Galston, another scholar to form unfavorable opinions of Rodalean methods is Emory University history professor J. Harvey Young, who has spent much of his career studying medical quackery and food faddism. He said: "I believe it possible for a lay person to become an authority on certain scientific fields by dint of deep immersion in the literature and a rational mind. In my judgment, Rodale did not so become. . . . [W]hat he did was seek to find things that bolstered his pre-existing set of beliefs. Because he published so much, Rodale did a great deal to create a set of myths about our food supply and what people should do about eating that I regard as harmful."

Two articles in *Reader's Digest* also attacked J.I.'s system of organiculture. The first was by R. I. Throckmorton, entitled "Organic Farming—Bunk!" (October 1952). His thesis was that the antichemical doctrine played on the words "natural" and "unnatural," and he asserted that any plant food, whether from organic matter or commercial fertilizer, came from nature; therefore, one is no more "natural" than the other (p. 46). The other *Reader's Digest* article (July 1962) was written by Harland Manchester and was called "The Great Organic Gardening Myth." As in the first article, stress was placed on the nondifference between organics and chemicals from a nutrition viewpoint, on the higher costs of organically produced material, and on the necessity of chemicals in providing a worldwide food supply (pp. 102-105).

As one might expect, the chemical companies are in complete disagreement with J.I. and his organiculture. Two examples will be sufficient to show the trend of the criticism. One is from the Woolfolk Chemical Works, Ltd., of Fort Valley, Georgia. Its representative, John C. Alden, said: "I do not think organic farming as Mr. Rodale advocates is practical. There has never been any scientific justification for it on a quality, nutritional or health basis. His criticism and condemnation of chemical fertilizers and pesticides is unjustified. Without the proper utilization of these chemicals, it would be impossible to grow the food necessary for our population without drastic changes in our standard of living. Because of these chemicals and mechanization and other advances of modern agriculture, it is now possible to feed 200 million Americans on the same acreage that fed 80 million Americans in 1910." The other example is from the Monsanto Company, which distributes a speaker's kit entitled "Plain Talk, Pesticides and the Environment." Included are excerpts from various science and general magazines that portray chemicals in a favorable light. Also, there are photographs of corn grown on "Nature's Acre" and corn grown on "Today's Acre." The former is said to have yielded only 25 to 30 bushels per acre, while the latter came to a whopping 130 bushels. The Monsanto material does not single out J.I. or any other personality in the organic movement, but it does take strong exception to those who object to chemical fertilizers, insecticides, and pesticides. Again, as with most other chemically inclined people, the message is that chemicals are indispensable in staving off world hunger, even famine.

It is this very appeal to feeding the world that gives the chemical way its most important justification. It is the appeal of keeping the world healthy through the food it eats that gives the organic movement its most attractive posture. J.I. frequently asserted that if *all* organic material were harnessed, there would be a sufficient amount with which to grow food. He constantly called for the government at least to establish some experimental programs along these lines and intimated that until this is done, there is no way the chemical proponents can disprove what the organicists are saying. Thus, the controversy continues.

J.I. believed that he was obliged to spread the organicultural message to as many corners of the land as he possibly could. His chief means of doing this was *Organic Gardening and Farming*, but he felt that experimental work should be done in organics as well. In 1947, therefore, he organized the Soil and Health Foundation to establish an experimental laboratory and to give grants to organically inclined individuals and institutions for research programs. J.I. set up a laboratory on his farm at Emmaus and appointed as its director Dr. William H. Eyster, who for several months had been the managing editor of *Organic Gardening and Farming*. A charter was obtained for the foundation, and funds were contributed to it by interested parties, primarily from the readers of *OGF*. The work at the laboratory, however, did not proceed as rapidly as J.I. desired, so he began more and more to give individual and institutional grants.

During the first several years of its existence, the Soil and Health Foundation was an almost total failure. J.I. could find very few universities and colleges to undertake organic experimentation. When J.I. offered grants, the educational institutions either bluntly refused or politely pointed to a schedule of priorities that prevented them from taking on any additional work. One exception, however, was the University of Missouri, which in 1950 accepted a $1,400 grant for experimentation in rock fertilizers, under the directorship of Professor William Albrecht. J.I. stated before the Delaney committee in December 1950: "At least this institution, the University of Missouri, has accepted a grant from us, whereas the others treat us, more or less, as crackpots, and refuse to do any experimental work."

J.I. had somewhat better luck in giving Soil and Health Foundation money to individuals than to institutions. For example, Dr. Ehrenfried Pfeiffer conducted mice-feeding experiments at his New York farm under the auspices of the Soil and Health Foundation. Pfeiffer's purpose was to determine whether there was a health difference between organic and chemical soils to those who ate their produce. He noted that the chemically fed mice became exceedingly nervous under various tests, whereas the organic ones remained calm and nonchalant.

Another notable recipient of Soil and Health Foundation grants was Dr. Albert Schaatz, who has spent much of his distinguished career in developing agricultural chelating agents. As Schaatz explained: "Now most of these [chelating agents] are synthetic compounds. They're chemically made. They don't occur in Nature. The use of chelating agents to provide a trace metal—iron, copper, cobalt, manganese, etc., in a soluble form . . . [is] a field . . . of tremendous importance. . . . [I]t turns out that soil organic matter or humus is probably the most important chelating agent in the soil."

Schaatz, one of J.I.'s most ardent admirers, related further that when he received his grants in the early 1950s, "I was in contact with people in chemical fertilizer companies and State Departments of Agriculture . . . and almost invariably they thought I had sold out to J.I., [and that] as a subservient grantee, I would deliver the goods. . . . There is no question that he was extremely interested in our findings, but on no occasion did he either covertly or overtly attempt to influence me. .... Now I have had considerable experience with drug companies which have tried to influence me, in fact, buy the results they wanted. That was never the case with the ... grants that we had from J.I. His objectivity equalled his interest."

J.I. frequently contacted individuals he heard about through various sources who had projects going that might possibly be subsidized by his grants. One such person was Associate Professor Leonard Hippchen of the School of Social Welfare at Florida State University. J.I. enlisted Hippchen's assistance in finding a student to investigate nutritional deficiencies in delinquents or criminals. Hippchen did find such a student, but before the experiment began, the student decided to complete his master's degree without rather than with a thesis. Thus, the project was dropped. "It was very difficult," Hippchen explained, "to find students who would do research in this area, partly because it is yet unpopular, and secondly, because it requires a team effort with help in the laboratory."

Though the Soil and Health Foundation operated quite minimally in its early years because of widespread rejection of its grants, it still had considerable funding. There, was, for example, one anonymous contribution of $15,000. This, plus other contributions, was invested in industrial and business corporations, and over the years the foundation's capital grew. By 1954, the foundation had grants operating in four different institutions of higher education: Antioch College in Antioch, Ohio; the National Agricultural College in Doylestown, Pennsylvania; the Horticultural School in Ambler, Pennsylvania; and Lavelle University in Quebec, Canada. Even so, the foundation had an extremely difficult task of granting its money. In recent times, as the organicultural idea has spread and as more and more people are accepting its philosophy, the Soil and Health Foundation has been reactivated in a strong way. A new newsletter is being published from Emmaus, giving full information on the updated version of the Soil and Health Foundation. J.I.'s son, Robert, president of Rodale Press, says: "I'm very optimistic that the Foundation can now be made into a great organization."

Quite apart from the Soil and Health Foundation, J.I. personally studied and experimented with various agricultural problems. In the files that he kept at his home in Emmaus, he had folders for each state of the Union. In many of these were descriptions of soil within certain parts of the country and short accounts of trips he took to several states and his agricultural impressions of them. In 1948, for example, he traveled to Alabama. There he gave speeches to groups of farmers and to state legislators and made extensive tours of the Piedmont Plateau. He believed that Alabama and the other southern states had excellent potential for organic farming, since cotton mill wastes suitable for composting were in such abundant supply. (On this trip, J.I., still interested in the English language, was amazed at some of the colloquialisms he heard. Alabama was the place, he said, where the word "ma'am" had two vowels, and each one was sounded separately. He was also intrigued by a food concoction he called a "little wad of cornmeal with an egg in it." He was, of course, describing a "hush puppy," a southern delicacy held dear by most Alabamans).

On his farm in Emmaus, one thought after another came to J.I. about experimentation. He rarely did any of the physical labor himself; instead, he was the "architect" for all these things, with farm employees to do the actual work. Indeed, he had little ability in identifying plants that grew on his farm and in surrounding areas. This embarrassed him occasionally as he escorted visitors through his farm, but he justified himself on the ground that plant identification was a specialized field within itself, and he asserted that he had no time to learn the names of plants, trees, and shrubs beyond the better-known ones.

In 1964 he worked out what he called his "Potato

Plan." He wanted President Lyndon B. Johnson to put the newly formed Job Corps to work on government-subsidized potato fields. Farmers, in return for giving their lands for this purpose, would receive bounties from the Department of Agriculture. The produce from this operation would be labeled "organic" in the markets where it was sold. J.I.'s "Potato Plan," he felt, would offer healthy foods to consumers and at the same time give training and employment to thousands of young people. Nothing ever came of the idea.

Since he opposed "vegetable factories," J.I. also lamented the methods employed by the poultry industry. He wrote a little play for the May 1962 edition of *OGF* called "The Egg and You," in which he condemned the practices of vaccination, tranquilization, and pill taking to push hens to increase amounts of production. It turned out that the farmer in this play produced sterile eggs only for the public; he kept his own private flock to obtain fertile eggs for himself and his family. J.I. apparently believed the old "needle trick" and felt it had potential importance for the poultry industry. For example, drink some water from a glass and then hold a needle suspended by eight inches of thread over it. If you are a male, said J.I., the needle will move in a clockwise rotation; if you are female, the needle will oscillate back and forth. J.I. conducted "needle experiments" on organically grown eggs and concluded that they were economically important. If it is a male egg, it could be sold immediately to the public; if female, it could be allowed to hatch. Also, he urged experiments to determine nutritional differences, if any, between male and female eggs.

J.I.'s experiments with eggs reflected his belief that atmospheric electricity greatly influenced the quantity and quality of things nature produced. He called the relationship between electricity and plants electroculture: "The soil is charged with electricity and so are the plants that grow in that soil. When a gardener pulls out a weed or touches the soil, he is either absorbing electricity or discharging an over-supply of it—which I do not know, but whichever it is it must be good." He planted small gardens of like vegetables side by side, but in one he placed rows of metal cans. Three weeks later he noted that the vegetables that had the benefit of the cans were vastly superior to those without. He also suspended metal hoops over growing plants, and metal wires as well. He was convinced that this metal conducted atmospheric electricity into the plant and gave it superiority over its nonelectrified neighbors. Plants grown in this condition, he stated, were extremely healthy and not too subject to attacks by insects and diseases. It is this sort of experimentation that drove many orthodox scientists to distraction about J.I. Rodale. They asserted that there is little, if anything, to the electroculture idea and that such experiments only proved that J.I. was a crank. In reply, J.I. began proclaiming: "Maybe so, but even the critics admit that it takes a crank to turn things."

Another thing J.I. did to produce superior plants was experiment with basalt rock powder, with which he first became familiar while on a trip to Holland and Germany. He made lengthy studies of the properties of basalt rock and of the places in the United States where it was found in abundance. He came to believe that basalt rock, in combination with humus, provided most of the fertilization that crops need. He was also interested in stone mulching and gave over several garden plots on his farm for experimentation in this practice. Stone slabs placed between rows of growing vegetables were instrumental in holding the earth's moisture and in keeping down the weed menace. J.I., in his "Thoughts and Comments" section of OGF, frequently mentioned the work of other gardeners in getting their plants to grow, though there were some experiments that even J.I. disbelieved. He heard, for example, from a teenager in Ithaca, New York, that her plants thrived on the music of the Beatles and of Anton Dvorák's "New World Symphony" and from a minister who wrote about the power of prayer to get his plants to flourish.

While J.I. never exactly denigrated everything orthodox science did, he was apparently willing, even anxious, to undertake those things usually spurned by traditional methods. He wrote endlessly about his rats on his farm at Emmaus; of how they had been emaciated before, when the farm had been operated chemically by its previous owners, and of how they became fat, healthy, "sassy," and unafraid of humans after they had eaten J.I.'s organic corn. If organiculture could do this for rats, J.I. was convinced that it would do the same for humans. He therefore followed his organicultural plan with a religious fervor, often to the astonishment, humor, and even anger of the orthodox scientific community.

J.I. predicted ultimate great success for his agricultural philosophy. In *Organic Front* he wrote: "Organiculture is a vigorous and growing movement, one that is destined to alter our conceptions of the farm and the garden and to revolutionize our methods of operating them in order to secure for ourselves and others more abundant and more perfect food" (p. 63). Another writer, Gurney Norman, agreed with this revolutionary aspect of organiculture. He wrote in the *Whole Earth Catalog* (Spring 1970): "It has occurred to me that if I were a dictator determined to control the national press, *Organic Gardening* [and *Farming*] would be the first publisher I'd squash, because it is the most subversive. ... I believe that organic gardeners are in the forefront of a serious effort to save the world by changing man's orientation to it, to move away from the collective, centrist, super-industrial state, toward a simpler, realer, one-to-one relationship with the earth itself."

Whether one agrees or not with J. I. Rodale's philosophy of organiculture, one must still admit that it has affected thousands, even millions, of people throughout the United States and the world. Certainly, J.I. was too hasty on numerous occasions in pronouncing judgments either against traditional science or for organiculture. He tended to rely too heavily on reader testimonials as scientific proof of what he was saying or doing. But the fact remains that he constantly attempted to enlist the aid of highly trained scientists in the area of organiculture, only to be soundly rejected for reasons that in themselves were quite unscientific. It was only toward the end of J.I.'s life that he began to see acceptance of his ideas and life style. Since his death, this acceptance seems to have grown considerably. Whether it will continue to do so, only time will tell.

CHAPTER 6

The Health Front

The telephone rang late one night in J. I. Rodale's home. The caller stated that he had been to a doctor a few hours earlier and had had his ailment diagnosed as cancer. The physician recommended immediate surgery. The caller, however, asked J.I. for advice on how to avoid the surgery and wanted J.I. to prescribe a regimen of natural foods that would cure the cancer. J.I. refused.

Such a call, while not exactly typical, was not uncommon. As in many instances, the caller did not give his name, leading J.I. to believe that some of his enemies were attempting to get him to practice medicine without a license. Though he probably did, at several stages of his life, have ambitions of becoming a doctor, he assiduously avoided giving curative advice. He was not beyond suggesting a proper diet to a friend on ways to keep hair from falling out of someone's head, but he always counseled seriously ill people to get proper medical diagnosis and treatment for the things that bothered them. He did believe that modern society had too great an inclination to run to a doctor when there was no need because, he felt, physicians were too interested in the curative rather than the preventive aspects of medicine; but as witnessed by his own experience of patronizing medical doctors, he did not counsel against them.

By far the most controversial and questionable aspect of J. I. Rodale's life was his connection with health matters. As related in a previous chapter, if he had stayed solely within the area of organiculture, he never would have become the center of controversy that he ultimately did. Health consciousness with J.I., however, was something that did not come to him suddenly. As a young man, he had pondered on the question of why some people are sickly and others are not. These feelings had been amplified by the early deaths of his father and of several of his brothers and sisters. A heart murmur in J.I. himself had furthered these thoughts of what produces a healthy body. He ultimately became convinced that the best health secret of all is prevention: to realize the relation between soil and health; to avoid such unhealthy practices as smoking and drinking to excess; to take adequate exercise; and finally to add several natural food supplements to one's daily regimen.

He used his own press—Rodale Books, Inc.—to get his points across to his readers. Each month in *Prevention* magazine, he wrote an editorial on some subject of health; and often, he penned long series of articles on particular subjects that he thought interesting and important. Also, he published several compendia of health articles, gleaned mostly from what had previously appeared in *Prevention*. Such books as *An Encyclopedia of Common Diseases*, *Health Secrets of Famous Doctors*, *Health Secrets of Famous People*, *Health Secrets from Foreign Lands*, *Complete Book of Food and Nutrition*, and *The Health Finder* rolled off the Rodale presses and were sent to readers anxious to peruse them. J.I.'s relation to preventive and nutritional health may be divided into several categories. What follows, therefore, are the chief areas of health with which he was concerned.

Though he wrote about human ailments that ranged all the way from acne and constipation to trench mouth and bed-wetting, there were a few subjects with which J.I. seemed to be preoccupied. Arthritis and rheumatism were such topics. He frequently asserted that sufferers of these maladies were especially vulnerable to medical quackery but that many of the quacks were medical doctors themselves. He recommended, nevertheless, medical treatments interspersed with visits to chiropractors for these ills.

One field of health that apparently interested J.I. more than any other was blood pressure and its relation to the heart. In many books and articles he described how, through a rigorous, personal routine of physical exercise, he kept his pulse at a satisfactory level. His heart became a major health factor to him in 1937, worsening after years of experiencing a murmur, and he concluded that he must take steps to protect himself. Some useful methods to lower the pulse, he found, were to reduce the quantity of food taken in per day, to avoid emotional stress, and to become involved in some sort of progressively more difficult exercise. For J.I. the latter was accomplished by walking. He began this exercise in a modest way and gradually worked up to hill walking. He marveled at the good he believed this did his heart, and sometimes he wrote purple prose about the beauty and mystery of this vital organ of the human body: while it should not be overworked, inactivity was the worst possible thing for it.

J.I. kept elaborate statistics on his pulse. He took it before and after walks, and sometimes (though he generally frowned on hard drinks) he deliberately drank a Scotch and soda just to see how it affected it. In his diary, and in several articles and in long book passages, he gave a "history of J. I. Rodale's pulse," in which he divided months into days, days into hours, and hours into minutes and copiously recorded his pulse at any given moment, with detailed descriptions of the circumstances under which it was taken. He finally got his pulse down to between 55 and 70, a condition that pleased him very much.

The validity of J.I.'s pulse experiments was hotly disputed by various physicians and medical societies. For example, in Allentown, Pennsylvania, there is a group known as the Lehigh Valley Committee Against Health Fraud, Inc. (LVCAHF), which condemned not only J.I.'s pulse studies but almost everything else he did as well. It is impossible, said one member of the LVCAHF, to take one's own pulse accurately. The mere act of taking it probably increases the count. He also asserted that if J.I.'s pulse actually did go down, it was probably because J.I. was walking downhill and did not divulge this fact to his readers. Even if the pulse changed, the next step, scientifically, would be to test a larger group of people, to take their pulses under varied circumstances, preferably without their knowing they were being tested, and to form a concensus of the value of the various experiments. The physicians, therefore, rejected J.I.'s findings on his own pulse on the grounds that they are unscientific.

Another subject of special interest to J.I. was cancer. Again, it must be asserted that he never offered any cure for cancer, but his writings were saturated with suggestions on how to prevent it. He was firmly convinced that the increase of cancer in recent years was directly connected to the ingestion of commercial foods that had been permeated by chemicals. He believed, too, as he pointed out in a November 1966 *Prevention* article, "Happy People Rarely Get Cancer," that one's state of mind was instrumental in preventing that dread disease. Organic gardeners, he found, were less susceptible to cancer than others for two reasons: gardening put man into a direct relationship with nature and fostered emotional stability, and also gave him healthful food. J.I. was dead-set against the practice of smoking, and he wrote such books as *Smoke and Die; Quit and Live!, If You Must Smoke, Twenty Ways to Stop Smoking,* and *The Nutritional Way to Stop Smoking.* His antitobacco work drew praise even from one of his strongest critics. A spokesman for the LVCAHF stated that the best articles showing the dangers of smoking had appeared in *Prevention.*

Other specific ailments with which J.I. was particularly concerned included prostate difficulties and eye troubles. He wrote books and scores of articles on these subjects, with suggestions of how, through good nutritional practices, one could prevent their occurrence. Prostates and eyes were especially receptive, he believed, to preventive measures. He argued that most sufferers from prostate troubles were too hasty in going into surgery; a diet that featured large intakes of pumpkin seeds, with generous amounts of amino acids and magnesium chloride, was instrumental in preventing prostatic hypertrophy.

From his earliest days, J.I. had been interested in eye protection; he had been rejected for military service in World War I because of his own sight difficulties. In a *Prevention* article of August 1960, "Your Eyesight Depends on Your Nutrition," he pointed to the importance of protein to good eyesight. Too, he discussed the value to eyes of vitamins A, B, C, D, and E, as well as the beneficial effects of rutin, calcium, and sunflower seeds. He stressed the fact that a majority of Russians ate sunflower seeds, and he believed that it was no mere coincidence that less than 10 percent of the adult Russian population wore eyeglasses as compared to 60 percent of the adults in the United States. These statistics caused him to ask: "In the event of war between the United States and Russia does this fact have some significance?" (p. 21).

A great thrust of J.I.'s health message was an indictment of certain foods and cooking practices that were highly popular with the American people. The first of these was the widespread use of sugar. He believed that overindulgence in sugar intake produced many of the world's problems. He wrote several books, a few plays, and countless articles to get across his antisugar stand. He stated that sugar produced unfavorable levels of blood sugar in the body that ultimately caused unhappy mental reactions. Adolf Hitler, for example, had been a fanatic on sweets, as had been Napoleon and Ivan the Terrible, and he wondered if their bellicose impulses had been formed as a result. J.I. maintained that he would probably realize his goal of living to be 102 years old unless he was struck down by some New York taxi driver who was a "sugar drunkard."

In 1968 J.I. wrote a book called *Natural Health, Sugar and the Criminal Mind.* He sent a complimentary copy of this book to California Governor Ronald Reagan, who had long ago taken up eating jellybeans as a substitute for smoking. J.I. told Reagan that he could go down in history as the first governor to adopt an honest attitude on nutrition and offered to suggest a course of reading that would enable Reagan "to stay in government, not be senile, or get eight heart attacks until you're 100." There is no evidence that Governor Reagan took up J.I.'s proposals.

In *Natural Health . . .* , J.I. related that he and his wife, Anna, had once written a cookbook called *Sweet Without Sugar.* Two large publishers were interested, he said, until they apparently concluded that they would anger the sugar interests by publication. "In one case," J.I. reported, "the managing editor stated honestly that he did not wish to offend the sugar-candy-soft-drink-ice-cream-bakery interests. Nowhere along the line were there questions of bribery or coercion involved, no threats of boycott, no strong-arm tactics. It was a matter of business judgment not to offend interests that operate in billions of dollars a year. I am not accusing the sugar interests of exercising any form of *direct* censorship, restraint of freedom of publication, or pressure. Subtle forces are always more effective" (p. 109).

In this book, *Natural Health . . .* , J.I. expressed the opinion that public advertisements for high sugar content foods should be banned by the federal government. He felt that candy stores in cities with high delinquency rates should be subsidized by the government *if* they began selling heathful foods. He believed that all people on welfare rolls should be required to take their meals at public feeding points and told that "unless they can keep their blood-sugar at a proper level [by avoiding sweets] they will be removed from the roll" (pp. 179-180). He felt that law courts, prisons, reform schools, high schools, and colleges should each have a resident M.D. to make blood-sugar counts on a regular basis, because "it would be interesting to study these school blood-sugar reports in connection with problem students" (p. 35).

As in his statements on pulse and other matters, J.I. was severely taken to task by orthodox nutritionists for his condemnation of sugar. Frederick Stare of Harvard University has long been an opponent of Rodalean methods, calling the Rodale enterprise one of the "leading purveyors of nutritional nonsense." J.I. mentioned Stare in *Natural Health* . . . : ". . . Stare is very active in a campaign to belittle food faddism, and since I am the number one American food faddist, I take it as a personal challenge" (p. 25). J.I. was scored, too, by the Food and Drug Administration. The FDA undertook a plan in 1963 to regulate the fast-growing health-food business in the United States. In his opposition, J.I. suggested a connection between a highly refined carbohydrate diet and juvenile delinquency. FDA Commissioner George Larrick responded by calling J.I.'s assertion highly speculative and by saying that no recognized nutrition authority would agree with this thesis. J.I. gave in *Natural Health* . . . what almost became his stock answer to criticisms of this sort: "I have always maintained that one of the greatest blunders of modern civilization is the placing of our health completely in the hands of the medical profession. I do not say we should ignore doctors when we are sick. But sickness and health are two entirely different things, and each one should have its own specialized treatment. Doctors should be in charge of disease, not health" (p. 176).

Another food that J.I. inveighed against was white bread. He thought it was instrumental in causing colds, and he argued that wheat was a naturally dangerous product because it contained gliadin and adenosine, two of nature's harmful elements. J.I. was opposed even to organically grown wheat products, saying that he was waging a "one-man war" against wheat. This "war," of course, caused him to counsel against wheat breakfast cereals of all types: they contained not only the two natural dangers but "tons" of artificial additives as well.

Sugar and white bread (as well as milk, because it made people grow too tall) were the food products that J.I. opposed. Two widely used cooking appurtenances also came in for his attacks. The first of these was plastic utensils. His initial article against plastics appeared in the August 1951 edition of *Prevention* and was followed by books and pamphlets on the subject during the next several years. The most offending element in plastic, he said, is formaldehyde, an antiseptic, "which definitely should not come into contact with food, not to mention hot coffee." J.I. feared that the formaldehyde of plastic cups would come into contact with the chlorinated water used by many Americans to make coffee. He noted that even the plastic manufacturers stated that chlorine compounds were "not friendly" to plastic surfaces. This produced, in J.I.'s opinion, "two chemicals at each other's throat with the public in between! How is such a thing permitted?" He urged readers to write to hospitals, restaurants, railroads, the Army, and the Navy to protest the use of plastic cooking and food-serving utensils.

Another practice that J.I. disliked because he thought it dangerous to health was the use of aluminum utensils in cooking. As early as 1941 he showed his disdain for aluminum by allowing a review of Mark Clement's book *Aluminum—A Menace to Health*, to be published in *Health Guide*. This review was one of the first instances that brought J.I. and his publications to the attention of the American Medical Association. In May 1941 Stuart Swensson of the Aluminum Association in Pittsburgh wrote to Dr. Paul Barton of the AMA, complaining about the *Health Guide* review. From this point forward, the AMA began to collect material on the Rodale enterprises, which finally amounted to several sizable volumes.

In 1955 J.I. wrote a short book, *Poison in Your Pots and Pans,* in which he stated his case not only against aluminum but against tin, copper, lead, and silver polish as well. It was the chemical properties of these materials coming into contact with those things from which human consumption occurred that disturbed J.I. In this book, he mentioned that all his previous articles on the subject had solicited "caustic" letters from several branches of the Better Business Bureau and from aluminum companies trying to intimidate him. He closed the book, however, by saying of such pressures: "Say what they [presumably the aluminum companies] will, howl as loud as they feel they must, I will continue to preach the truth that while aluminum is something wonderful to put on your car, it is poison for your porridge."

If the foregoing activities disturbed traditional practitioners of health and nutrition, J.I.'s recommendation of certain foods, minerals, and vitamins often angered them. For example, in addition to the benefits of sunflower seeds, J.I. believed that hawthorne berries were valuable as well. In his little book *The Hawthorne Berry for the Heart* (1971), J.I. asserted that around 1915 ". . . the whole run of botanical drugs, good, bad and indifferent, were shunted into a category [by whom he did not say] of old witch remedies, characterized as charlatanism and quackery. . . . From what I have learned about it [the hawthorne berry] I would say that together with Vitamin E we have an unbeatable combination to combat heart diseases" (p. 2). He was also highly complimentary of magnesium, which he called "the miracle mineral." Magnesium was a preventive, he said, against tooth cavities, migraine headaches, high levels of cholesterol, alcoholism, body odors, polio, and stones of the kidney and gallbladder. He derived these opinions about magnesium from the writings of several medical doctors and from the less reliable source of reader testimonials.

J.I. was convinced that primitive man was healthier than modern man because of dietary factors. For example, primitive people chewed up bones, ate whole fish including the internal organs, and consumed other matter deemed unacceptable by modern society. Yet these primitive foods were rich in vitamins and minerals, and J.I. believed they could be produced in tablet form and made palatable to citizens of the twentieth century. He always referred to these units of bone meal, fish liver oil, rose hips, desiccated liver, and so on as "food" and objected to their designation by some people as "pills" or "pseudodrugs." J.I. also continually emphasized the point that not all the nutritive substances in this world had been found and identified. If additional and more intense studies could be fostered toward discovery and utilization of all these natural substances, perhaps the national diet could be rescued from the hold that processed and synthetic foods had upon it.

By far the most controversial supplement that J.I. advocated was bone meal. The controversy was heightened by the connection made between bone meal and fluoridation of municipal water supplies. In this area, he earned the enmity of dentists all over the country. J.I. believed that bone meal was effective in preventing tooth cavities, and, if taken with vitamins A and D, was a useful safeguard against asthma. He described himself as a long-time user of bone meal, a practice, he said, that materially strengthened his bone structure. He frequently told audiences about the time he fell down a long flight of stairs and his bones were so strong "that I laughed all the way down, and enjoyed the ride."

J.I. asserted in scores of *Prevention* articles and a few books that bone meal was much superior to fluoridation in protecting teeth: "Not one dentist will ever be put out of business on account of fluoridation, but thousands of them would have to shut their offices if every individual took some bone meal tablets every day." He lamented the "faddist" label given to bone meal by many people. Often these same people, he declared, used not only bone meal but other supplements as well, except under different names; he said that Armour and Company, for instance, had been marketing bone meal for years under the name of calcium phosphate.

In the early 1960s a long and often embittered controversy raged in Allentown, Pennsylvania, over the effects of fluoridating the local water supply. J.I. had long opposed chemicals of any kind in eating and drinking supplies; accordingly, he headed the antifluoridation campaign in the Allentown area. He called fluoridation the "stupidity department," because it only "helps children up to about 10 to 12 years of age. It is estimated that children drink less than 1/20 of one per cent of all the water that goes through the water works. So—close to 100 per cent of the water is fluoridated without the fluoride in it meaning anything to the teeth of the children." He claimed that "for every $10,000 spent to fluoridate a city's water, $5 worth actually goes into the children at whom it is aimed," and he wanted to know "what kind of crazy finance is this?" He maintained that most fluoridated water wound up in sewers, from which it was ultimately transported to rivers, thus becoming a major and costly pollutant.

The opposition led by the Rodale groups (Citizens Group Against Fluoridation and Lehigh Valley Health Club, for example) was sufficient to defeat the fluoridation issues in Allentown. In the late 1960s and into the 1970s the controversy was revived with emotions on both sides reaching a high peak.

The Lehigh Valley Committee Against Health Fraud undertook its own campaign for fluoridation and against the Rodale enterprises. Its chairman, Dr. Stephen Barrett, wrote a letter in September 1970 to the Federal Trade Commission objecting to advertisements for bone meal and articles laudatory of bone meal appearing in the same edition of *Prevention*. Also, in January 1971 Barrett pointed out in a letter to the Allentown City Council that "[I]n articles and editorials, *Prevention* advises its readers that eating bone meal tablets is a sensational way to prevent dental cavities. During a recent one year period, bone meal advertising occupied more than $50,000 worth of advertising space [though Rodale figures put it at $26,000]. *Prevention* also carries ads for filters which are supposed to remove fluorides from water. The more people can be frightened about fluoridation, the more people will be interested in buying fluoride filters and the more likely it will be that filter companies will advertise in *Prevention* for $2850 per full page ad." Another member of the LVCAHF, Dr. H. William Gross, stoutly refuted claims for bone meal that J.I. made in the June 1971 edition of *Penthouse*. In a subsequent issue of the magazine, Gross said: "The ridiculousness of the claim by J.I. Rodale (June) that bone meal products prevent tooth decay or that it should be accepted as a health measure is only surpassed by the absurdity of the claim that bone meal 'heals' cavities already started. . . . Bone meal manufacturers could not and do not make these health claims since they could not document them to meet government regulations."

During the controversy, there were a few direct confrontations between J.I. and the profluoridation forces. One, as stated by the LVCAHF, was a challenge for Dr. Gross to debate with J.I., but Gross declined because, he asserted, J.I. was not qualified. Reportedly, however, a young Allentown housewife did debate J.I., and during the debate's course, he stated that none of the dentists in Allentown were any good and that he had to go to New York for his own dental work. The obvious question about this assertion was why wasn't his bone meal intake keeping him away from all dentists? J.I. apparently did not respond to the question but changed the subject, making some of those present doubt the sincerity of his arguments. On the other hand, J.I. reported in his book *My Own Technique of Eating for Health* (1969) a fluoridation debate with an Allentown dentist he did not name: "I took the side against fluoridation. In the course of the proceedings the dentist, a poorly nourished man I am sure, called me a liar. I sat there smiling, twiddling my thumbs. Excitement ran around the room. A newspaper reporter came over and expressed his admiration at my calmness. Instead of getting angry, I answered that dentist with facts about fluoridation." The program chairman later wanted to know if J.I. desired a public apology for the way he had been treated. J.I. declined by saying that he was not vindictive: "I am a happy, tolerant man, and for it I give a great deal of credit to my diet" (pp. 41-42).

According to some reports of his critics, J.I. stopped taking bone meal products about ten years before his death because he discovered that they were radioactive but continued to advertise them in his magazines because the ads were so profitable. Yet on the day of his death, J.I. stated before a large audience on the Dick Cavett Show that he had been a continuous user of bone meal tablets for thirty years. J.I. did write several articles about the strontium 90 content in bone meal but found that it was considerably lower than in most usually accepted foods consumed by the public.

The LVCAHF has in its possession a sworn affidavit, dated January 23, 1973, from a former Rodale employee relating to J.I.'s treatment of strontium 90 and bone meal. It is reproduced here in its entirety:

"I am a former employee of Rodale Press. In June, 1961, I overheard a conversation among J.I. Rodale, Ruth Adams and Marshall Ackerman [*Prevention* editor and advertising manager, respectively] about bone meal and advertising.

"As I recall, an article had been written for *Prevention* magazine [presumably this is the article that appeared in December 1961] based on the fact that nuclear fall-out in the mid-western plains was causing strontium 90 to appear in the milk of cows grazing in that area. This was one more reason, according to the *Prevention* plan, why parents should not allow their children to drink milk.

"Miss Adams, then an editor of *Prevention*, was concerned about the strontium 90 level in bone meal. She believed that strontium 90 might be present in the bones of cattle and would therefore be present in bone meal. She thought that *Prevention* should therefore stop carrying bone meal ads.

"There was a long discussion of the problem. It was decided that *Prevention*'s approach would be that bone meal was an antidote for strontium 90.

"Bone meal advertising continued in the magazine. Ruth Adams quit her job at *Prevention*, but resumed work for Rodale Press a few years ago."

The Rodale personnel mentioned in the affidavit remember the events surrounding the bone meal controversy. Adams stated that the strontium 90 question regarding bone meal began with the rash of atomic testing that occurred in this country in the early 1960s. ". . . I began a thorough search of every piece of relevant literature I could find. I wrote hundreds of letters to world-famous experts all over the world. No one could give me any answers. I talked to J.I. about it every day, literally. . . . I would turn up a piece of evidence that seemed to support my point of view. Then Jerry [J.I.] would come in with something that seemed to support his viewpoint. . . . We wrote memos to one another and to Bob [J.I.'s son], because we were both very troubled. But each of us respected the other's integrity and we both knew that this was an honest divergence of views which simply could not be settled with the knowledge we had at that time." At no time during the discussions of bone meal at *Prevention*, said Adams, was there a question of continuing to promote bone meal while secretly knowing that it was harmful. Nor was there ever any question of profits involved. "There are as many mineral supplements available as

Cheerful J.I. poses
in a tractor tire.

A young J.I. Rodale poses in
front of the Capitol Building
in Washington, D.C. He was
about 20 years old when this
photo was taken.

J.I. as a young man, about 25 years old.

J.I. Rodale and wife Anna. Photo taken around 1927.

J.I. guides a tour of interested people through his Emmaus farm.

J.I. listens to a question from former Vice-President Henry Wallace.

J.I. makes a point with Mr. Wallace.

J.I. listens to a point made by Gloria Swanson. Anna is second from left.

J.I. shows some friends a copy of his new book, *The Healthy Hunzas*.

"Family portrait." From left to right, J.I., Nina, Robert, Ruth, Anna.

J.I. dances with daughter
Ruth on her wedding day.

J.I. and daughter Nina on
her wedding day.

Generations of Rodales. At left, middle row, is Robert.
Fourth from left is J.I.'s daughter Ruth. Anna is on right,
middle row. First left, back row is J.I. Fifth left is daughter
Nina.

At left is J.I. Third from left is Senator Wayne Morse of Oregon.

J.I. and his British press representative, William Green.

J.I. boarding a plane for one of his European trips.

J.I. putting the finishing touches on a manuscript.

J.I. at work in one of his studies at his Emmaus home.

J.I. and his son Robert. Photo was taken in the late 60s.

J.I. and two of the performers in one of his plays. This photo was taken not long before his death.

there are people to put them together. . . . Refusing to advertise bone meal would not have made a scrap of difference to any advertiser. They could advertise some other mineral supplement. . . . And I would like to point out, too, that never, in all the years I was writing and editing *Prevention*, was I ever told by Jerry Rodale or anyone else that I had to take this-or-that editorial position because of what some advertiser might do or think."

Ackerman pointed out that there was "at no time a conflict of interest between our editorial concern and the advertising acceptability standards. . . . If we had felt that animal bone meal was hazardous, we would have stopped accepting such advertising. . . ." The statements of Adams and Ackerman indicate that the bone meal question was one of honest disagreement between J.I. and his *Prevention* editor. Adams felt uncomfortable writing about bone meal when the nuclear tests made so many things uncertain about it. J.I. was convinced that the strontium 90 content in bone meal was lower than in most other foods and was thus willing to continue patronizing it. The disagreement was the basis for Adams' resignation, but there does not appear to have been any unfriendly connotations in the act, as implied in the affidavit.

On November 27, 1961, Robert Rodale sent a memorandum to *Prevention* advertisers on the subject of bone meal. It read, in part, "You are no doubt familiar with the question of strontium 90 in animal bone meal. We have done research on this subject in the literature and have consulted several authorities on radiation biology and have concluded that we are on firm ground in stating that animal bone meal is a safe food and food supplement. There is strontium 90 in bone meal, of course, but with its average strontium unit of 5, it is at least as safe a food as milk, which has a value of about 6 and is safer than grains and vegetables, which average about 20 strontium units."

Apparently, the Rodaleans knew about the radioac-

tivity in bone meal a long time before certain professionals did. In a letter of October 6, 1970, from Barrett
of the LVCAHF to Oliver Field of the AMA, Barrett
stated: "Incidentally, bone meal tablets, as tested at
Lehigh University, turned out to be radioactive! We do
not know how significant this will turn out to be, but
the local agent seems quite excited about this." Barrett
went on to say that his committee was timing the publication of radioactive tests on bone meal with its overall
fluoridation campaign. The battle over Allentown fluoridation is continuing even today, months after J.I.'s
death. Though optimistic about the ultimate outcome,
the profluoridationists say that because of Rodalean opposition, Allentown will probably be the last city in the
United States to have fluoridated water supplies.

In summary, the chief points of J.I.'s critics are:

- His system is unworkable.
- He promoted food supplements that are worthless.
- He was unscientific, mistaking the coincidence for
  the pattern; he prejudged everything, forcing the "ailment" to correspond to the "cure" or the "preventive" he had in mind at any given moment.
- He was profit- rather than health-minded. Though no
  evidence exists that he was ever a member of the National Health Federation (founded in Monrovia,
  California, in 1955, the federation is both antifluoridation and anti-immunization), his foes claim that he
  acted as though he were.

J.I.'s policy of advertising always brought the
greatest protests from those who disagreed with him. In
a typical issue of Prevention, for instance, several bone
meal and vitamin E ads were inserted alongside articles
favorable to the use of these supplements. The advertisers could make no specific claim for their products,
but the Prevention articles could, for they were protected by the First Amendment. This practice of advertisements for supplements and articles laudatory of the

supplements disturbed not only the medical societies but the Food and Drug Administration as well. A member of the FDA staff recently wrote: "In addition to the articles which have so much potential to mislead and misinform the untrained individual, the [Rodale] magazines carry a great bulk of advertising which further contributes to the questionable interpretations and postulates of the articles" (letter to the writer, March 20, 1973).

As early as 1953, J.I. was confronted with advertising questions. In *The New Yorker*, March 7, 1953, a reader asked about *Prevention* advertising practices. In reply, J.I. said that at first he had not intended to accept ads for *Prevention*. For the first eight months of its existence, *Prevention* offered only one small ad, he said, and that was for "unpoison-sprayed" organically produced food. But then queries about bone meal, vitamin E, wheat germ, and so on became so numerous at the *Prevention* offices that advertisng was resorted to. J.I. said: "We had come to the conclusion that the cost of paper and printing being what it was, and that it being unpatriotic not to help pay off the Government's bonded debt by paying income tax, *Prevention* must take paid ads." In 1961, J.I. deferred slightly to his critics. After running an article about vitamin E on one page and an advertisement for it on the next, he wrote: "It does look unethical, I admit, but if you know a better way, tell it to me, and my heart will always be toward you."

A New York University student, Dorothy Manuche, however, saw little irregularity in *Prevention* advertising. Her studies involved her in a comparison of several health magazines, including *Prevention*. The unpublished paper she wrote of her research was titled "Today's Health and Prevention: A Propaganda Analysis." She found that a typical issue of *Prevention* contained fifty-one full-page food-supplement advertisements, twenty-nine of them merely statements of the merchandise available. Of the other ads, eight came with a distinct message aimed at some particular group—as for example, those seeking natural food to prevent cholesterol build-up. The remaining full-page ads, while making no specific claims for health, stated the general, overall benefits the food-supplement companies believe their products capable of giving. Manuche believed that *Prevention* advertising "is in perfect harmony with the text and constitutes in fact a valuable supplement to the text."

Efforts to increase *Prevention's* circulation led its advertising staff once to buy space in several other journals around the country, including the AMA-supported *Today's Health* and *The American Journal of Public Health*. The *Prevention* advertisement brought a storm of protests from the readers of the medical journals. Patrick Flanagan of the American Public Health Association described the situation in a letter to Barrett: "The *AJPH* carries ads for advertisements for nutritional products and birth control devices which have many times come under close scrutiny from government regulatory officials and appropriate professional groups. Where they advertise has never been a consideration in these deliberations as to whether or not these products should remain on the market. . . . On the basis of the mail we are now receiving, our attempt to be fair has obviously met with a great deal of criticism from the membership." The criticisms were sufficient to cause the health journal editors to discontinue the *Prevention* advertising. "*Where they advertise has never been a consideration in these deliberations as to whether or not these products should remain on the market*" (writer's italics): The statement was perhaps an unwitting justification of all the advertising done by the Rodale journals that was so heavily scored by some members of the medical community.

In 1952, a year or so after he started *Prevention*, J.I. exchanged a series of letters with Dr. Austin Smith of the AMA. On February 29, 1952, J.I. told Smith: "I would like to have you take into consideration the fact that *Prevention* magazine is a friend of the MDs. When we began publishing about a year and a half ago, we decided on a policy. We would quote only from conservative MDs' sources. We would print no articles about chiropractic and osteopathy. We definitely would not print anything by Naturopaths." J.I. went on to explain that he favored socialized medicine, but he knew of the AMA's opposition; therefore, he asserted that he would refrain from writing about it in *Prevention*. He said, however, that the AMA would occasionally find *Prevention* to be critical in general of the medical profession: "I say . . . it is a good thing for any science to have a little gentle criticism so as to keep things stirred up a bit. You will find our criticism rare and when it comes, it will be dignified and gentle." Then, J.I. asked Smith for permission to quote three or four lines occasionally from the various AMA journals: "This will give you good publicity. Most of our readers have so much confidence in us that when they see us quoting from the AMA, it makes them feel that it is a good publication."

Smith replied to J.I. on March 4, 1952: "I am indeed pleased to read that you would like to turn to authentic medical sources for medical information. I am sure that such information is generally available." Then in this letter, as in previous ones, Smith denied J.I. permission to quote AMA articles because of copyright complications.

The Rodale-Smith correspondence was the first major argument between the Rodaleans and the AMA—an argument that is still in progress. J.I.'s disclaimer toward criticizing the AMA was apparently soon forgotten, as attested to by the editorial guns of subsequent issues of *Prevention*. The cockiness of J.I.'s offer to give publicity to AMA journals through the pages of *Prevention* was equaled by the condescension of Smith's refusal. Thus, as time passed, J.I.'s antagonisms toward the AMA grew almost as fast as the AMA's file on Rodale. J.I. poked derision at the AMA and its constituents, and the AMA proved that it could do the same. In one of the AMA folders is an article by J.I. in which he identified himself as the author of a play called The Goose. Someone inserted into the margin: "Autobiography, no doubt!"

J.I. also subsequently abandoned his earlier inclinations not publicly to support socialized medicine in deference to the AMA. He strongly endorsed the various congressional proposals that ultimately led to Medicare in 1965. He was for the King-Anderson version that appeared in 1962, saying that the Social Security tax was the appropriate financing agency. He referred to the AMA stand against Medicare as "selfish" and labeled local Allentown ads against the bill as being close to the "Stalin-Hitler-Khrushchev technique of the 'big lie.'" AMA was devoting its energies, he said, to "scare gimmicks" against Medicare. Though he did not push the idea, it was clear that J.I. favored socialized medicine, not only for the elderly in this country but for all citizens as well. This fact, quite apart from his support of natural food supplements and unorthodox medical practices, was quite sufficient to earn him the undying hostility of the AMA.

It is regrettable that quarrels of this nature developed between the AMA and the Rodale group. It appears that almost from the beginning the AMA and its constituent organizations labeled J.I. as a fraud, a charlatan, and a quack, without making a thorough study of his activities or of even the things he printed in his various magazines. Much of the AMA's knowledge of J.I. and what he did is apparently based on letters from interested readers around the country—a process that is not really different from the "testimonials" J.I. used in his magazines as "proof" of his methods. Such incompleteness by the AMA encourages the widely held conception that the medical community in this country is indeed a closed corporation.

J.I. stated on several occasions, and there is no reason here to doubt his accuracy, that Prevention had the second-highest circulation of any health magazine in the United States—second only to the journal published by the AMA. (In the late 1960s, J.I. said that *Prevention* was the most widely circulated popular health journal in the world although, according to reports, a health magazine in Russia has a much larger circulation than *Prevention*.) Whatever the AMA's opinion of J.I. was, and is, the fact remains that there were times during the AMA-Rodalean confrontation that the AMA could have seized the opportunity and could possibly have turned *Prevention* into a magazine more acceptable to its philosophy. This possibility is amply indicated in some of J.I.'s letters, cocky and self-serving though they were, to the AMA. Despite AMA charges against him, and despite the extremely high circulation of *Prevention*, the chief historian of twentieth-century medical frauds, James Harvey Young, in *The Medical Messiahs*, does not mention J.I. Rodale.

On the other hand, J.I. was not blameless—especially in intensifying the argument once it was started. He frequently came on too strong in a field that was obviously "sacred ground" to thousands of medical practitioners. He often adopted a "preaching stance" and made it appear that the doctors were possessed with the same characteristics of charlatanism that they attributed to him. As related in an earlier chapter, J.I. put more stock in experience than in formal training, and this attitude often gave him an anti-intellectual posture. Perhaps he could have accomplished more by toning down his constant jibes at people who had "more education than good sense." His style of writing did not endear him, either, to many persons who might otherwise have joined him. He often included references to what were obviously "inside jokes" and sometimes to the jargon of his childhood days. These statements, though perfectly understandable to J.I., often left his readers wondering what he meant.

Despite everything, a considerable portion of J.I.'s critics credit him with sincerity in his activities. A statement from the LVCAHF begins: "We believe that J.I. Rodale was sincere in his views on health but was confused and misguided. Clearly, the scientific method of experimentation was not used to test his theories." The statement continued by asserting that "*Prevention* contains some articles which appear authoritative and well-written, such as the one on the dangers of smoking. This lends an air of respectability to the magazine and confuses many people about its nature. . . . The 'health' food approach is one which gives people false hopes and false feelings of security in return for their money. Often, the people who are most influenced are the ones who can least afford the 'luxury' of unnecessary nutrients."

Even if J.I. was "confused and misguided" in his health theories (and there is evidence to show that he was in some instances), any fair appraisal of him cannot put him into the category of the common medical quack. The quack *knows* that he is delivering false products: the quack also lays claims to curative powers; the quack is generally lacking sincerity about his beliefs and activities. All people of goodwill applaud when such malefactors are brought to justice. But one should not confuse lack of education, pointed criticisms, and bull-headed disagreements—especially when the objective is preventing illnesses—with quackery. As James S. Turner said in *Chemical Feast* (1970): "The vitamin and health food business, which may not be a fraud at all, was called 'the most widespread and expensive type of quackery in the United States' by former FDA Commissioner George Larrick at the 1961 Conference on Medical Quackery. But this 'fraud' is minor compared to the routine practices of other segments of the food industry (pp. 43-44)."

J.I. wrote several books to show the effects of these "routine practices" which, according to Turner, caused the FDA to proclaim the American food supply as "the best in the world" (*Chemical Feast*, p. 67). One such book was *Are We Really Living Longer?* (1955). Here he relied on his accounting background to challenge statements about man's supposed increased longevity in the twentieth century. Statistics always emphasized reductions in contagious rather than degenerative diseases; thus, medical advances had been greatly neutralized by increasing deaths from heart diseases, cancer, and other degenerative conditions. A man of 40 today as compared with a century ago has an increased advantage in life expectancy of only 2.7 years; a man of 50, 2 years. J.I. stated that for the 60-70 age bracket, "we have actually lost ground. The death rates in 1850 were better than those today." The falling death rate of infants gives the impression that we are becoming a healthier nation, creating a false sense of security and causing people to think: "I can do as I please, because, don't the figures show that we are living longer?" (p. 61). But something happens between the ages of 0 and 50 to slow down the rate of increase in life expectancy.

J.I. wondered if it were possible "that the very techniques [vaccinations, and so on] that are effective in preventing deaths at younger ages, may cause an increasing disposition towards the degenerative diseases later?" (p. 46). Then, too, he firmly believed that the increased use of chemical fertilizers and additives and of pesticides and insecticides took a heavy toll on a cumulative basis. He expressed the opinion that "it is time to give us food faddists a chance at the mortality figures." He felt that if organic methods of nutrition could be applied across the nation, within a very few years "there would be a turn-around, a going of the other way, in the degenerative category" (p. 46).

In countless articles and books, J.I. described his nutritional way to obtain what he believed would be superior health. He disagreed with the widely held thesis that life in America has become "faster" in the twentieth century; on the contrary, man is "dying because of a destructive inactivity" (*This Pace Is Not Killing Us*, 1954, p. 48). The inactivity was brought on, he believed, by profit-minded businessmen and gullible citizens. Although he wanted no return to the so-called good old days, he did urge people to eat properly and to get exercise. In such urgings, he certainly was not at variance with medical doctors in this country; it was not the ends that differed between J.I. and the medical profession—only the means.

In addition to writing about nutrition, J.I. also supported it in several speeches, mostly to local groups such as Parent-Teacher Associations and to cultural organizations. In these talks, he lamented the lack of attention given to nutrition throughout the country. He felt universities should increase their offerings in nutrition, that trucking firms and other transportation media should stress nutrition as a means of preventing accidents, and that some notice should be given to the relation between mental health and nutritional qualities. On the whole, he felt that our intelligence was in a state of decline, a decline that could possibly be reversed by proper nutrition habits.

J.I.'s relation with the subjects of food and nutrition is the most difficult aspect of his activities to analyze. He laid himself open to criticism much more readily in this field than in any other because he trod upon the ground of scientific specialists throughout the country and the world. His encyclopedic mind enabled him to integrate the diverse information he gleaned from the two dozen or so medical journals that he read each month. This integration often produced results that—if not helpful from an orthodox medical viewpoint—at least were not harmful. The integration caused him also to overreact on numerous occasions against the traditional practitioners and sometimes to make exaggerated and unfounded claims for his system of health. Perhaps he should have been criticized for his health-food ideas, but, if so, the medical community attacked him for the wrong things. It said primarily that he was a businessman and a book publisher without formal training in medicine and asked why he was interested in the subject. Profit, said his detractors, but this explanation stopped far short of what the criticisms should have entailed, causing the gist of the criticisms merely to be that of a profession that had acquired value systems far beyond the calling of medicine.

It must once again be stated that J.I. was not a healer and did not claim to be. He was wary of the speed with which many citizens ran to the doctor at even the slightest provocation; but then, many doctors are wary of this propensity themselves. Never did J.I. counsel against the patronage of doctors, but he did want to bring them down, as a group, from their godlike pedestals and to protest the separation of medical scientists as well as other types of scientists from society as a whole. These attempts made it completely predictable that J.I. Rodale would become a controversial person and would remain one long after his death.

CHAPTER 7

The FTC Takes a Look

In 1948, according to J. I. Rodale, Dr. Benjamin P. Sandler announced that, through a high-protein diet that avoided refined sugar and starches, he could establish immunity against polio within twenty-four hours. J.I. subsequently began printing articles about Sandler's claim, one of which was titled "The Cause of Polio Discovered." This article ultimately drew the attention of the U.S. Government's Federal Trade Commission.

On the grounds of financial incapabilities and of desiring to avoid adverse publicity, J.I. signed a cease-and-desist decree against the polio articles. A letter from J.I. to Millard W. Cron of the FTC, January 22, 1952, however, indicated that J.I. was not "repentant": "I am absolutely convinced that according to the work of Dr. Sandler, a person can condition himself against polio within twenty-four hours. This is the record of medical publications. I'm willing to go to court on that basis. And I know that between Dr. Sandler and myself, and the ten or twenty physicians that we can get, based on correspondence with them, I could present a favorable case to a federal court." Instead of seeking litigation, J.I. signed on May 26, 1952, an affidavit of discontinuance of the polio articles and the matter was dropped.

Some two years after this run-in with the FTC, J.I. published three books: *The Health Finder* (1954), a huge book of nearly a thousand pages that dealt with almost the whole gamut of medical subjects from a preventive viewpoint; *This Pace Is Not Killing Us* (1954), in which he argued that inactivity was one of modern man's most dangerous indulgences; and *How to Eat for* a *Healthy Heart* (1954), in which he urged, among other things, avoidance of certain foods if one wished to keep his heart functioning properly. The latter two books were combined into one volume and offered as a bonus to purchasers of *The Health Finder*. *The Health Finder* did not attract much medical attention, but that which it did was generally hostile. A review of it in the winter issue of London's *New Health: Quarterly Journal of Health and Diet* called it a "scrapbook of assorted information" that was misnamed "encyclopedia."

The books were widely advertised through the mails and other outlets, and they enjoyed a brisk sale throughout the mid- and late 1950s. In 1956, J.I. issued an eight-page yellow brochure to prospective customers around the country. Here the contents of the books were divulged, and some reader testimonials were used. In 1960, J.I. discontinued the yellow advertising brochure, substituting for it a green one that eliminated some of the statements in the earlier advertising. He kept the green one in circulation until 1963.

In October 1959, five years after the initial publication of *The Health Finder, This Pace Is Not Killing Us,* and *How to Eat for a Healthy Heart,* a staff member of the FTC visited the Rodale enterprise and said that a complaint had been made to the FTC (by whom he did not say) about the books' advertising. On this occasion, the FTC member asked for copies of the books and of all the advertising for them. The Rodales complied. On April 28, 1961, the FTC sent a letter to Rodale Books, Inc., requesting one copy of each magazine J.I. published so that the advertisements in them could be studied. Nothing more was said until October 1962, when the Rodales had another visit from the FTC. The agent reported that the matter of *The Health Finder* and the other two books was once again being looked into because of another complaint (again, he did not identify the source).

In the meantime, Rodale Press had virtually exhausted its supply of *The Health Finder*. After selling approximately 137,000 copies, it had slightly over 200 left in stock. *How to Eat for a Healthy Heart* and *This Pace Is Not Killing Us* had gone out of print in the early 1960s. In 1963, the last of the advertising for the books, the green brochure, was abandoned.

Throughout much of 1963, the FTC reviewed all Rodale publications and advertising, including *The Health Finder* and its discontinued advertising. No objections were made to other Rodale activities, but the FTC did decide to challenge the old advertising for *The Health Finder*, essentially because it allegedly represented ideas and suggestions in the book that were false and misleading. Several people raised the question of why the FTC made its move at this late date—almost a decade after the book first came out.

The Rodales and their attorney, Morton J. Simon, wondered if there were any connection between the FTC action and testimony given at a meeting of the U.S. Senate Special Committee on Aging. The theme of this meeting was "Frauds and Quackery Affecting the Older Citizen." On January 15, 1963, Dr. Robert Shank, chairman of the AMA Council on Foods and Nutrition, testified. He mentioned a book that J.I. had published in 1961 called *The Complete Book of Food and Nutrition*, in which J.I. extolled the virtues of brewer's yeast and desiccated liver for preventing various human ailments. Shank expressed the opinion that this book, along with a host of others by different authors, constituted medical fraud and quackery. He also stated that the AMA was working with the FTC "to combat food and nutrition frauds and faddism" (*Senate Committee on Aging*, p. 44). This testimony of Shank and of other AMA personnel, the Rodales believed, induced the FTC action against *The Health Finder*. This belief, however, is probably not well grounded. In the first place, Shank did not "single out" the Rodale publication in his testimony before the Senate committee but included it among several other books and articles that he thought deceptive from a medical viewpoint. Second, the FTC had already inquired into Rodale publications in 1959. Third, it did not issue its formal complaint against The Health Finder until over a year after the special Senate hearings on aging.

There were, instead, two fairly solid reasons why the FTC acted at this time. First, its investigation of The Health Finder since 1959 had been delayed by budgetary problems. It had no desire in 1964 to begin new procedures with emphasis on another Rodale publication. Second, the FTC considered advertising for The Health Finder as more "hard sell" than for current Rodale publications. Restricting The Health Finder advertising would have a much more severe effect on Rodale publications as a whole than any restriction of a current title. (And it was clear from the beginning that though the FTC moved ostensibly against The Health Finder, it had in mind the entire Rodale operation.)

On April 3, 1964, the Federal Trade Commission handed down its complaint against The Health Finder on the grounds that its advertising repeated ideas and suggestions in the book that were false and deceptive. The charge was divided into two areas. First was the general one that The Health Finder advertising assured the book's readers of a longer life, more energy, medical savings, feeling better, preventing illnesses like the common cold, and finding answers to health problems. The second division dealt with specific points such as preventing cancer, heart disease, tuberculosis, and several other maladies. Apparently, the FTC offered to let J.I. "off the hook" if he would sign a consent order against the advertising that had already been discontinued. Apparently, also, the FTC move caught one of its top officials by surprise. He told a Rodale attorney just before the hearings began that he did not know that the allegedly offensive advertising long ago had been discontinued. If he had known, the official averred, no FTC action would have been taken.

J.I. had more standing and more power in 1964 than in 1952, when he had bowed to the FTC. He believed

that the FTC charge was an attempted invasion of the
rights of publishers generally, and he was strongly convinced that the FTC effort was mostly a move to
discredit the whole philosophy of organic and preventive methods. If he accepted the consent order, he felt
he would "let down his readers," as well as the entire
organic and preventive movement. He therefore decided to contest the FTC's action.

At first J.I. wanted to defend himself, rejecting the
time-honored dictum that "he who acts as his own lawyer has a fool for a client." He was, however, ultimately convinced that his best interest demanded the
performance of highly trained counsel. He thus enlisted
the services of one of the country's most distinguished
practitioners of the law, Thurman W. Arnold. Even so,
J.I. probably never lost his desire to act as his own attorney. He attended the first day of the hearings, sitting
in the audience, and passed notes to Arnold on how to
handle the case. When Arnold rejected J.I.'s proferred
advice, J.I. became a bit upset and left Washington altogether. He never appeared as a witness before the
FTC proceedings.

Prehearing conferences were held on July 22 and
October 5, 1964. It was decided that the case would be
placed before an FTC examiner, John Lewis. On
November 9 and 19 and December 3, 1964, the Rodale attorneys unsuccessfully tried to get the charges dismissed. They argued that the questions before the FTC
were moot because the books and their advertising had
long ago ceased circulation; thus, the hearings would be
a waste of the commission's time and finances. The appeals were denied on the grounds that, although the
FTC was aware of the "alleged" discontinuance of the
challenged advertising, it believed that Rodale's present
advertising (presumably of all his other publications)
"suffered from the same basic deceptive themes as did
the earlier advertising" (*Federal Trade Commission Decisions*, Vol. 66, p. 1583). The denial to dismiss charges asserted that the FTC's move was not against the

books but only against the impressions in their advertising that by using them one could add years to one's life, prevent many diseases, and save money on medical and dental bills.

Again, on January 25, 1965, efforts by the Rodale attorneys to dismiss the charges failed. In all the FTC denials, one commissioner, Philip Elman, gave vigorous dissents. He felt that advertisements for a book could rightfully repeat the ideas and suggestions in the book itself. Therefore, the advertising in this case was as fully protected by the First Amendment as the book. Elman asserted that "what is challenged here, essentially, is the book and the ideas in it. These ideas may be silly or senseless; but Rodale has a constitutional right to disseminate them. The Commission is saying, in substance, that Rodale may have a constitutional right to publish *The Health Finder*, but it has no right to advertise the book, even truthfully, because the 'ideas and suggestions' contained in the book are not 'effective.' . . . Congress did not create this Commission to act as a censor of unorthodox ideas and theories in books, whether they deal with politics or health. We should not forget that, in both fields, today's heresy may become tomorrow's dogma" (*Federal Trade Commission Decisions*, Vol. 66, pp. 1584-1585).

Examiner Lewis convened the Rodale hearings on November 30, 1964, in Washington, D.C. Each side called a lengthy array of witnesses to testify for its contentions. For the Rodales, this was a rather costly procedure for, in addition to paying attorneys' fees, each witness for the Rodales cost between $200 and $300 a day. In a letter of October 2, 1964, Arnold described to Garland Ferguson, an attorney for the FTC, the role of prospective witnesses: "In sum our position will be that while the testimony of the government witnesses no doubt reflects their sincere opinions, there are other experts who similarly hold opinions supporting the validity of the information contained in these publications. We will contend that the FTC is not authorized to decide which of these different medical opinions is correct. The FTC cannot arbitrate between different schools of medical thought."

Some of the major witnesses for the government were Dr. Modestino Crisctiello of Georgetown University, Dr. Thomas A. Waldman of the National Cancer Institute, and Dr. Frank Finnerty, a practicing physician and graduate of Georgetown University. Very quickly the proceedings centered around *The Health Finder* statements that dealt with the common cold, constipation, ulcers, fatigue, high blood pressure, uses of salt, cancer, tuberculosis, polio, heart disease, arthritis, and mental health.

On the first day of the hearings, November 30, 1964, FTC attorney Ferguson asked Crisctiello his opinion of *How to Eat for a Healthy Heart* and *This Pace Is Not Killing Us*. Ferguson wanted to know if there was information in these books that would benefit readers in the prevention, treatment, or cure of heart maladies. Arnold objected, insisting that the issue was whether the books as a whole were beneficial to readers who followed their advice. He believed Crisctiello had read only those portions that related to heart disease; therefore, in his opinion Crisctiello was not a competent witness.

Crisctiello, however, asserted that he had read all the books in question in their entirety and felt he was capable of judging them from a medical standpoint: "I feel that in reviewing this book [that is, *How to Eat for a Healthy Heart* and *This Pace Is Not Killing Us*] which is a combination of two, there is information which under many circumstances, definitely would not be helpful and conceivably harmful to a patient with heart disease. . . . If a patient with congenital heart disease were to follow the advice in this book, very conceivably he would fail to approach a physician for a proper diagnosis, with recommendation for the proper surgical treatment. He might therefore continue with his heart disease over an extended period of time, relying on dietary measures alone which would be grossly inadequate. . . . With respect to the administration of the particular vitamins listed, I personally do not feel that there is any great benefit to be gained in the various forms of heart disease by administration of the various agents" (*Transcript of FTC Proceedings*, Docket 8619, pp. 139-150).

In his cross-examination of Crisctiello, Arnold claimed that the doctor's chief criticism of the books was that they might keep someone from seeing a physician. Crisctiello, according to Arnold, knew nothing "about the effect of reading these books on the ordinary person who might be deterred from going to a physician. That is the only harm this book can do." Crisctiello responded to Arnold's statements: "Most of the patients I see are in fact quite ill and are referred specifically to me for their heart problems. There are a number of patients I've seen in the past, and continue to see once they are improved and follow them along when they come to me for their regular physical examination, and they often will bring up questions that have occurred as a result of reading in the newspapers and magazines about problems of general health, and ask me those specific questions. In other words, not something related to an acute illness at the time, but to the maintenance of their health over a period of time" (*Transcripts*, p. 160).

Waldman's testimony covered a wide range of subjects. Asked if he thought *The Health Finder* contained an effective preventive for the common cold, Waldman replied negatively: "I think the common cold has been shown to be due to a multiplicity by now at least of seventy virile agents, and that there is no manner known to medicine that can assure one of avoiding the common cold short of completely isolating oneself from humanity. Irrespective of the dietary management which is suggested by the book, there is no way of assuring one's avoiding a common cold" (*Transcripts*, p.

209). Waldman went on to attack *The Health Finder's* ideas on constipation by calling them incomplete because of a lack of reference to the danger points of constipation that would cause a sufferer to seek the advice of a physician. Also, said the witness, there was no known cause for ulcers, cancer victims could be lulled into a false sense of security by *The Health Finder*, the garlic preventive for tuberculosis was unfounded, and there was nothing in the books that was efficacious in preventing arthritis.

With Waldman, Finnerty, and several other government witnesses, Arnold hammered away at the idea that their condemnation of *The Health Finder, How to Eat for a Healthy Heart*, and *This Pace Is Not Killing Us* must not be based on their narrow fields of specialization but upon the books as a whole. He attempted to have one witness take a pencil and mark through the books' areas with which he disagreed. This brought a strenuous objection from FTC's Ferguson that was sustained by Examiner Lewis. Arnold then referred to a recent pamphlet that had been distributed by the government that promised its readers "stamina, strength, and flexibility." This reference brought on a rather sharp exchange between Arnold and Lewis.

The examiner said there was no relationship between the Rodale books and the government's pamphlet: "It may be that the U.S. [government] puts out publications that are inaccurate. That does not justify a private person to do the same thing. We are trying this case, not that of the U.S. government." Arnold responded: "Your honor is holding that even if following the general instructions of this book [Rodale's] would cause, or if there is a likelihood of its readers living longer and feeling better, nevertheless if there are mistakes in the book, then that advertising becomes false. That is your position?"

Lewis avoided Arnold's "trap" by asserting: "I am not holding anything yet. I am hearing this case. That is your position. The government's position is to the contrary."

ARNOLD: That seems to be . . .

LEWIS: Wait a minute. I'm going to decide which position is legally right. But we have a question here, a technical question of cross-examination, and you are trying to use this witness to sustain your legal position, namely that the legal issue is whether the book as a whole . . .

ARNOLD: I am trying to do this . . .

LEWIS: I'm not finished yet. Whether the correct legal position is that we have to look at the book as a whole and determine whether the ideas in it as a whole are helpful.

ARNOLD: I'm trying to establish through cross-examination that this advertisement [for the Rodale books] is true as a matter of fact, and I'm entitled to do that, and your position in preventing that cross-examination [by sustaining the objection to have the witness mark out specific areas of the Rodale books with which he disagreed] necessarily means that if there are mistakes in the book, then the advertising is no longer true, that is the way I see it, and if that is your position, all right.

LEWIS: You are trying to put words in my mouth. We have, aside from the general question of whether the book will assure better health and a longer life, we have the question of whether the book is incorrect in certain specific aspects with reference to certain specific diseases which the advertisement assures. It is contended that the advertisement assures that the ideas in the book will be helpful in the prevention and cure of the specific conditions, and a general question of the type that you have indicated as to whether there are or are not ideas in the book that will be helpful, does not it seems to me, respond to the testimony of this witness.

ARNOLD: If your honor thinks whether there are mistakes in the book, then your ruling is correct, whether the advertising is true, then your honor is incorrect as to whether that is the question.

LEWIS: We will take a ten minute recess.

The Rodales' long-time attorney, Morton J. Simon of Philadelphia, assisting Arnold in the case, asserted that the stress of commission testimony was that "this chapter or that chapter was incomplete, did not go far enough, applying to a great many portions of the case, but not in this or that or the other type as conditions of goiters or ulcers, or whatever it was." Lewis disagreed with Simon's characterization of the commission's witnesses, saying that he (Lewis) had personally read all the advertisements for the Rodale books and thus felt that the government witnesses' testimonies were not fragmentary.

Arnold was in complete agreement with Simon on this point, claiming time after time that the Rodale books must not be judged piecemeal but as an entity. In a long letter to Simon, May 2, 1965, Arnold stated his beliefs about the matter. Since it portrays Arnold's stand so succinctly, the letter deserves extensive quotation:

"We argued to no avail to the Examiner and before the Commission on interlocutory appeal that this was censorship run riot. The only other instance in American jurisprudence where both advertisements of books and the books themselves may be banned from the mail were on the cases of obscenity. In such cases, the book as a whole must be judged. Excerpts from the books may not be used, however vile the language, to establish the book as obscene. Therefore, having established that the book [Rodale's] as a whole was a valuable one, we thought that if the Commission was sincere in its efforts to prevent the dissemination of quack books, that showing should be sufficient. We proved to be wrong. . . . Whether this case further demonstrates that in making his decision, the Examiner [Lewis] will inevitably decide in favor of conventional ideas which are generally accepted as true, he will not have the temerity to doubt the authority of the American Medical Association. The record further establishes that in a case where the AMA does not like a book and makes a public attack on it, a prosecution will be initiated by the staff [presumably of the FTC] on the flimsiest excuse even when the book is practically out of print and the advertising discontinued."

Among the Rodale witnesses were Dr. Blaine McLoughlin, chairman of the Department of Psychiatry at the University of North Dakota, and Dr. Theron C. Randolph, a practicing physician from Chicago.

McLoughlin said: "I would be an idiot indeed if I said there wasn't some harm done by every piece of learning put out. I know for instance that authors sometimes do harm to people with the best of intentions by saying things. I've done this myself. Every lecture done on the body, some people on the extreme fringes might be harmed. But if we tend to repress everything that could harm some extreme person, we tend to suppress the process of education on all levels. Because there is a danger in all education, we must start with the person as he is. The book [Rodale's] and the advertising enters into a certain segment of the population. It does not apply to any person in the room [at the Rodale hearings,] really, but it does apply to millions of people and I think that within that framework, it is a useful book in our health and health education areas." Randolph was complimentary of *The Health Finder* for pointing out the dangers of chemical insecticides which were in wide use throughout the country.

Possibly the most significant witness for the Rodales was Dr. Louis Lasagna, then an associate professor of medicine at Johns Hopkins University School of Medicine. Frequently in the past Lasagna had served as a commission witness on several matters and intermittently had been a research consultant for the government agency. He was, however, a strong believer in the free expression of ideas and opinions, not only in the medical community but in other areas as well. Therefore, on this occasion Lasagna offered to help the Rodales in all possible ways. He testified that *The Health Finder* "made a number of admirable recommendations in the field of diet and nutrition and in suggesting the avoidance of excessive reliance on drugs . . ." He did say, however, that some portions of the book exaggerated "the benefits of dietary manipulation." Lasagna's testimony, believed the defense attorneys, "turned the tide" in several important respects for the Rodales. They felt that Lasagna's words were instrumental in influencing Examiner Lewis later to dismiss some of the general charges in the complaint.

The most controversial witness for the Rodale side was Robert Rodale, J.I.'s son and president of Rodale Press, Inc. Arnold stated that originally he intended to call J.I. as a witness but then decided J.I.'s and Robert's testimony would overlap and thus "burden the record."

Ferguson asked Rodale if *The Health Finder* was still listed in their current catalogs. Rodale replied: "We put out a lot of things. We are a pretty big company, and I am not the advertising manager. I am the President of the Company, and I cannot put my finger exactly on where it might be listed. But I presume, I believe, that somewhere in our operations, we have listed this as being available."

Ferguson then produced the November 1964 edition of *Prevention*, where, on page 58, there was a listing of *The Health Finder* as a current and available Rodale publication. The Rodale attorneys immediately objected to connecting *The Health Finder* with *Prevention*, stating that the facts were not related in this instance. Ferguson, however, continued his questioning of Rodale: ". . . I will ask you whether or not the book *The Complete Book of Food and Nutrition*, is a book which is being currently sold and advertised by your company?" (This was the Rodale book mentioned by Dr. Shank at the Senate Special Committee on Aging in January 1963.) Rodale replied: "It is being currently sold. Whether it is being currently advertised, I cannot give you an exact answer. We have advertised it in the past, and in the recent past, let us say, and it may be that it will not be advertised again, or it may be that it will. I just cannot say."

Ferguson's aim, he said, was to show that the books in question were still being advertised, not in mailing brochures but in current Rodale publications. He then pointed to page 57 of the *Prevention* issue, where there was a reference to *How to Eat for a Healthy Heart*. In parenthesis, it was stated: "Rodale Books, $1.00." Before the Rodale attorneys could object to Ferguson's questions, Examiner Lewis interrupted with the exclamation: "That is the fire alarm bell. We will have to vacate."

On Lewis' announcement, defense and government witnesses, attorneys, and Lewis himself headed for the elevator on the office building's eleventh floor. Naturally, they pushed the "down" button, but the elevator went up instead for, understandably, someone on the twelfth floor also wanted to escape the danger of any fire. As it turned out the fire was only a small one in an air duct.

Shortly after the question of the physical fire was settled, the group returned for a resumption of the verbal fireworks. Arnold's partner, Stuart Land, raised a strong objection to the introduction of *Prevention, The Complete Book of Food and Nutrition*, and other Rodale publications, on the grounds that they were irrelevant to the FTC proceedings. "The allegations of the complaint make no challenge to the ideas and suggestions contained in that book, nor do they make any references to any allegations in the advertising of that book." Lewis, however, gave some indication that when he made his trial ruling, he would not really confine himself to *The Health Finder, How to Eat for a Healthy Heart*, and *This Pace Is Not Killing Us* but would assess any other Rodale publication he desired to.

The FTC Rodale hearings concluded on March 5, 1965, almost a year after the initial complaint had been made. Dozens of witnesses had appeared at the hearings, giving testimony that, in transcript, amounted to several thousand pages. The cost to both sides was extremely high. The FTC did not divulge its expenses, but the Rodales estimated that their cost ran well in excess of $150,000. There was actually no great amount of publicity about the case from the nation's newspapers and magazines. *The New York Times*, December 13, 1964, included a brief article about it but confined itself primarily to Commissioner Elman's dissent. The Allentown (Pa.) *Morning Call*, January 20, 1965, speculated that the case would ultimately go before the United States Supreme Court, which would decide how far a government agency could go in banning advertisements regardless of subject matter or ideas.

Examiner Lewis took from March 5 to April 16, 1965, to prepare his final report for recommendations to the full Federal Trade Commission. The most noted precedent he had to rely on was the Witkower case, which had been heard by the commission in the mid- and late 1950s. Don Dale Alexander, president of the Witkower Press of Hartford, Connecticut, had written a book, *Arthritis and Common Sense*, which ultimately became a runaway best seller, with well over half a million copies sold. According to the FTC, in the advertisements for the book Witkower Press had promised effective treatments of arthritis and rheumatism, as well as legitimate advice on how to prevent those illnesses. The advertisements had been sent through the mails, thus crossing state lines, and had been carried over numerous radio and television stations whose listening and viewing audiences were in several states. Because of the interstate character of Witkower (and subsequently Rodale) advertising, the FTC claimed full authority to inspect its activities.

In its conclusions on the Witkower case, the FTC had made it clear that it was making no judgment on Alexander's privilege of writing a book or deciding what should be in it. The FTC's only interest was in the advertisements for the book, and the government agency maintained that advertisements, unlike the book itself, were not protected by the Constitution's First Amendment. The FTC accordingly ordered that Witkower Press "do forthwith cease and desist from representing, directly or indirectly" that *Arthritis and Common Sense* was adequate, effective, and reliable in giving relief to arthritic and rheumatoid sufferers. Alexander and Bernard Witkower, secretary-treasurer of Witkower Press, had accepted the FTC ruling, and had not appealed the case to a higher authority.

The first part of Examiner John Lewis' initial decision, April 16, 1965, established that Rodale's business of publishing health books and advertising them through the federal mails and of competing with other health publishers justified the FTC's intervention into his activities. He also reasserted the FTC's case against Rodale that "respondents have used false, misleading and deceptive advertising in connection with the sale of certain of their books and pamphlets ... based principally on mailer advertisements sent to potential purchasers of their book *The Health Finder*."

Next, Lewis took up the subject of the yellow advertising brochure, which had been used between 1956 and 1960. He classified the "messages" of the brochure under four different categories: "A. General statement regarding the importance of good health. B. General description of the book, *The Health Finder*. C. Statement concerning the value of the ideas contained in the book. D. Statement concerning specific diseases or subjects discussed in the book, with references to pages in the book where such subjects are discussed."

Category A was about the value of good health in general, and the giving of impressions that *The Health Finder* could help one discover it. Category B identified

The Health Finder as an encyclopedia of health information from the preventive standpoint and asserted that *The Health Finder* answers health problems. Category C was not emphasized in Lewis' findings. Category D concerned itself with recommendations for a winter free of the common cold, preventives and cures for constipation, connections between cancer and nutrition, and other matters dealing with ulcers, heart diseases, polio, TB, goiter, and fatigue.

Lewis noted that the green advertising brochure that replaced the yellow one in 1960 eliminated several of the more flamboyant statements and reader testimonials of the earlier advertisements. Despite the changes, FTC counsel still maintained that all advertising for *The Health Finder, How to Eat for a Healthy Heart,* and *This Pace Is Not Killing Us* was deceptive and misleading. Lewis also noted that the Rodale book *The Complete Book of Food and Nutrition,* currently being advertised by a red brochure, contained many of the same ideas and suggestions as *The Health Finder.* Lewis rejected the Rodale position that the FTC hearings contravened the First Amendment and that the public good would not be served because the allegedly offensive advertising had long ago been discontinued.

The first finding of Examiner Lewis favored the Rodale position. FTC counsel had argued that advertisements for *The Health Finder* and the two bonus books had assured prospective purchasers, among other things, an increased life span, more energy, and savings on medical and dental expenditures. The closest the Rodales came to "assurance," said Lewis, was in the yellow brochure. Even there, however, no "assurance" in the sense of a guarantee was ever given. Lewis wrote: "A number of the medical witnesses called in support of the complaint who had testified that the ideas in the book would 'assure' these benefits, conceded that the book contained information which, if followed, would probably result in the reader's living longer, feeling better or achieving certain health benefits." Thus, the charge against J.I. of his books' "assurance" was dropped by Lewis. He was also of the opinion that *The Health Finder* statements about garlic treatment for TB and vitamin B for mental illness did not give assurances of efficacy in preventing these two sicknesses. The charges in respect to TB and mental health, therefore, were dropped.

Lewis' second finding also favored the Rodales. In connection with category B, created by Lewis for convenience, he repeated the statement used by Rodale advertising for *The Health Finder*: "Answers health problems." FTC counsel had contended that implicit in this statement was the word "all," which, if correct, would make the statement read: "Answers all health problems." Lewis disagreed with this interpretation: "It is the opinion and finding of the Examiner that this portion of respondent's advertising cannot be fairly interpreted as representing that the reader will find in the book the answers to 'all' his health problems."

Having ruled for Rodale in these respects, Lewis then turned his attention to specific diseases and ailments listed in *The Health Finder*. Lewis used category D to identify and judge these various subjects.

The first topic was the common cold. J.I. had used several reader testimonials in the yellow brochure, and Lewis believed that these meant that J.I. intended for the public to believe that *The Health Finder* advice was useful in preventing colds. He disregarded the recommended diet, which was heavy on vitamin A in cold prevention. Instead, he asserted: "According to the greater weight of the credible medical evidence in the record, persons following the recommendations in the book will not be able to avoid getting a cold" (*Federal Trade Commission Decisions*, Vol. 68, p. 1201). There were changes in the wording of the advertising from the yellow to the green brochure, but Lewis still found that, on the common cold, "there would be members of the public who would interpret respondents' advertising to mean that the book will tell them how to avoid or deal with the common cold."

The yellow brochure had asked: "What is the most successful preventative and cure for constipation?" The green brochure omitted references to "cure," but Lewis still found against *The Health Finder* ads on constipation. *The Health Finder* had emphasized the tremendous importance of diet in preventing constipation. Lewis claimed, however, that there were many types of constipation problems that had nothing to do with diet.

On ulcers, J.I. had ruled out emotional factors as causative. Examiner Lewis disagreed. In the yellow brochure, the subject was discussed as "Prevention of ulcers." In the green brochure, the subject was simply "Ulcers." Lewis believed that the cause of ulcers is not entirely understood and that the change of wording from one brochure to another did not eliminate the risk that some members of the public would be led to think that in the pages of *The Health Finder* they could discover how either to prevent or to cure ulcers. Therefore, in respect to ulcers, Lewis ruled against the Rodales.

Desiccated liver for the prevention of general bodily fatigue came in next for Lewis' scrutiny. Again, he found the "greater weight of credible medical evidence" to dictate against the value of desiccated liver. The same was true with the prevention of goiter.

Lewis objected also to the testimonials in Rodale ads on high blood pressure. He found deceptive several statements to the effect that elimination of salt from one's diet would help to prevent high blood pressure. He rejected cancer testimonials and references to "experiments" and "laboratory experiments" in connection with prevention of cancer. Lewis also faulted *The Health Finder* statements about diet manipulation for preventing polio and vitamin E for the heart, as well as testimonials on arthritis. In all these instances, Lewis appealed to the "greater weight of credible medical evidence" and expressed the belief that there would be members of the public who would be led astray by the Rodale advertising.

Examiner Lewis was completely opposed to the advertising for the two bonus books, *How to Eat for a Healthy Heart* and *This Pace Is Not Killing Us*. He said the ads for all the books were "false, misleading and deceptive in a number of material respects." Such advertisements have "the tendency and capacity to mislead and deceive members of the purchasing public into the erroneous and mistaken belief that such statements were, and are, true . . ."

In the concluding portion of his decision, Lewis pointed out again that the FTC was not attacking the books per se but only the advertisements of them. "Respondents are free to advance any theory they wish in their publication, no matter how ill-conceived and misguided. However, if they wish to advance the sale of their publication, as a commercial product, and to induce the public to purchase it, then they have no right to falsely advertise the therapeutic benefits which purchasers of their product will receive, merely because that product is a book." On the Rodale claim that the FTC move should not have occurred because the advertising of the books had been discontinued, Lewis said: "In cases of asserted abandonment of a practice, it must appear that the practice has been 'surely stopped' and that it is not likely to be renewed."

Lewis' recommended order to the full FTC was for Rodale advertising for *The Health Finder, How to Eat for a Healthy Heart, This Pace Is Not Killing Us,* and any other books with similar content to cease and desist. Obviously, if this order had stood, the entire Rodale organization would have been destroyed. Attorneys for both sides quickly indicated that they would appeal Lewis' findings. FTC counsel believed he had not gone far enough against Rodale advertising; Rodale counsel believed he had overstepped his authority, especially in respect to the First Amendment.

Press coverage on Lewis' findings and recommended

order was somewhat greater than it had been when the case was first brought up. Both The Wall Street Journal and The New York Times featured short articles about it. The newsman who gave it most attention was a correspondent for the Washington Star Syndicate, James Jackson Kilpatrick, whose column appeared in more than fifty newspapers throughout the United States. Calling J.I. an "apostle of nonconformity," Kilpatrick said that J.I. was fighting a "lonesome and exhausting battle that merits the support of free men everywhere." He called Lewis' order "extraordinary and ominous" and said that every person interested in freedom had a stake in the case. Kilpatrick closed his article by asserting: "If the publisher of unconventional ideas cannot advertise his unconventional ideas, his freedom is assuredly abridged. And if the First Amendment fails to protect an advocate of desiccated liver, whatever that is, the First Amendment is suffering a fatigue that demands better doctors."

Thurman Arnold and the other lawyers who had represented J.I. in the FTC hearings were disappointed at the findings. In his May 2, 1965, letter to Simon, Arnold showed his disgust when he said that the FTC was willing to have its processes used to cast public discredit upon the Rodale books. He said: "In this case a release was issued and presumably sent through the mail emphasizing the absurd finding of the Examiner that readers of this book [The Health Finder] might lose their health and even their lives. The AMA reprinted this finding, and without the sanction of the Commission, the [medical] Association could have been sued for libel. But since it acted under the official sanction of the Commission, it is being published by the AMA with complete immunity. We submit that the opportunities for the abuse of the Commission's newly claimed power portrayed in this record, demonstrate that Congress could not have intended to lodge that power with a body so ill qualified to exercise it and so indifferent to the consequences to publisher and author. If it be assumed that Congress has authority to forbid the use of the mail for a summary of opinions in medical books, where such opinions are regarded as unsound and Congress decided to pass a law to suppress medical quackery, it is impossible to believe that it would not choose the Public Health Service.

Probably everyone involved in the case knew that Examiner Lewis' decision was at best a stopgap measure. Regardless of which way his decision went, the case undoubtedly would have gone on to the full commission. Indeed, it was cross-appealed by counsel for both sides. Machinery for the full hearing was set in motion during the closing months of 1965. The Rodale case at the hands of the full commission created some more twists and turns in the effort to keep Justice a blind figure.

CHAPTER 8

Short of the First Amendment

A few weeks after Examiner John Lewis gave his decision against the Rodales, the American Civil Liberties Union entered the case. On September 27, 1965, the FTC gave permission to the ACLU to act as amicus curiae, allowing ACLU counsel ten minutes on the opening date of the appeal, September 28, to present its views and opinions.

The ACLU brief urged the commission to set aside the examiner's decision because it was in violation of the First Amendment. The examiner's decision, said the ACLU, did not really rest upon the accuracy or inaccuracy of the advertising for the books in question but upon the supposed scientific invalidity of the ideas and opinions expressed therein. "Hence, it must be assumed on this appeal that the advertising is an accurate reflection of the opinion content of the book, and no more. It follows that the Commission is squarely presented with the question of whether or not it can condemn truthful advertising of a book on the sole ground that the opinions expressed in the book are incorrect or not accepted by majority opinion."

A bookseller cannot be held responsible, the ACLU brief continued, in advertising his ideas, as long as he reports the ideas with reasonable accuracy. The First Amendment, in guaranteeing freedom of speech, did not categorize its subjects; it did not say that we may have freedom of speech on this subject but not on that one. It said, plainly, freedom of speech. Therefore, medical thoughts and ideas were just as protected as any other. The brief concluded with the speculation that the commission may have been led inadvertently into the "forbidden territory" of the First Amendment. Thus, the ACLU hoped that "when the Commission recognizes the full implication of such activity, it will conclude that it is contrary to the First Amendment of the United States Constitution, to sound administration of the trade regulation laws, and to the general public interest."

The commission, as we shall see, apparently paid some attention to the ACLU argument, but in doing so it created additional problems. The appeal in the case started on September 28, 1965, and the decision of the full commission was not rendered until June 20, 1967. At the commission hearings there were no witnesses as there had been before Examiner Lewis, only oral arguments from the opposing attorneys.

The Federal Trade Commission was composed of five members. Its chairman since 1961 was Paul Rand Dixon, a native of Nashville, Tennessee, with an AB from Vanderbilt University and an LL.B. from the University of Florida. He had been a trial attorney for the FTC for several years before his appointment as chairman. One of Dixon's colleagues was Philip Elman, a former law clerk to Justice Felix Frankfurter of the United States Supreme Court and a Kennedy (1961) appointment to the FTC. Elman turned out to be the "maverick" in the Rodale case, giving at least three strong dissenting opinions during the course of the proceedings. The other members of the Commission were Everette MacIntyre, John R. Reilly, and Mary Gardiner Jones.

Oral arguments in the Rodale case before the commission were fewer than when Lewis conducted the initial hearings. A few excerpts, however, are in order, to show their general trend and also to point out that some commission members seemed to be a bit confused about the issues.

DIXON: This complaint did not challenge what was said in the book, did it?

FERGUSON: It challenged the advertising statements as being false. They represented certain benefits.
DIXON: Advertising about the book is challenged?
FERGUSON: That is correct.

At this point, Commissioner Jones wanted to know if Ferguson had determined whether the advertising "merely tracked and described" what the book said. Ferguson answered in the negative, whereupon Jones wanted to know specifically what the commission was concerned with here—whether it was what the book had said or what the advertiser said the book said. Ferguson then referred to the Witkower case, stating that it and the Rodale case were identical. Commissioner Elman said that the "Witkower case didn't charge the advertising was false because it departed from what was in the book—because it followed what was in the book. That is also true here, isn't it?" Ferguson replied, "I believe the two complaints are similar."

At one session, Elman stated that several years ago he read a book by Oswald Jacoby, *How to Win at Poker*, and had faithfully followed the advice therein, "and I can testify as a witness that I have not won at poker. Does that justify our issuing a cease and desist order against the advertising of that book?" Ferguson said the test would have to be more than one person's winning or losing. Elman claimed that he could qualify as an expert, "certainly on losing."

During the time his case was being deliberated, J.I. generally stayed away from Washington, putting his interests in the capable hands of Thurman Arnold, Stuart Land, and Morton Simon. He did follow closely what was happening, and he began reporting the events to his readers in the pages of his magazines and occasionally in special "news bulletins." According to a family friend, the Rodales "kept their readers advised of the progress of the case as it moved through the FTC. . . . They wrote about the unhappy developments just as much as about the happier aspects. In short, they were good reporters." This reporting elicited hundreds of letters both to the Rodales and to the FTC. A typical one was from Myra Nell Silton of Boston, who wrote to FTC Chairman Dixon on October 7, 1965: "The FTC in this proceeding is dangerously close to thought control. One cannot help but question your judgment in moving against advertising alleged not to have been used for at least five years."

Also, while the proceedings against him continued, J.I. apparently became a subscriber to an FTC newsletter. In a release of November 4, 1966, the commission announced its intention to undertake a study of smoking to determine a reliable test for checking tar and nicotine content in cigarettes. The Commission invited interested persons to submit their suggestions. J.I. was most definitely an interested person. He therefore wrote to the commission, asking it to look into the large quantities of pesticides used on each year's tobacco crops, which subsequently affected not only cigarettes but cigars, pipe tobacco, chewing tobacco, and snuff as well. He requested permission to appear before the commission and testify on this important matter. He claimed that he could present his case in less than half an hour. J.I. received a letter on November 25, 1966, from the FTC's Francis J. Charlton. J.I.'s submission of ideas, the letter said, related only to the problem of pesticide residues in tobacco products and did not come within the purview of the "limited purposes" of the FTC hearings on smoking. On behalf of the FTC Charlton did, however, extend his thanks to J.I. for his interest. At no time during the exchange of letters was the subject mentioned that at this precise time J.I. himself was under FTC investigation. Critics could argue that J.I.'s offer to help the FTC in its study of smoking was just another example of his cocky and perhaps self-righteous attitude. It could just as easily be maintained, however, that he was convinced that he had, through the years, gathered important knowledge that could be useful and that he should share it regardless of any other existent situation.

The findings of the commission, in large part, vacated the recommended orders of Examiner Lewis. The original complaint was that Rodale's advertising repeated ideas and suggestions in *The Health Finder* that were deceptive and misleading, and Lewis had found that in most instances the charges were true. The commission, however, apparently very quickly noted the danger Lewis was running in regard to the First Amendment. If the advertising merely repeated the ideas and suggestions in the book, then the advertising was just as much a part of free speech as the book and thus was protected by the First Amendment to the U.S. Constitution. The commission therefore spent quite a bit of time in efforts to justify a restraining order against the Rodales and still remain within the confines of constitutional protection.

In regard to the specific illnesses—colds, constipation, ulcers, polio, cancer, arthritis, goiters and so on—the commission supported Lewis' findings that the advertisements had the capacity to mislead the purchasing public. But, in upholding Lewis in this respect, the commission went beyond the original complaint that the advertising *repeated* ideas and suggestions in *The Health Finder* that were deceptive. It found instead that the advertising was characterized by "puffery," by "hyperbole," by "flamboyance," and by "exaggeration." But the book itself, the commission found, was written in guarded tones. The author-editor (J.I.) had been very careful to note that there was no known preventive for the common cold and that the diet manipulation he recommended for the other maladies had no distinct preventive or curative qualities. (Indeed, the commission specifically dismissed the charge by complaint counsel that *The Health Finder* offered a treatment and cure for cancer, polio, and mental illness.) There was, therefore, in the commission's opinion a distinct difference between what was promised in the advertising and what was delivered in the book. Because of this difference, the commission asserted its right to investigate Rodale activities and to give any orders that it thought necessary to protect the public good.

Commissioner Jones delivered the commission's majority opinion. Regarding the First Amendment, the opinion asserted that "freedom of speech" is not, and never has been, regarded as "absolute." ". . . [T]he constitutionality of regulatory statutes [in this case, the FTC] has been sustained [by the courts] against attacks even where their impact resulted in some restraint of the exercise of constitutional freedoms." Precedent had established that "slight impairments of speech" would always have to give way to the "need to protect the public from deception." Moreover, the commission found, Rodale's advertising was not intended to spread J.I.'s ideas and thoughts about health to the general public but only to sell his books. Thus, the Rodale position that the advertising was merely an extension of the book was rejected. The commission insisted that the advertising was advertising and not speech and that therefore the advertising was not constitutionally protected.

The test used to interpret advertising, said the majority opinion, was the "net impression" it might make on the general populace. "Where an advertisement is subject to two interpretations, one of which is false, the Commission is not bound to assume that the truthful interpretation is the only one which will be left on the mind of every reader." The opinion continued that "the Commission's mandate from the courts is to protect the 'ignorant, the unthinking, and the credulous'" (which in one way or another, covers just about all of us). Since the "very language of this advertising makes the representation of an affirmative promise of therapeutic benefits," the commission felt impelled to protect the "ignorant, the unthinking, and the credulous" elements of American society.

Most of the commission disagreed with the Rodale

claim that the advertising was done in qualified terms. "If a limited claim is in fact intended then the claims must be exactly delineated by express qualifying language. We will not imply such qualifying language in our interpretation of such claims, nor indeed do we think the ordinary casual reader would do so. . . . Literalness and exactitude—and perhaps understatement— must be the earmarks of promotions connected with health remedies."

Despite its unwillingness to interpret what was claimed to be qualifying language in this respect, the commission showed that it had no qualms about interpreting in the other direction. When Examiner Lewis had heard the case, complaint counsel had attempted to prove that the sentence in the advertising "Answers health problems" had in fact meant "Answers all health problems." Lewis had ruled against this contention. The commission, however, stated that Rodale's labeling his book as an "encyclopedia," his sentence of "Answers health problems," his inclusion of a checklist of diseases that readers might want to know about, and the reader testimonials "would certainly be interpreted by the reader as a representation that the book in fact furnishes answers to any and all health problems." The absence of "all" or "each" from the advertising "does not avoid the representation to the public that all health problems are answered. It would ignore reality to hold that the omission of these words must of necessity imply something less than 'all' or 'each' to the reader." Examiner Lewis' earlier finding was therefore vacated by the full commission.

The commission continued its propensity for speculation when it looked into the point made by the Rodales that the case should never have occurred because the alleged offensive advertising had been discontinued and The Health Finder was almost out of print. The majority simply could not believe that The Health Finder would be consigned to "the junk heap." Ignoring the "literalness" and "exactitude" that it demanded in advertising, the commission said: "It is more likely that respondents intend to bring it [*The Health Finder*] out in the future in some new edition. Thus the advertising of the publications in our judgment could not in any sense be said to be 'moot.'" Also, the Rodales had not shown themselves to be "repentant advertisers," because there was no way of assuring that if the publications were updated the questioned advertising of other Rodale publications would be accurate and correct. (In the ruling, however, the commission restricted itself only to the Rodale books in question and did not inquire into other Rodale publications.)

In summary, the material differences between Examiner John Lewis' findings and those of the commission were: Lewis found that the advertising repeated ideas and suggestions in the book that were false, deceptive, and misleading; whereas the commission found that the advertising was an exaggeration of what was in the book. This finding was quite inconsistent with the content of the original complaint and was a postulate different from the one upon which Lewis first heard the case.

Commissioner MacIntyre dissented from the finding but concurred in the result of the commission's hearing. He claimed that the commission, in trying to skirt the First Amendment, had emphasized "discrepancies between the content of the book and the challenged advertising. The complaint did not make that distinction." The commission's opinion, said MacIntyre, "conveniently" avoided the Rodale claim that the challenged advertising was within the scope of the First Amendment. The commission, moreover, was running the possible danger of throttling any future similar decisions because "[I]n another case, where equally false claims are made in the advertising, such promotion would be insulated from Commission action as long as it coincided neatly with the advertised book." Though he voted with the majority, it was clear that Commissioner Mac-

Intyre would have preferred a sustainment of Lewis' findings.

The most heated dissent came from Commissioner Elman, who throughout the Rodale proceedings had protested the commission's moves. He began by stating that in discussing the First Amendment the commission had demolished a straw man. It was axiomatic to him that an author had the right to write and publish a book and advertise it to the public and to repeat his opinions and beliefs regardless of their "truth" or "falsity" in the book's advertising.

The commission's opinion, claimed Elman, did not so much as mention the one "all-fours" precedent that it had in deliberating the complaint against Rodale—the Witkower case. In that case, it may be recalled, the commission decided against "false promises of therapeutic benefits in the advertising for a book when such advertising statements derive from or reflect like views or information contained in the publication itself." Until the day of the commission's opinion, the charge against Rodale was exactly like the charge had been against Witkower.

But now, Elman declared, "all this is turned upside down. According to the majority opinion, respondent's [Rodale's] advertisements were deceptive because they made claims which did not repeat but exceeded those to be found in the book. This marks a 180 degree reversal of the theory of the case, as alleged in the complaint, tried before the hearing examiner, argued on appeal to the commission." The commission's action in trying to satisfy First Amendment problems created Fifth Amendment questions by adding a new and different charge (that the advertising was an exaggeration of the content of the book) and by convicting the Rodales without so much as a notice or hearing on that new and different charge.

As he had done previously in an earlier stage of the Rodale hearings, Elman said that Congress did not establish the FTC to censor unorthodox ideas. "It is the glory of a free society that a man can write a book contending that the earth is flat, or that the moon is made of green cheese, or that God is dead, without having to 'substantiate' or 'prove' his claims to the satisfaction of some public official or agency. Such an inquisition is intolerable. It is no less so because the inquisition is justified as an attempt to forbid deceptive advertising."

No exception of subjects, even health, should be made in protecting constitutional rights. Elman recalled the derision with which the ideas of Pasteur and Semmelweis had been greeted and also that it had not been too long ago that patients were bled for conditions treated today by transfusions. "If the suggestion had been made, in the not too distant past, that a cardiac patient should take up bicycle riding, the medical experts would have regarded it as homicidal. Or if it had been suggested that a patient should get out of bed the same day he had undergone major surgery. How can we know which medical 'ideas and suggestions' that are universally accepted today will not be discarded tomorrow? It is arrogance to presume that in any field of knowledge whether dealing with health or otherwise, all the answers are now in. How can we be sure that the 'nut' of today will not be hailed as a genius tomorrow? And vice versa."

The FTC order, by a 4-to-1 decision, decreed that the Rodales "cease and desist" from advertising, directly or by implication, that readers of *The Health Finder* and its subsequent editions will: (1) add years to their lives; (2) gain more energy; (3) save on medical and dental bills; (4) feel better than ever before; (5) prevent the common cold, constipation, ulcers, fatigue, goiter, heart disease, arthritis, and mental illness; and (6) find answers to all health problems.

The order also enjoined the advertising for *How to Eat for a Healthy Heart* and *This Pace Is Not Killing Us* from promising therapeutic benefits for any stated disease or health problem. Shortly after the decision Rodale Press received a letter from the FTC stating that reports of compliance with its order "must consist of a full statement showing the manner and form" of compliance. Mere statements of nonviolation were not sufficient.

As with the initial finding of Examiner Lewis, press coverage of the FTC Rodale order was spotty. *Publisher's Weekly* featured a long article giving a detailed history of the case. The newsman who gave the FTC ruling the most attention was again columnist Kilpatrick. A glimpse at the tone of his article, which appeared in scores of newspapers, may be seen by the headings that some editors put on it: "A Typical Great Society Happening," "Who Is Going to Regulate the Regulators?" and "When Bureaucracy Bangs on the Little Guys."

Kilpatrick's article began: "It passed unnoticed in the news, but the FTC handed down a decision on June 20 that should stand as a landmark for years to come in the outrages of a bureaucracy. . . . Lovers of freedom will be sick." Kilpatrick averred that the Rodales had stood up "to the moguls" of the AMA, "and now and then literally they have cried 'nuts.'" The columnist closed his article by saying that the FTC had "picked on an unorthodox, redoubtable little publishing house, marketing unconventional but harmless ideas and crucified it. What price freedom in the forums of bureaucracy?"

In all likelihood, even if the FTC had fully upheld Lewis' findings, Arnold and his colleagues would have favored an appeal to a higher authority. When the FTC changed the initial complaint by adding a new and different charge against the Rodales, an appeal was certain.

Apparently, J.I. wanted to bring before the judges of the U.S. Court of Appeals, District of Columbia circuit, that he had once signed an FTC cease-and-desist order. Arnold, in a letter to Robert Rodale, January 23, 1968, advised against it: "I can't see what possible good it would do to inform the Court of the fact that your father signed a stipulation consenting to an order of the FTC. [Presumably, J.I. had in mind here the 1952 order against his articles on polio.] It is completely irrelevant and if we could get it in, it would do more harm than good." Arnold and his colleagues completed their work on the appeals brief by mid-February 1968. He told Robert, "If we lose [before the Court of Appeals] I'm going to appeal to the Supreme Court of the United States as a matter of principle . . ."

In the brief that Arnold presented to the Court of Appeals, he seemed anxious to test the Rodale case only on the virtues of the First Amendment, using the adjective "absurd" to describe his opinion of the commission's finding and order. He adopted Commissioner Elman's dissenting opinions as his major argument in the appeal. Censorship of the book was the commission's first endeavor, said Arnold. If the advertisements of the book merely repeated the "ideas and suggestions" of the book itself, then efforts to repress the advertising were violative of constitutional privileges. That was the point upon which Arnold believed the Court of Appeals would make its decision.

Arnold felt, therefore, that the Fifth Amendment question that the commission had interpolated into the case would never be reached by the court. Also, he speculated that the court would make its decision before it came to the difference between the examiner and the commission on the use of the words "all" and "assure." (The examiner, it may be recalled, had ruled against complaint counsel's contention that *The Health Finder* answered "all" health problems and "assured" health success to its readers. The commission had vacated the examiner's findings on these charges.) Nor did Arnold believe that the court would have to decide the mootness of the FTC's attack against advertising that had not been used for four years. It was amply clear from Arnold's appeal brief that he expected and hoped that the court would make its ruling only on the First

Amendment aspects of the case. Such, however, was not to be.

Sitting on the Court of Appeals for the District of Columbia circuit were three judges. Two, Spottswood W. Robinson III and Carl McGowan, had come to the court from legal backgrounds. The third, Edward A. Tamm, was a former FBI agent who had never practiced law. They heard arguments on the Rodale case on February 13, 1968.

In a letter written on the day of the arguments, Arnold described to the regular Rodale attorney, Morton J. Simon, some of the events that transpired before the court. "The arguments went over very well. I was asked particularly about the mootness point and also on the issue of sending the case back [to the FTC]. I explained both points, but told the Court that neither one of these . . . ought to be reached because I was so convinced that the authority exercised by the Commission was unconstitutional. . . . When counsel for the Commission got up to explain the theory of the Commission's case, he ran into all kinds of trouble. . . . Judge McGowan kept putting to the Commission's counsel various types of advertising, and asking him whether the Commission would approve or disapprove. At the end of ten minutes of such questions and attempted distinction between one ad and another, the Commission's counsel got completely mixed up. So I think the case looks pretty good, but of course, you can never tell."

Between the time of the court's hearing of the Rodale arguments and its final decision, an article about the case appeared in the *Harvard Law Review*. Arnold's opinion of the article was that it was a "thoroughly lousy and superficial treatment" of the case. Arnold liked, however, the article's supposition that some agency other than the FTC could and should be a more capable censor of promotional advertising.

The Court of Appeals rendered its decision on October 18, 1968, four years, six months, and fifteen days after the initial complaint was made. Judge Tamm gave the court's opinion. It dealt very quickly with the charges of "all" and "assurance." Tamm said: "I fail to see how even those easily duped would have interpreted the quoted material as an assurance of longer life, more energy, etc." In the absence of absolute terms like "all" in the advertising, Tamm felt that it was "unfair and unreasonable to interpret advertisements as representing that the books contained a panacea." Thus, the commission's findings on "assurance" and "all" were overturned. On the mootness of the issue, the court stated that "while there is some authority for a deceptive practices proceeding on discontinued advertising, there is obviously an outer limit to the Commission's discretion. At some point, the balance between the public interest and fundamental fairness to respondents must be weighed . . ." Judge McGowan, in this respect, stated that one of two alternatives could be taken—that of reappraising the examiner's findings or opening new FTC hearings. The "staleness" of the whole matter, however, raised "a substantial question as to whether either alternative is wholly the part of wisdom."

The court virtually ignored the First Amendment aspects of the case. Judge Robinson asserted that "our function . . . stops short of constitutional determinations not imperatively required . . ." Thus, the court went straight to the Fifth Amendment question, possibly because this was the obvious thing to do. This action, however, disappointed Arnold and others who wanted the court to face squarely the issues of the First Amendment.

It is well settled, said the court, "that an agency may not change theories in midstream without giving respondents reasonable notice of the change." Thus, the Rodales had been denied due process; they must be given the opportunity to present argument against the FTC's new theory of violation. The court then vacated the commission's order and remanded the case to the FTC for further hearings and arguments.

The next question was what the FTC would do.

Would it reopen hearings on its new charges, or would it reappraise Lewis' findings, or would it drop the matter altogether? Much more publicity was given to the court's decision than to either the examiner's or the commission's findings. Newspaper stories about it appeared throughout the country and in several publishers' trade journals. Simon feared that the publicity might have an adverse effect, as he wrote to Arnold on November 4, 1968: "The Commission is so deeply involved and the case has received so much publicity that the Commission may force the issue once again." Therefore, Simon sugested that the defense attorneys reexamine carefully the approach, if any, that they might take if the commission again brought up the charges.

Attorney Simon's fears, however, were unfounded. A news release from the FTC stated that on December 4, 1968, the complaint against the Rodales was dropped. "Acting on a remand of the case to the Commission by the United States Court of Appeals, the Commission stated in its order of dismissal, further continuation of these proceedings at this time appearing not to be in the public interest, and the possibility appearing remote that the practice challenged in the complaint would be resumed in the future, the complaint is dismissed with respect to all respondents." The last clause of the FTC statement angered Arnold and his colleagues because it made it appear that the court had acquiesced in the FTC's original order, when in fact the court had only offered to the FTC a face-saving device.

Arnold, though disappointed that the court had stopped short of considering the First Amendment implications, was pleased with the outcome. He felt that the court, in essence, had warned the commission that if it retried the case, "it may lose on its own merits." He was still outraged at the wording of the final FTC statement in the matter, and on February 7, 1969, in a long, detailed letter, he gave his opinions to Robert Rodale. This could very well be one of the last extensive letters that Thurman Arnold ever wrote to anybody, for he died in November 1969. (Arnold had stated during the Rodale trial that this was to be his last major case before retirement.) Because of its thrust and its possible historical significance, the letter is reproduced here almost in its entirety.

"There were two grounds on which the Court of Appeals could have dismissed the case. First was that Federal Trade grossly exceeded its jurisdiction in changing the whole theory of the case during the trial. The other was the substantive ground that even if your advertising had been an exaggeration of the claim in the book, it was nevertheless an unconstitutional exercise of the Commission's power to suppress it. The substantive reason for reversal was never reached. The opinion in effect says the Commission mistried the case against you, which entitled you to a new trial. The opinion then goes on to advise the Commission that the whole case against you was so flimsy that it should never have been brought in the first place. . . .

"Unfortunately there is nothing whatever you can do about the libelous statements contained in the Commission's proceedings against you. Since you have won the case you cannot appeal because the ground for dismissal is misrepresented in the Commission's motion. The language of the [FTC] motion [of dismissal] is thoroughly dishonest, but you have no legal remedy. You may take satisfaction in the fact that the Commission did not have the nerve to issue a public release with respect to its motion to dismiss as it did in the outrageous release which was copied by the AMA [of Examiner Lewis' findings]. This is because the Commission knew from the opinion of the Court of Appeals that its ruling had been repudiated.

"What the Commission set out to do was to put pressure on you to sign a consent decree which would have repudiated the integrity of your books. Unquestionably, you could have obtained the decree which would have been easy to live with as far as your future publications were concerned. The Commission would then have issued a public release to the general effect that the contents of your books were medical quackery and that in signing the decree you had admitted it. Had you done this, I do not think the Commission would have bothered you in the future. You chose to fight for the integrity of your book rather than make the admission the Commission wanted. I am very proud that you did so. . . .

"The only face saving device left for the Commission [after the court ruling] was to assert in the motion that it had suddenly found that there was no danger that you would repeat the advertising. . . . But in my practice before the Commission I have become so used to the libelous statements in the pleadings that I do not pay much attention to them so long as they do not appear in a public release.

"This poses the question of what, if anything, you can do about it. Only two things occur to me. The first is that you write a letter to the Commission telling it what you think of its procedure. This would do no harm, nor would it do any good. I cannot write such a letter because I am an attorney in the case and am not in a position to adversely criticize any court or commission before which I am appearing.

"You personally are not bound by such a rule. Nevertheless, I counsel against your writing the Commission. . . . The best way to deal with the Commission is to get someone to write an article about the case. I'm inclined to think that if such an article was written, it could be published in a magazine of general circulation.

"On the whole, you came out very well indeed. I do not think the FTC is going to bother you anymore. The case has been expensive, but I am very proud that your father did not give in and sign a consent decree that your book was quackery."

After the hearings were finally over, Robert walked into J.I.'s living room and said, "Well, we won. How do you feel now?" J.I. replied, "I still think I should have defended myself. It would have been cheaper, for we wouldn't have had to pay all those lawyers and doctors." The FTC case brought J.I. and his son, Robert, very close, for in a sense they both felt they were being persecuted by the government.

Just after the FTC case finally ended, J.I. left the country for a short vacation. On the plane, he brought along some "light" literature; the entire testimony of the FTC hearings and a book by Horatio Alger titled *Brave and Bold*. He unabashedly admitted to enjoying the latter more than the former. "The more I read the more convinced I was that the FTC was bold but not brave in the sense of the word as I would like to remember it by. Also I would recommend that all the Horatio Alger books be brought back for the enjoyment and edification or even education of modern youth. Yes daddio, of this I am serious. Give our kids less sugar and more Horatio Alger, and spare the rod." Clearly, despite the FTC, J.I. was off to his next adventure.

J.I.'s confrontation with the FTC raises several questions and observations. First, what was the FTC's motive in bringing up the question? Second, should it have pursued the matter at all? Third, was it really sincere in its prosecution or was it just "looking around" for an extension of the Witkower case and found the Rodales to be convenient?

The motive probably never will be known because both sides have their own version of it, and one is just as credible as the other. The FTC is a governmental regulating agency with the express charge of protecting consumer interests in this country. Thus, if it sincerely feels that deception has occurred, it has not only the right but the duty to investigate the matter. It was not the ends sought, then, that created any criticism of the FTC, but the means it used and its apparent inability to correctly define its role. Even though it is a regulatory body, it cannot, as shown by the Court of Appeals decision, flaunt the basic law of the land—the Constitution.

In the initial hearings it was apparent that Examiner Lewis gave greater weight to the government's medical witnesses than to Rodale's. Also, he frequently overruled Arnold's objections and sustained those of complaint counsel. The net impression that one receives from reading the transcript is that the decision was made long before the hearings ended. Lewis relied almost completely on the Witkower model, in which it had been ruled that the repetition in advertising of ideas and suggestions in a book that were false and misleading were subject to the commission's rule. There had been no appeal to the courts in the Witkower case.

Apparently, however, the full commission had rethought its position on Witkower. When the commission saw that Lewis had put it under the burden of the First Amendment in the Rodale matter and that an appeal to the courts under these conditions was a certainty, the commission obviously sought to extricate itself from the situation by vacating Lewis' findings and making some of its own.

But the Fifth Amendment, granting among other things the right of due process, is no less a part of the Constitution than the First. Thus, by trying to square itself with the First, the commission became entangled in the Fifth. The mind boggles at such proceedings. How four out of five commissioners could suddenly switch the theory of the case and add a new and different charge—and then think they could get away with it—is almost incomprehensible. Such procedures did not "protect" the citizen from anything, least of all his tax dollar. Perhaps the commission thought the matter would drop right there—that the Rodales, while they would appeal on the First Amendment, would not do so on the Fifth. When the appeal was made, it was done on the grounds of both.

It is regrettable that the Court of Appeals did not make a ruling on the First Amendment—that it did not hand down a decision on just how far the FTC could go in regulating the advertising for a book. Five years after the Rodale decision, the matter was apparently still open for some future litigation.

There were some reports that about 1971 the commission itself had written a policy statement on book advertising that in general agreed with the Rodale position in the FTC hearings. According to these reports, the FTC will not censor advertising whose source is a book and that purely represents the views of the author. Gerald Thain, FTC's assistant director for national advertising, however, says that the commission has not issued any such formal statement.

Nevertheless, the commission apparently now agrees with the Rodale premise, for as Thain's letter (to the writer, January 26, 1973) points out: "The Commission staff has not recommended formal action where the advertising for a publication only purports to express the opinion of the author. Similarly, the staff has not sought to proceed against parties whose advertising accurately quotes portions of a publication, provided that it fairly discloses the sources of any such quotation. In such instances, the staff does not normally consider it necessary to determine whether the claims stated in the advertising are, in fact, valid."

J.I. bore no grudge against the FTC, and the feeling was mutual. In later years, FTC staff members consulted from time to time with the Rodale organization on how best to deal with misrepresentations of the word "organic" that were perpetrated by various people around the country. The FTC apparently came to believe that the Rodale enterprise could offer the most legitimate definition of that word.

All confrontations—whether they are fought on false or true premises—have their value. All parties to them generally learn something. The FTC in this case undoubtedly learned, as the court said, that there are indeed outer limits to its discretion. And assuredly J.I.

Rodale learned—not that he didn't already know it (and possibly the FTC too)—that the First and Fifth Amendments to the United States Constitution do not contain mere idle phrases.

CHAPTER 9

Rodale: Playwright and Patron of the Arts

"There was this mother cat who was walking along the road with her four kittens following behind her. All of a sudden there was this vicious bulldog right in front of her. She gathers her wits and shouts 'woof! woof!' The dog is so frightened that he runs away. The mother cat then looks triumphantly at her kittens and says, 'Do you see the advantage of knowing another language?'"

This story, related in J.I. Rodale's play *How to Choose a Marriage Partner* (formerly *Silence at the Zoo*), may have explained his own situation better than he realized. He was constantly on the watch for media to get his messages across. He used his regular journals, his books, and his attempted novels, but it was the play that finally gave J.I. "another language."

In all likelihood, J.I.'s propensity for writing plays developed from his desire to become a novelist—and he did write a number of novels, which he published himself. He apparently came to believe that he could put on plays easier than he could persuade other publishers to accept his novels. Also, he could see his creations "come to life" before his eyes. He had always been fond of attending plays and of writing skits and conversations for his publications, so it seemed predictable that his peripatetic mind would lead him to playwriting.

It must be noted, too, that he did not begin this new career until he was in his mid-fifties. By that time, Robert had taken over much of the Rodale publishing activities. This left J.I. with a certain amount of time on his hands—time that he had never had before. But he was, he believed, much too young to retire. Therefore, playwriting became a natural outlet for him.

He began, even as early as the 1940s, to collect and read books on the technicalities of the art and to keep a card index on those subjects, lines, and words that he believed would make an audience laugh. He lined his bookshelves with volumes dealing with the best plays of the 1960s, plays for holidays, modern humor, and guides to great plays. In the margin of several of these, he made copious notes and comments. Therefore, although he was not the most accomplished playwright in the world, he certainly was not totally ignorant of playwriting techniques. To be sure, many people faulted him for going into playwriting for the same reasons he had been criticized for addressing himself to fields of health; no formal training in an acceptable institution. If this lack of formal education had not stopped J.I. in other fields, it was inconceivable to think it would do so in writing for the stage.

Altogether, he wrote more than forty plays, many of which were staged—not only by himself but by universities and colleges, high schools, community groups, and summer stock companies. His plays may be divided into four rather loosely constructed categories. First was the health and organic area: he thought he could teach audiences the value of good nutrition and the importance of avoiding certain foods. Second was the adaptation. Here he took short stories of authors like Pirandello and Dumas fils and plays by Molière, Feydeau, and Chekhov and presented them in condensed versions. He justified his adaptations on the grounds that modern temperament, unlike that of the 1890s, would not wait several hours for a play's denouement to occur. Adaptations of the classics had become not only acceptable but fashionable, he believed, and he cited instances of adaptations other than his own, such as George Bernard Shaw's *Pygmalion* being turned into *My Fair Lady*. As we shall note, J.I.'s penchant for adaptation did not sit very well with the purists among New York's literary critics.

The third category, and the most difficult to define, can, for want of a better phrase, be called "unstructured tutoring." In these plays, motive was either lacking altogether or quite difficult to discern unless, perhaps, the reader or viewer was familiar with "inside" Jewish words and phrases and was knowledgeable about "New Yorkese" or "Brooklynese." These plays, though they did sometimes try to show how to conjugate a verb in Latin, had little logic of sequence or character and plot development. They were frequently a hodge podge of the Marx Brothers, Don Rickles, and movies like *Hellzapoppin* and *Mad Mad World*.

The fourth category was "history," loosely defined. Here J.I. turned his attention to such historical figures as James McNeil Whistler, Benjamin Franklin, and John Hancock.

J.I. wrote several playlets for inclusion in *Prevention, Organic Gardening and Farming*, and some of his other publications. In 1958 he came out with *Skits and Conversations Toward Better Health*, which he called "an experiment in health education through comedy." Hoping they would be performed mostly by high school groups, J.I. created *Skits* revolving around imaginary conversations between himself and a Mr. Barrett (most assuredly not Dr. Barrett of the Lehigh Valley Committee Against Health Fraud, Inc.). At first Barrett was a skeptic about organic methods and preventive procedures in health. But as the book progressed through Rodale's discussions about health in general, properly raising chickens, how chemical fertilizers are dangerous, and the value of vitamins, Barrett became less of a "doubting Thomas" and was well on the road to conversion.

J.I.'s next major venture was a play entitled *The Girl and the Teenager* (1958). He was primarily concerned here with the juvenile delinquency problem. His play, therefore, centered around how the young derelict oc-

cupants of a low-rent housing district in New York became model citizens after they eliminated sugar from
their diets. In writing this play, J.I. felt a sense of urgency: "It [the play] was done in frantic haste in the
hope that it would be in time, that it would throw some
light on causes [of juvenile delinquency] other than
broken up homes, and shaken-up families. . . .
[R]esearch and experimentation must begin at once
to ascertain the part that good nutrition can play in
rehabilitating these unfortunate youngsters, and preventing the younger ones from ever entering into the
ranks of these confused young people. . . . What you
are going to witness now [the play] is a combination of
a lecture and a play, but essentially it is a lecture—nothing more or less, although it will be dressed up in the
trappings of the theatre, with its comedy and drama. In
judging it therefore please bear in mind that basically
The Girl and the Teenager is actually a lecture—a
sugar-coated one—easy to take, we hope. In that spirit
we will ask the curtain to rise" (pp. 5-6).

The play was performed a few times by small community groups, mostly in the Allentown area, but J.I.
had his eye on bigger things. By early 1960, he had
rewritten the play and had retitled it The Goose. It
opened at the off-Broadway Sullivan Street Playhouse
in March 1960. If J.I. ever believed that the AMA was
down on him for his health ideas, he probably came to
believe that its criticisms were nought in comparison to
New York's drama critics'. One gave the opinion that
J.I. might as well have titled the play The Turkey, in
view of the egg it laid. Donald Malcolm, writing in The
New Yorker, March 26, 1960, was even more sarcas-
tic: "In this rough world, there are few things indeed
that oblige one to speak of perfection. To any current
list of such things we now may add J.I. Rodale's 'The
Goose,' a drama of nutrition that opened last week at
the Sullivan Street Playhouse. It is perfectly awful. It is
supremely inept. It is magnificently foolish. It is sub-
limely, heroically, breathtakingly dreadful. It inspires a

sacred terror. It is beyond criticism. So much for civilities." Critic Malcolm then went on to give the play's plot—its condemnation of sugar, especially in doughnuts and sodas, and its references to Hitler's aberrations because he was a "sugar drunkard." He closed by facetiously expressing gratitude to the cast and assuring them that "the secret of their identities is safe with me."

As the audience filed out of the theater after seeing *The Goose*, they were handed a pamphlet entitled "The Proofs of Claims Made in the Play . . ." Here, J.I. reprinted doctors' statements about the dangers of sugar, particularly that by Dr. E. M. Abrahamson in *Body, Mind and Sugar* regarding Hitler's addictions to sweets and all the unseemly things his habit made him do. In July 1960, J.I. reprinted "The Proofs . . ." in *Prevention*, and September 1960, in the same magazine, he discussed some of the reactions to *The Goose*. It was a "trial balloon," he said, "sent up in an attempt to discover what the attitude of a New York theatre critic would be towards a play that attempts to teach health" (p. 18). *The Goose* ran for five weeks in March and April 1960 and then was suspended. Thus ended J.I. Rodale's first major venture into the field of playwriting.

Undaunted by the unfriendly reception that the critics gave *The Goose*, J.I. forged ahead with another theatrical undertaking. This time it was an adaptation of Jean Baptiste Molière's *Le Malade Imaginaire*, which went through several titles before it was staged. It was first *The Streets of Confusion*, then *The Healthy Invalid*, then *Toinette*, and more recently *The Malade Who Was Imaginary*. While it was still called *The Healthy Invalid*, actress Barbra Streisand became interested in it. In an undated letter to J.I., she wrote, " 'The Healthy Invalid' is quite an improvement over 'The Streets of Confusion.' It is very interesting. It needs rewriting, of course, but on the whole I enjoyed reading it. I would also like very much to play the part of Toinette. She is the best written character in it."

Streisand's complimentary remark about the play's leading female character may have been instrumental in J.I.'s decision to rename it Toinette. It made its debut in summer stock in 1961 at Fishkill, New York. On November 20, 1961, Toinette opened at Theatre Marquee on 59th Street in New York City, a small off-Broadway playhouse that was once the apartment of famed dancer Isadora Duncan.

J.I.'s rendition of Molière's work was a spoof on the medical profession. In one part of the play, with the help of Dede Meyer, he had physicians making judgments about the treatment of Argan, the "imaginary invalid":

> Our neglect may help kill 'em,
> But we won't neglect to bill 'em,
> This is one mistake we doctors never make!

Shortly after this recitation, a character said of a doctor that he "doesn't know his liver from a hole in the wall." In his instructions to the director, J.I. pointed out that if the play were performed off-Broadway, it would be acceptable to replace "from a hole in the wall" with "from his asshole" (although it is certain that this phrase was not unknown to Broadway audiences of that time).

If The Goose suffered from torrid reviews, Toinette was practically slain. Howard Taubman, in The New York Times of November 21, 1961, wrote: "There must be a lesson in a disaster like the witless, tasteless 'Toinette,' an alleged musical comedy, which was allowed into Theatre Marquee last night. How about a punishment to fit the crime of invoking the name of the great dead? How about a stiff penalty for helping oneself to a work in the public domain and then doing it violence? There would be a justice of sorts in such an arrangement."

The penalty for the author of this "noisome, contemporary affair," Taubman said, should be a payment of at least ten times the rates he would owe Molière if the latter were still alive and his work protected by copyright. For the actors in J.I.'s version of the play, if desperate for work, "they should be sent to a sunny beach for a holiday, to heal their wounds and recover their self-esteem." For the critics, Taubman declared, earplugs and opaque glasses should be issued "that would enable them to ignore every offensive word, sound and gesture on the stage."

New York's drama critics led J.I. to something that his health detractors had never been able to produce: an angry reaction in public. On November 29, 1961, J.I. took out a two-thirds-page advertisement in *The New York Times* entitled " 'Toinette,' A New Musical Comedy, The Playwright Vs. the Critics." He cited favorable reviews of *Toinette's* run in Fishkill and noted particularly that the critics liked Ellie Wood, who played the lead role. He also gleaned complimentary remarks about it from the Associated Press, *World Telegram*, *New York Daily News*, and the *New York Post*. The critics for these journals, however, had found certain aspects of the play they disliked and had said so in no uncertain terms, leading J.I. to exclaim that the critics were being picayune and nitpicking.

J.I. was especially incensed when one of the critics referred to him as a "noted lawyer." He responded by saying, "I am not even an un-noted lawyer." He stated that many newspaper and magazine articles complained of the stagnancy of modern theater, urging that "new blood" be infused into it. "And yet when a really new idea comes forth, what do the critics do? They get out their sledge hammers and clobber the innocent victim."

He declared that if he were a newspaper editor, he would have each of his critics medically checked before letting them write reviews. If any of them had heart or kidney problems, he would transfer them to another department.

On the day of J.I.'s advertisement, *The Times* ran a news story about it titled "Toinette's Sponsor Rebukes Its Critics." The article gave an accurate description of the ad and J.I.'s opinion that the critics did not really judge the play, but him. This, he said, was largely because he was the editor of *Prevention*, "the largest circulating popular health magazine in the world, a magazine that, because it is telling the truth, is a menace to certain powerful and industrial interests."

The Times staff contacted a spokesman for the play, who defended J.I.'s production against the critics. The spokesman stated that *Toinette* would continue at Theatre Marquee indefinitely. In this case, however, "indefinitely" turned out to be twenty-one days. Louis Calta, in *The Times*, December 19, 1961, stated that J.I. had "temporarily" suspended *Toinette* after thirty-one performances. "Mr. Rodale explained yesterday that his musical will be re-written and will be open in mid-March at another off-Broadway playhouse, which he plans to acquire soon. 'What I'm trying to do is add another forty laughs to the show,' he said."

J.I. was convinced that his large advertisement in *The Times* created positive effects. In *Organic Gardening and Farming*, February 1962, he stated that after the ad, radio managers were quite kind to him, as were several newspaper editors. He said also that his volume of mail grew steadily after the ad—mostly favorably. *Toinette* and its later version, *The Malade Who Was Imaginary*, played before audiences at several high schools and colleges and community acting groups through the remainder of the 1960s. In 1970, at a testimonial dinner given in honor of J.I.'s seventy-second birthday, excerpts from *The Malade Who Was Imaginary* were read. Clearly, though the critics bent the play considerably, they did not break it.

It was characteristic of J.I. that whenever he felt strongly about something, he would make every effort to achieve it. Therefore, sometime in 1960 he bought an old building on East 4th Street in New York and made plans to convert it into his own theater. The building had been constructed in 1873 and was used as a meeting place for various clubs until about 1913. From 1913 to 1919, it was a dancehall, restaurant, and lodging place. It remained empty for the next several years. In 1923 it was used for baking and meat packing. It stayed vacant from 1957 to 1960, when J.I. bought it. The local name for the structure, which delighted several critics, was "the baloney building." At first, J.I. named his new property Rodale's Theatre, but he soon changed it to Theatre 62, in honor of his favorite school when he was growing up, Public School 62, on Norfolk Street.

J.I. never disclosed the price of Theatre 62, but he did point out that he planned to spend over $100,000 to get it ready for operation. Theatre 62 seated 149 persons and featured a three-quarter arena-style stage on the first floor. But he did not think of the building merely as housing a platform where performances could take place. A *New York Times* story of July 11, 1962, showed that he intended for his building to serve multiple purposes. He announced the creation of the "Rodale School of Theatre Arts," to be housed upstairs in Theatre 62, where actors, directors, and technicians could train, work, and experiment, free of any tuition charges. "The first semester will be for ten weeks. Alex Kameny, Lonny Chapman and Alex Ansara have been announced as instructors. They will supervise courses in acting, directing, theory, and movement. Mr. Rodale estimated that 100 students, none of whom will be required to have professional background, will be accepted. But, he added, 'they should show some promise.' The first workshop group is expected to get underway next week."

Though the "Rodale School of Theatre Arts" never really materialized, primarily because of a lack of students and instructors, it is nevertheless true that J.I. befriended several young actors and actresses on their way up, including Barbra Streisand, Peter Fonda, and

Dustin Hoffman. J.I. arranged discounts for other young thespians at natural food and vitamin stores in New York. Sometimes, he loaned them money or treated them to a meal, not expecting or wanting repayment. Frequently, he invited entire groups to his home in Emmaus, where he fed them natural vitamins and organically grown food from a large lazy Susan in his dining room. Many of these people today speak with awe and reverence of J.I. Rodale—that he believed in them when few other people were willing to do so.

The theater opened in April 1962, and with its repertory of skits and several one-act plays, it at once began fulfilling J.I.'s ambition, as reported by Louis Calta in *The Times*, of presenting plays "that are 'helpful, beneficial, and that teach something, and that tie in with character development, improvement and education.'" Between the opening date in 1962 and the closing date in 1965, some fifteen of J.I.'s plays were performed in Theatre 62. Generally, admission to these performances was free, and at times J.I. was not beyond chartering a bus, filling it with Allentown citizens, and taking them to New York to witness the current performance. J.I. paid for his own productions, sometimes going as high as $50,000 for the run of a single play.

While Theatre 62 operated in New York City, J.I. was busier than ever turning out plays at high schools, colleges and universities, community groups, and summer stock companies. He began a rather heavy travel schedule, going from one place to another to see his plays performed. His main subject, at least through the mid-1960s, was health and nutrition.

Lost and Found Psychodrama concerned a man who had lost his integrity and had come seeking it at a municipal lost-found bureau. Finally, the clerk discovered that the man worked at a candy factory, and he obviously had lost his sincerity and integrity because of all the tooth cavities he caused. *The Yugoslav Medical Mystery*, based, said J.I., on an actual occurrence, dealt with efforts to trace lead poisoning that affected over half of the population in a tiny village in Yugoslavia. Only one person, old Vojislav, had escaped the sickness. When it was found that he had not eaten bread for twenty years, the local wheat mill came under suspicion. Sure enough, the investigators discovered tiny bits of lead-bearing stone eluding the sifters and getting into the flour. Thus, the mystery was solved.

The Devil and the Nails had Satan appearing on earth and inveighing against the practice of smoking. The more people smoked, the more carbon dioxide was created. Too much carbon dioxide put out fires, and where would the Devil be if this happened? J.I. wrote this play in 1963, around the time that he was first confronting the Federal Trade Commission about *The Health Finder*. One of J.I.'s characters in this play asserted that the FTC had been acting like a circus "in some of their recent cases." J.I. attacked "parthenogenesis" (the process of producing infertile eggs) in his play *Can a Hen Lay an Egg Without a Rooster?* He concluded that it could, but ought not to. The grocer in the story who explained the evils of "parthenogenesis" to a woman customer donned the cap and gown of a college professor so his "lecture" would sound authoritative.

Even the lowly cockroach was defended by J.I.'s pen in *The Cockroach Who Wanted to Go Steady*. The girl cockroach could not get the boy cockroach interested in her because of her inability to produce eggs. This inability was brought on by an excessive exposure to DDT. Dr. Klonk saved the day by administering electrical treatments to offset the effects of the DDT. Once the girl cockroach could lay eggs, the boy cockroach warmed up to her, but only temporarily, "because cockroach relations are broken after seven days anyway." *Moon Over Taurus* was about an astrology-maddened dean of a medical school who tried to rob one of his students of a valuable medical discovery. "In science," the student was told, "the professional standing of the person who discovers something is of terrific importance." The student had no standing, but the dean did. It turned out that "digimaxin," the student's drug that was supposed to prevent heart attacks, actually caused them. The dean wound up thoroughly disgraced.

Another of J.I.'s "nature" productions was *A Series of Ecological Comedy Skits*. Included here were three short plays: *The Man Who Kicked the Bucket*, *The Earthworm and The Cockroach* and *The Floodwatcher*. The first showed a man sitting by a river holding a bucket of its water. The man had come to the river to commit suicide, but after seeing the river's polluted condition, he changed his mind because he wanted to drown, not suffocate. Therefore, he "kicked the bucket," but not in the way he originally envisioned it. The second play was a conversation between an earthworm and a cockroach on the baneful effects of chemicals. *The Floodwatcher* took the point of view that if farmers and people in general would use organic methods, there would be little danger of the disastrous floodings that tormented the country from time to time.

Despite the flailings that J.I. took from the critics, especially for *Toinette*, he continued to write adaptations of short stories and classical plays. After *Toinette*, J.I.'s next adaptation was *Uncle Vanya*, by Anton Chekhov. Originally this play was done in four acts, with four different scenes. J.I. condensed it to one act and one scene. He eliminated many of the long, drawn-out speeches that Chekhov gave to the original characters. Also, J.I. simplified some of the Russian names. In Chekhov's version, for example, Uncle Vanya was also called "Ivan Petrovich" and "Voynitski." In J.I.'s version, "Uncle Vanya" was used throughout.

To complement *Uncle Vanya* and to be performed at the same program, was J.I.'s rendition of Chekhov's *The Cherry Orchard*. Again, J.I. employed the one-act format, but in *The Cherry Orchard*, unlike *Uncle Vanya*, he eliminated some of the characters. He justified this elimination on grounds that the theme "is about the cherry orchard, and by eliminating secondary actions, and retaining every word pertaining to the orchard, it comes into sharper focus." The presentation of *Uncle Vanya* and *The Cherry Orchard* in one performance gave an opportunity, J.I. believed, to compare two works of one author. *Uncle Vanya* had rather serious themes, while *The Cherry Orchard* was lighter, enabling the audience to see Chekhov in different moods and styles. Seeing the two together might also encourage conversations and exchanges of opinion on the part of the audience.

The French playwright Georges Feydeau also came in for J.I.'s scrutiny. In 1969, J.I. adapted one of his plays and called it *This Mania for Running Around Half-Naked*. It was a farcical treatment of how a French politician named Ventroux appealed to his wife, Clarisse, to wear something more than a shift in front of important guests. Ventroux's political colleague, Clemenceau, was such a blabbermouth that Ventroux believed he would spread scandal and destroy Ventroux's career. This seemed likely as the play closed with Clemenceau looking into a window and finding Clarisse and Roman de Jaival, a reporter for *Figaro*, in the process of getting to know each other. *The Railroad Ticket* was another of J.I.'s one-act adaptations of a French play. It concerned the problem faced by a commuter whose wife has swallowed his train ticket.

In addition to adapting various plays, J.I. rewrote short stories for presentation on the stage. One such was Guy de Maupassant's story "The Umbrella." In the story Mme. Oreille had humbly asked an insurance company to pay for damages that had been done to her umbrella, and in the first part of J.I.'s adaptation, he followed closely the story's developments. Then, J.I. added a second part in which Mme. Oreille haughtily presented a bill for forty francs to the insurance man for the repair of her umbrella. She was practically thrown out of the office because the insurance company was insulted that someone would want a paltry forty francs. The agent told Mme. Oreille to go burn down her house so she could present a *real* insurance claim.

A little-known story, "The Pigeon Prize" by Alexandre Dumas, fils, the illegitimate son of Alexandre Dumas, was turned into a play by J.I. in 1969. The story revolved around M. Leon, who wanted the hand of Julia Lebron, but before her father would assent, Leon had to earn a substantial sum of money. In London, Leon became the central figure in an experiment being conducted by the Scientific Society of London. He had to eat roast pigeon for dinner thirty-one days in a row, because the society was interested in "determining the capacities of the human body." When he succeeded, but only barely, Leon not only collected 60,000 francs and visited the King but also became a public celebrity who could "hardly be protected from the enthusiasm of the multitudes." The story proved that "pigeon is a heavy meat," that "fortune has strange ways of helping man," and that the British have a society for every purpose.

Luigi Pirandello's short story "The Miser's Coffin" was also adapted for the stage by J.I. A lawyer's dog had absconded with a farmer's sausage. The farmer visited the lawyer and asked, in general terms, what the law said about reparations for such a deed. The lawyer looked into his books and found that the owner of the dog was responsible. Triumphantly, the farmer then announced that it was the lawyer's dog who caused the trouble and demanded a payment of four lire. The lawyer quickly agreed, then billed the farmer ten lire for legal advice. At the height of the confrontation, Mendola, the tax collector, entered with a coffin (which the lawyer had secretly had made for himself) to show that the lawyer had not paid all of his property taxes. The lawyer clutched his chest in a massive heart seizure, fell straightway into his coffin, and the play ended.

Adaptations did not seem to be as popular with J.I. as his nutrition plays, nor with those that, on the surface at least, were sheer nonsense. Heading the list in this category is *The Cop and the Robber*, a mixture of Laurel and Hardy and Charles Chaplin chase scenes, with a would-be robbery victim talking to his assailant about health. Others here included *The $19.00 Actress*, *The Flower Thief, Some Sweeping Remarks, A Bull Fight, The Cat and the Rumanian, 20 Years From Now* (when people shake hands with their legs, and when national attention is focused on President Doolittle, who kept running away from the White House; he promised to go back if he could raise and lower the flag each day, asserting that "those horrid soldiers won't let me do it"), and *Funeral Jazz*. These plays, while no doubt humorous and enjoyable when seen on the stage, were nevertheless disjointed affairs, with no apparent structure, form, or balance behind them. They were full of "bathroom humor" with jokes that turned on the baser side of human nature. It was this very baseness, though, that J.I. thought we should be able to joke about.

One play in this category, however, ultimately became J.I.'s pride and joy. *The Hairy Falsetto* which opened at his theater in mid-December 1964, was far and away the most successful creation in J.I.'s playwriting career. It was based on the "Little Red Riding Hood" fairy tale. In his research for the play, J.I. said that he discovered twenty-one different versions of the tale. His play attempted to show that the wolf was largely an innocent creature and that deceptive Little Red Riding Hood had framed him all along. J.I. told Richard Shepard of *The New York Times*: "In my play, the wolf is brought to trial à la Eichmann. . . . I have a lot of laughs in it, even a good one about the [electrical] black-out [in New York City.] . . . The play shows the foolishness of people and, in the end, it turns out Little Red Riding Hood committed the crimes." When writing the play, J.I. sent a draft of it to his friend and attorney, Morton J. Simon, for some "legal talk" to be interpolated into it. In a letter to Jean

Neese of Mobile, Alabama in 1969, J.I. stated that he intended for the wolf in the play to symbolize the travails of the American Negro. In one of the productions of The Hairy Falsetto, a black man played the role of the Southern judge, who apparently knew only one word: "Guilty!" In another performance the judge was played by an actor who was adept at impersonating the voices and actions of Lyndon B. Johnson, Hubert Humphrey, and Richard Nixon, all to the delight of the audience.

Apparently, The Hairy Falsetto was the first performance at Theatre 62 in some time. When he first began playwriting, J.I. was obviously ready and willing to match the critics' invective, point by point. But as he got more into it, he was increasingly sickened by the critics' rebukes, so much so that he once gave up playwriting for half a year. His absence on the New York scene was noted by columnist James Davis, December 6, 1964, writing for the Sunday Daily News. "A vanity playwright we miss the most is J.I. Rodale, who set out to correct the nation's health by writing plays given over to the evils of sugar, the benefits of organic gardening, and the eagerness of surgeons to remove valuable organs from patients." J.I. had written to columnist Davis a few days before Davis' article appeared, hinting that his new play marked a turning point in his career: "I have completed 'The Hairy Falsetto,' a nonhealth comedy. . . . The critics were right: you can't teach people about sugar in a play." Davis concluded his article with the opinion that "perhaps it is just as well that Rodale has mellowed and has abandoned his preventive crusade [in playwriting only]. The plays he put on for several thousand dollars a few years ago would perhaps cost ten times as much today."

Reviews of The Hairy Falsetto were essentially noncommittal from the major critics and highly complimentary from the less-circulated journals. The Village Voice, December 10, 1964, said of the play: "The courtroom scene works well. Mr. Rodale's one-line jokes are for the most part laugh-getting, his serious writing is for the most part inoffensive, and his quotes are for the most part well chosen." Similar reviews came from *The Villager*, *Backstage*, and *Show Business*. *The Hairy Falsetto* ultimately became J.I.'s most performed play. In 1968 it was produced at Marquette University in Milwaukee, Wisconsin, and at nine other colleges and universities. Its record for 1969, through May, was thirteen performances at colleges, universities, high schools, and community acting groups. This play, which was translated into French as *Le Fausset Velu*, more than any other caused J.I. to believe that he had "arrived" as a playwright. By the early 1970s it had gone through fifteen printings.

The final category of J.I.'s plays fits into "history," broadly defined. In his records, J.I. kept a file on the "ifs" of history and also of close-up, practically forgotten facts of history that had been subordinated to major events. Most of the things J.I. described in his "history" plays were true in one way or another, but he did exercise dramatic license on more than one occasion.

He was fascinated by the great Benjamin Franklin and wrote three plays about him. One was *Franklin and Mr. Gout*, in which gout appeared before Franklin as an apparition and chastised him for the slothful habits of living to which he had degenerated in his old age. Neglect of proper diet and exercise was the chief cause, said Mr. Gout, of his frequent visits to Dr. Franklin.

The next Franklin story concerned his inability to keep a secret. Called *Talkative Franklin*, it showed Jonathan Dayton of New Jersey accompanying Franklin wherever he went to keep him from divulging the secrets of the 1787 constitutional convention, then in progress. Franklin became so upset with Dayton's constant presence that he told a friend, "I'm going to kill that Mr. Dayton!" The friend replied, "No, don't kill him! Just tell him to go fly a kite." The third play about Franklin was *Franklin and Mme. Brillon*, in which Franklin declared that Mme. Brillon's withholding of her favors had given him the gout.

J.I. continued his interest in colonial history as he turned his attention to John Hancock. His first play here was initially called *The Boston Tea Potty, or the Indian Who Didn't Want to Go*. He changed it later to *The Boston Tea Party . . .*, probably because he allowed schools to perform it free of royalty and perhaps "potty" might turn off some directors. The play was mostly about a colonial man named Enoch who believed that Hancock was a first-rate scoundrel, causing unnecessary friction between the colonies and the Mother Country. As the other characters get dressed for the Boston Tea Party, which was to start promptly at 11 A.M., Enoch declared his intention to take no part in it.

John Hancock, Portrait of an Empty Barrel, was apparently the last play J.I. ever wrote. He included here a bibliography to show what a bounder Hancock really was. He stated that in 1884 the Hancock family engaged a writer for a biography of their kinsman. The writer gathered so much incriminating material that the family paid him $1,000 to abandon the project. J.I.'s play depicted Hancock as a social snob ("One thing I learned at school was to sign my name in a manner befitting a gentleman"), a detractor of George Washington as commanding general of the revolutionary army, and an embezzler of funds from Harvard University. He even commented on Hancock's references to the immortal words of Captain Prescott at the Battle of Bunker Hill: In Hancock's words, "Prescott didn't say, 'Don't fire till you see the whites of their eyes.' " He actually said, "Aim for the bastards' bellies and try to pick off the officers." Throughout his life, J.I. had been a debunker, and he certainly proved it with the Hancock stories.

J.I. was intrigued by the career of American painter James McNeil Whistler. One of his plays about Whistler was called *Whistler Vs. Ruskin*. Whistler had painted "Falling Rockets," and John Ruskin, the famous Victorian and Slade Professor of Art at Oxford University, had said that it was "flinging a lot of paint in the public's face." Whistler sued for slander. Ruskin was found guilty by the judge but was fined only one farthing for his "transgression." The legal fees incurred by Whistler led to his bankruptcy.

Young *Whistler at Paris* was mostly a collection of reminiscences about the artist's school days. At West Point, he said, he and his classmates were once lined up on their horses ready to practice a charge: "My mount suddenly kicked up his hind legs and threw me forward, right over his head. My professor commented that that was the only time I was at the head of my class." In this play, too, J.I. had Whistler talking about the new art form of Impressionism and how it would take the public some time to accept it. In correspondence with his daughter Nina, J.I. expressed the belief that one of his Whistler plays would make Broadway. None ever did.

As J.I.'s playwriting became more known and accepted, he and his wife, Anna, began to travel far and wide to see his productions staged. J.I. was certainly not beyond applying a bit of pressure on behalf of his plays. He once received an invitation from the Palm Beach, Florida, Roundtable, a discussion group, to participate in a program about natural foods. J.I. made his acceptance conditional upon the Roundtable's efforts to stage one or more of his plays while he was in the area. He told the Roundtable directors: "I am not an amateur playwright. My work has been done by over sixty colleges, high-schools and community theaters in the last twenty months." The Roundtable acceded to his request.

Another visit that J.I. and Anna made, one that no doubt brought back nostalgic memories to J.I., was to Kentucky. (As related in Chapter 2, while working for the IRS, J.I. visited Kentucky and was so charmed by the Commonwealth that his desire to farm became more intense than ever.) Several of his plays were performed during the 1969 season in Kentucky, at places like Morehead State University, Eastern Kentucky University and Danville's Pioneer Playhouse, under the direction of Gerald Honaker.

J.I.'s plays that were performed at Danville were *20 Years From Now*, *The Cat and the Rumanian*, and *The Hairy Falsetto*. He made a hit with the actors and actresses in the plays by faithfully attending all the rehearsals and making copious notes, especially of any improvisations that were made. He frequently wrote the ad-lib lines of the performers into new editions of his plays. This is why there are so many editions of J.I.'s plays—each time he heard an actor or actress or, for that matter, a director improvise a line he liked, he would incorporate it into a new edition. Though J.I. made a hit with the performers and directors at Danville, he still came in for the scrutiny of reviewers. In the Louisville (Ky.) *Times*, reviewer Dudley Saunders had some rather caustic remarks about J.I.'s plays, which had been billed as "An Evening With Rodale." Saunders said: "[J.I.'s plays] are a hodgepodge of good jokes, bad jokes, ancient jokes, pointless jokes, collegiate antics, spotty sight-gags and lame topical humor. All of it is rolled together in a bland, imitative, warmed-over style that wanders from avant-garde to burlesque." He went on to say, however, that "some of Rodale's stuff is very good and extremely funny, but most of the time we are laughing at its campy ineptness, rather than at its humor or its ideas and attitudes."

While in the Bluegrass State, J.I. received the highest honor that can be bestowed on an outsider: he was commissioned as a Kentucky Colonel by Governor Louie B. Nunn. Shortly after this investment, J.I. wrote to his friend Mrs. Ingebourg T. Frank: "I spent three weeks in Kentucky . . . and the Governor of the State honored me by appointing me to be a Kentucky Colonel, although I'm practically a pacifist." He went on to say that since he was now a Kentucky Colonel, if Kentucky declared war against Ohio, he would have to enlist in the Kentucky militia. What Governor Nunn did not know, however, Colonel Rodale declared, was that J.I. had numerous kinsmen in Ohio; thus, in the event of hostilities, serious conflicts of interest would arise.

It was perhaps this extended travel causing long absences from New York that, in part, caused J.I. to discontinue Theatre 62. In 1965 he moved his operations to Philadelphia's 40th Street, where he once again established Rodale's Theatre. Still later, around 1968, he transferred his theatrical productions to Emmaus, where he set up Rodale's Comedy Theatre. Theatre 62 in New York was bought by another concern and renamed The Fortune; Rodale's Theatre in Philadelphia became a church. Not only did J.I. organize a theater for the Allentown area; he also bought an old church, with the intention of turning it into a movie theater. The desire to make movies became one of his chief interests toward the end of his life.

A man of J.I.'s temperament would never have been satisfied merely with running a theater of his own, hopping around the country to see his plays performed, and being a benefactor to young actors and actresses. Among other things, J.I. wanted to break into the international scene, not so much with his own plays but with ones he sponsored. This led him into a lengthy correspondence with James Verner, Ltd., in London, about producing a play called *Eat the Cake and Have It*, with Norman Wisdom in the role of Rupert. The play was finally staged for a short time at a West End theater. Although Verner accepted and represented *Eat the Cake and Have It*, he turned down J.I.'s request for arranging performances for *John Hancock, Portrait of an Empty Barrel* (perhaps J.I. thought this would sit well with English audiences) on the grounds that it was not enough of a play to warrant his involvement.

J.I. also, along with Ira Eaker and Allen Zwerdling of New York, became a co-publisher of *Backstage*. In this magazine, J.I. wrote a regular column, "In The Theatre With J. I. Rodale." There, he spoke sometimes about his own plays, especially *The Goose* and its short life off-Broadway. Other subjects included the disrespect that audiences sometimes showed actors by not responding properly to the emotional impact that was intended and by applauding too soon; the history of the word "thespian"; the various atmospheres that a theater performance could create; and the inconveniences one experiences in Dutch and German theaters where there are no center aisles. In short, J.I.'s column in *Backstage* was mostly shoptalk about the major plays he witnessed in New York and elsewhere, interspersed with a few short reviews.

One of *Backstage's* activities, in addition to reporting and assessing current stage fare, was sponsorship of a playwriting contest. After the announcements for the contest were made in 1961, two dozen applications were received immediately. Ultimately, only six scripts were received, and only two of those turned out to be halfway decent. No evidence exists that any prizes were ever awarded in *Backstage's* competition. J.I. did not long remain a co-publisher of *Backstage*. He left it to start his own magazine, *Theatre Crafts*.

J.I. became involved with university affairs on a higher level than having them perform his plays when he began the sponsorship of the Brandeis University Creative Arts Award, a $15,000 cash award that he underwrote for several consecutive years. The famous silent-screen film star Charles Chaplin was one of the recipients of the Brandeis award—at its fifteenth annual presentation ceremony. At one of the Brandeis ceremonies, held at New York's Whitney Museum, J.I. was a bit miffed because his speaking time was limited by the program chairman. He took the attitude in his three-minute speech that while the university was unlimited in its ability to take his money, it did not want to hear too much from him. Even so, in his limited time, he managed to talk about health foods and the evils of sugar.

Additionally, J.I. arranged for his own enterprises at Emmaus to give awards to outstanding and deserving students of the arts. One such recipient was Arlene Love of Temple University's Tyler School of Arts, who wrote to J.I. in May 1970: "Often people ask me how does such a little girl manage to do such big sculpture? I smile and answer, I take vitamins, and they think I'm joking." J.I. was also a major sponsor of the Allentown Art Museum. Once he suggested to its director that a "history of the cow" be painted on the walls of one of the museum's rooms. The director, Richard Hirsch, found J.I.'s proposal "udderly fantastic" but made no move to implement it. Too, J.I. contributed money to various private schools. One was the Lincoln Square Academy in New York. Once he was invited to become a director of this school, but he declined because of pressing schedules elsewhere. J.I.'s work of writing plays, co-sponsoring magazines, and supporting actors and actresses through cash awards and moral support gave him much joy in his later days.

At one point he considered, and even planned on becoming an actor himself. In a letter to Jean Neese in March 1969 he said: "I can't work as an actor. I have a nervous habit of clearing my throat, but maybe acting would cure it. I'm going to take lessons from the Lessak people in New York. They work on actors to improve their voice. They claim to get results by enlarging the oral clarity through certain exercises." It would have been a most interesting activity to follow J.I.'s career as an actor, and also his career as "Sam Green," the pseudonym he intended to use for some of his "racier" productions. There is no evidence to show that he would have pursued these interests, but the events of June 7, 1971, clinched the fact that he would not.

In his movie enterprise in Emmaus, J.I. intended to start with organic and health subjects, then work toward other things. Undoubtedly he had in mind the filming of some of his plays. He had already written to a Hollywood producer to check the possibilities of filming *The Hairy Falsetto*. Whistler and ecology also would have been two of his early movie interests, as he explained in May 1971 to Mrs. Betty G. Franklin of Fairfax, California. None of these plans materialized.

One of his earliest movie ambitions was to turn *The Hairy Falsetto* into a film for high school audiences. Before filming could start, however, J.I. invested a considerable sum in a Broadway play, *Engagement Baby*, which closed after a few performances. Losing money on this play thwarted immediate plans for filming *The Hairy Falsetto*. J.I. was quite hurt by one reviewer of *Engagement Baby* who took the point of view that J.I.'s investment of $30,000 to $40,000 (of a total of around $250,000) had brought ruin to the performance—that when people learned that J.I. was a sponsor, they were repelled because of his odd way of life. It did not take long, however, for J.I.'s resilient spirit to recover from the inane remarks of the reviewer.

J.I.'s file cabinets in his home at Emmaus were packed full of letters and references to his plays, both complimentary and adverse. He took pride in the large numbers of people who viewed his performances. Such responses encouraged him to continue, to turn playwriting into a passion. He seems to have thought of little else during the last months of his life.

J.I. began writing plays because he thought the stage was an excellent education medium. Through humor and pointed remarks, people would come to understand the importance of good nutrition and the avoidance of bad habits. So he thought. Even if this supposition had been true, J.I. nevertheless would have sallied forth into other areas and subjects because it was in his nature to grow and expand. Creating a status quo in any field was for him an impossibility.

In the theater, as in other areas in the past, lack of

formal training was no barrier for him. It was fortunate that J.I. had enough money to buy all the costumes, to pay the cast, and even to purchase his own theater. It was the message that he deemed significant, regardless of what the costs might be.

Again, in his pursuit of the theater, he exhibited those same characteristics that had driven him in the fields of health and organic gardening: perseverance in the face of adverse circumstances to begin with, accompanied by ample amounts of optimism, stubbornness, and, after a while, even dogmatism and a bit of arrogance. In 1970, a woman named Anna Maria Dobinsky "analyzed" J.I.'s handwriting. She said: "Now I know that you are as great as I thought you were. There are rare occasions when you respond impulsively and may act without thinking." J.I., according to Dobinsky, had strong "vibrations" interlaced with feelings of inferiority. He harbored a few grudges but had the ability to forgive. He had a sense of humor and was generally able to "roll with the punches." He had a retentive memory that sometimes produced narrow-mindedness. He liked to receive a "pat on the back" for his efforts, but he doubted his ability to speak effectively. He possessed a "fine sense of idealism," with standards so high "that you feel inadequate in attaining them." Apparently Dobinsky studied J.I.'s handwriting from a distance, but it was obvious from the first line of her letter to J.I. that she was generally familiar with his career, so her handwriting analysis could fit easily into the knowledge of him that she already had. Certainly these characteristics, and more, applied to J.I. Rodale.

Did J.I. make a lasting impression on the theatrical world, or was he a transient who momentarily gave pause to the New York critics? As pointed out in Chapter 1, there have always been in this country hundreds of writers considered to be "subliterary" by sophisticated reviewers who nevertheless, through their zeal and enthusiasm, command a wide following. This was true of J.I. as a playwright. To a great extent, he and Anna were the number-one supporters of a "super fan club" to promote J.I.'s playwriting creations. Indeed, he often got his inspirations for a play from conversations with Anna, and she never failed to give him moral support when things looked darkest.

Regardless of whether or not J.I. was "sophisticated," it is still a fact that his plays—generally free of royalty—played at scores of institutions around the United States. His files are packed with letters from directors wanting a full list of his plays and the procedures for producing them. Thus, it is clear that after a time there was really no need for J.I. personally to promote his own plays; their broad initial exposure was their promotion.

Since J.I.'s passing, Anna has brought out new editions of all the plays J.I. wrote. She has also formed Rodale Theatrical Publishing to facilitate the performances. Apparently, then, J.I.'s plays are "alive and well" at high schools, colleges, universities, and community playhouses, an enviable circumstance for any playwright.

CHAPTER 10

The End of a Dream

On August 16, 1970, J.I. Rodale entered his seventy-second year. He was a happy man, for he sensed strongly that the message he had been spreading for the past thirty years was at last gaining wide acceptance. John Stuart Mill's dictum of ridicule, discussion, and acceptance of new ideas was, J.I. believed, just now coming into the third stage. The number of magazine articles about either the organic movement or J.I. himself, the invitations to J.I. for radio and television appearances, and the proliferation of organic farms throughout the country, run mostly by young people, showed that the agricultural and health changes he had been preaching were indeed in the making.

In the midst of this growing popularity, J.I. had no intention of stopping his manifold activities—retirement, for a man like J.I., was out of the question. If he was going to become the "grand old man" of organiculture, it was not going to be in a passive way. Noting that the organic movement was now riding a tidal wave of acceptance, J.I. said, "I thank God that I'm alive. And I say, gee whiz, another day. And I've got so many wonderful things I can start out with. I've got 60 million different things, any one of which I can do and enjoy immensely. I have a full program ahead. I'm just thinking every morning will I live to the year 2,000, because if I do I will be 102 years old, and will have lived in three different centuries. I was born in 1898, and I'm gonna do it." Since he mentioned it so frequently, and since he believed he would accomplish it because of his organic life, living to be 102 years old was apparently J.I.'s personal dream.

A testimonial dinner in celebration of J.I.'s seventy-second birthday was given by several Allentown and Emmaus citizens. At this meeting, excerpts from some of J.I.'s plays were presented and complimentary letters from widely scattered sources were read. One message of the evening was from Roderick Cameron, executive director of the Environmental Defense Fund. He said: "It is odd how history sometimes turns nuts into prophets. Mr. Rodale has been for far too long a lonely voice against the experts who insisted that the only way to grow things was with massive quantities of chemical fertilizers and pesticides. . . . There is some truth to the saying that a man can be known by his detractors. J.I. Rodale has the right ones. If we survive our present insanity, it will in part be due to the organic agricultural science J.I. Rodale has been so influential in developing."

Kind words are expected at testimonial dinners. But it was not just J.I.'s friends and associates who were now giving them. They were indeed coming from all directions. For example, free lance writers and environmental columnists began visiting J.I. at his Emmaus home on a frequent basis. On each of these occasions, J.I. took great pains to show the visitors every aspect of his experimental farm. Throughout March, April and May 1971, numerous articles gave full publicity to J.I.'s operations.

Mike Clark, writing for the *Philadelphia Enquirer*, April 18, 1971, titled his story "Nature's Way Gaining Favor, People From Emmaus Say." The article was a general one, with descriptions of J.I.'s organic activities and the operations of the Rodale Press. Another descriptive article appeared in *The Bulletin*, May 2, 1971, "A Son of the Ghetto Becomes Patriarch of Health Foods." *Barron's National Business and Financial Weekly*, May 10, 1971, featured an article about J.I. Its author, Margaret D. Pacey, called her piece "Nature's Bounty." It was a general discussion of the return to ecological considerations, to health food stores, and to organic movements. J.I.'s friend Betty Franklin had apparently expressed surprise at J.I.'s being the subject of a *Barron's* article. He wrote to her on May 25, 1971: "Regarding *Barron's* being such an unlikely publication, how would you like me in the current *Penthouse*, a nude magazine known as the skinny *Playboy*. A very fine, long rave article. The climate sure has changed. Imagine, 30 years of klobbering and now I have become respectable." *The National Observer*, May 31, printed Michael T. Malloy's article "The Nation Gobbles Organic Food." A letter from C. M. Wells, president of the California Food Retailer's Association, declared that it was irrelevant whether or not one agreed with J.I.'s philosophy: "The fact remains that he was directly responsible for introducing good nutrition to thousands of people and therefore was directly responsible for the tremendous growth of the health food industry."

The Smithsonian, May 1971, printed Wayne Barrett's article "The Organic Way of Gardening and Its Prophet." Here, Barrett spoke of the "new breed" of farmers coming into prominence around the country. They were mostly "long-haired, under 30, city bred, working in experimental plots on campuses, or tilling communal fields." They had turned their backs on insecticides, herbicides, and chemical fertilizers in favor of composts of cattle manure and rotting vegetation. "Jerome Rodale is looked upon as the elder statesman of the organic food votaries." The article went on to say that when J.I. first started his work, he was generally referred to as a faddist, but now he and his movement were viewed with much respect.

Early in June 1971, J.I. gave a lengthy interview to *Penthouse*. Here he touched on a multiplicity of subjects but dwelled primarily on his arguments through the years with the Food and Drug Administration, the American Medical Association, and the American Dental Society. He expressed the opinion that it will be the young people "who will save us. Before the young came to us, my magazines were being listened to by a very limited audience. . . . [S]uddenly these hippies and dropouts who had been making a lot of noise read my writings and found something real. There is so much truth in what we say that if you are not prejudiced, you must become convinced. They are buying land and growing food organically. Of course, when they taste the difference in the products they never want to go back."

In addition to the articles about him, J.I. began appearing as a guest on radio and television programs. In May 1971, he was a guest on a Philadelphia television show in which he gave the history and the philosophy of the organic movement. The publicity that seemed to please him most, however, was an article by Wade Green for *The New York Times Magazine* called "Guru of the Organic Food Cult" (June 6, 1971). On the eve of the article's appearance, J.I. told an audience in Allentown: "You know, I just want to say that on Sunday, tomorrow, Sunday, there's going to be a big article about me in the *Times*, a thing which is often written about millionaires." Later in this same speech, he said he wanted to put in a plug for himself: "My friends, my time has come. Years ago they heaped violence and poured ridicule upon my head. I was called a cultist and a crackpot. In the newer version, no less, the leader of a cult of misguided people relying on half truths and pseudo-science and emotions. That he preached a doctrine of pure speculation. . . . These are the people who have been attacking us for thirty years, claiming we were crackpots. But no longer, now even the chemical people have become respectful towards me and my manure ideology. I am suddenly becoming a prophet here on earth, and a prophet with profits." He closed his speech by giving his play schedules for the upcoming month and by announcing that soon he intended to take a long trip. Anna, from the first row in the audience, jokingly said, "Good-by."

Through his public relations man in New York, Max

Eisen, J.I. received advance copies of the Green article. Eisen reported to J.I. that the article was good—that it should be a capping to all the favorable publicity organic gardening and J.I. had been receiving in the past few months. Among the interested readers of Green's article were scouts for several major television talk shows. J.I. received a call from New York on the Sunday the article appeared. Would he come to New York for a guest appearance on the Dick Cavett Show? J.I. quickly accepted the invitation.

J.I. and Anna left Emmaus on Monday morning for their New York apartment on 58th Street, taking along as usual their regimen of natural food supplements. Included this time were ample quantities of asparagus (a favorite of J.I.'s since youth), loaves of rye bread, and a huge, organically produced goose egg, which he intended to display before the Cavett audience. After their arrival Anna conducted some of her business, leaving J.I. alone in the apartment. Shortly after she left, the phone rang. It was from the producers of Johnny Carson's Tonight Show, who had read the Green article and had heard that J.I. would appear at five that evening for the taping of the Cavett show. Would J.I. appear on Thursday, June 10, on the Carson show? J.I. was delighted, and he intimated that he would like to put on a few of his skits for the Carson audience. Then, exultant, J.I. left his apartment for a brisk walk down to 42nd Street and back. When he reached the apartment, Anna had returned. The first thing she told him was that a New York radio station had called for an interview.

Throughout the afternoon of that Monday, J.I. received numerous telephone calls from friends and well-wishers, bidding him good luck in his Cavett appearance and promising to watch the show, scheduled for eleven that night. In late afternoon, he and Anna dined on the food they had brought with them from Emmaus, then J.I. took a cool bath—one of several that day. Before dressing to go to the ABC studios, he had Anna give his mustache another trim, because he wanted to look his best. As he departed, he said to Anna, "Maybe you could come to see me on TV." She replied, "You might better do it alone." Then there was a quick, gentle kiss, and J.I. was off to another adventure. As it turned out, it was his last one.

At the studio, J.I. went through the formalities of make-up, giving his social security number, and signing a release for things he might say on the show. Backstage, J.I. sat close to his monitor, taking notes of the things said by other Cavett guests. J.I. met Marshall Effron, who was doing Ovaltine commercials that night, and asked for Effron's card because J.I. desired his help in making some amateur movies.

When Cavett introduced J.I., he said, "My next guest used to be known as a food freak. Now that he's rich and famous—a New York Times article about him called him 'Guru of the Food Cult'—a lot more people are listening to him. J. I. Rodale is his name. He's an unusual man with a lot of opinions which the U.S. Department of Agriculture, to mention one, doesn't agree with." As J.I. walked across the stage to greet Cavett, the band struck up "Doing What Comes Naturally." J.I. quickly told Cavett that his name was accented on the first syllable and, as he had jokingly told friends in the past, the name was Rodale, not Rawdeal.

Cavett wanted J.I. to start with a good definition of organic gardening. J.I. responded: "Organic gardening is using natural fertilizers like manure. I should say animal manure; manure is an all comprehensive term. Even a leaf is manure. So we use animal manure, vegetable manure, we don't spray; we use ground up rocks, powdered rocks—a lot of it is my development. . . . The whole thing is a trying or an attempt to be natural and not too synthetic. We have had a movement too fast forward, and it has assumed dangerous proportions, I think."

Cavett inquired whether J.I. had ever been called a crackpot. Amid laughter from the audience, J.I. declared that "crackpot" was mild; more usually, it was "manure worshiper." J.I. mentioned Sir Albert Howard, giving him credit for the organic idea. Then he began talking about carrots, taking the viewpoint that where a carrot, or anything else for that matter, grows does indeed have a bearing on its nutritional content. He felt that the whole idea of modern nutrition was defective, that medical schools studied symptoms and palliations but "the average doctor was not taught nutrition."

Upon Cavett's questioning about the insect menace, J.I. repeated a statement that was axiomatic with him: "The insect is the censor of Nature to destroy unwanted vegetation." If a plant were healthy to begin with, it would not be nearly as susceptible to insect attacks as it otherwise would be.

In the next sentence, J.I. took over the show by asking Cavett, "When do we start with the jokes?" Cavett replied, "What for?" J.I. stated that he really didn't know—that "I didn't come prepared with any. Did you?" He said he did not wish to disappoint Cavett's readers, then corrected himself to say viewers. Cavett assured J.I. that it was not necessary to get a laugh.

After this exchange an intermission soon occurred, during which the band played "I'm Beginning to See the Light." Then J.I. spoke about undesirable tallness in American people and attributed it in part to their drinking milk. They moved back then to organic foods in general, with J.I.'s opinion that "I don't care if you do eat organic food. It's the way you handle it in your kitchen. . . . I believe in the vitamins and the minerals and the supplements that *Prevention* recommends. Like for instance bone meal. I've taken bone meal for thirty years and haven't had a single cavity for thirty years."

At this point, Cavett asked, "How old are you? Mind my asking?"

J.I. replied, "I will be seventy-three in August," a remark that drew applause from the audience. J.I. continued, "I am so healthy that I expect to live on and on. I have no aches or pains. I'm full of energy. If you want me to do—not a flip—but kicking my heels up—not this time, the next time—I want to get to know you first. What was I talking about? Headaches? Bone meal?"

Inevitably, J.I. got onto his favorite kick—sugar—which he called his *bête noir*. He believed the cake for Tricia Nixon's recent wedding was scandalous: "Did you see the enormous amount of sugar that went into that blender?" He felt President Nixon should have seized the opportunity of his daughter's wedding to point out to the American people the dangers of over-consumption of sugar and wheat products.

When Cavett asked about the U.S. Department of Agriculture, J.I. gave a short essay: ". . . [T]he chemical fertilizing companies subsidize all the agricultural colleges in the country. And there is an unwritten law that on every agricultural college board must sit one representative of a chemical fertilizer company, and this ought to be stopped. For they furnish so much money that naturally they've got the poor professors scared to death. They are afraid to do anything that would cast a shadow on chemical fertilizers." Cavett asked J.I. about the AMA: "They don't love me, I'll tell you that."

Here, J.I. brought out his raw asparagus, and he and Cavett had a snack. J.I. stated that the value of raw vegetables was the intake of enzymes, which were destroyed by cooking. He said that in cancerous tissues there was always a lack of enzymes, and he wondered if more studies should be made of any possible relationship between cancer and the degree to which food is cooked. A medical doctor had told him once that cancer is nature's revenge on man for living artificially. Cooking vegetables, to a large extent, produced such artificiality.

In the last segment of J.I.'s interview, he expounded at length on the values of electricity to health and life:

"I went to a lot of trouble and I accumulated over forty old textbooks on electricity in the human body, and electrical treatment. And around 1890 and 1900 it was the thing. . . . Then around 1920 or 1930 when the pharmaceutical idea came in and they could get a lot of money for these drugs, all these [electrical treatment] departments were thrown out and the AMA said crackpots, quackery. Well, I intend to start a series in *Prevention* that will show how wonderful it is to have this electrical treatment. . . . The whole body runs on electricity. Every cell in our body has a positive and negative charge. We consist of billions of batteries. . . . But as you get older, some of the electricity drains out. And I know that when I reached the age of about seventy, I got a little tired here and there, so by taking these electrical treatments it gives me more electrical energy. This I know." The electrical machine J.I. used was called a Theramak, which he first saw in a doctor's office in Florida. Getting a medical prescription from the doctor, J.I. paid $2,700 for his Theramak. He mentioned, however, that a new electrical machine called Seratome, costing $500, was now on the market and was as efficient as Theramak.

When Cavett mused that J.I. "had a million interests," J.I. replied, "Well, not quite a million; a hundred thousand." Then J.I. brought out his huge, fertile goose egg and used it as an example of the superiority of the organic system. After joking for a while about J.I.'s "exhibit," Cavett announced a commercial break.

The commercial over, Cavett began chatting with a new guest. Suddenly he saw that J.I. had slumped over in his chair, with his head in a nodding position and his beard slightly resting on his chest. The guest, newsman Pete Hamill, heard J.I. make a low, whooping sound, "like a bad imitation of a seal." Everyone at first thought J.I. was feigning sleep out of boredom with the show. The audience laughed as Cavett asked, "Mr. Rodale, are you all right?" It took only seconds for Cavett to see that J.I. was not feigning anything. Cavett jumped to his feet and asked any physicians in the audience to come to the stage.

Drs. Eric White and Richard Kaslow of Columbia Presbyterian and Mount Sinai Hospitals, respectively, were attending the Cavett show with their wives and were seated on one of the back rows of the balcony. When J.I. was first seized, the two doctors stared at each other for a moment, both thinking that surely a physician would go to J.I. from the orchestra seats below. Simultaneously, however, they realized that they were the only two persons in the house with medical training. They rose from their seats and ran to the orchestra level and up onto the stage.

J.I. appeared an ashen gray to the doctors, who realized immediately that, for whatever reason, his blood pressure had dropped and he was approaching unconsciousness. Kaslow took J.I.'s pulse and found none; White noted that the pupils of J.I.'s eyes were constricted, indicating that his nervous system was still functioning. Then the two doctors concluded that J.I. was suffering from a cardiac arrest. Kaslow gave him a sharp blow in the chest in an effort to restore cardiac action. The audience, hushed to this point, gasped at the blow, for most of them did not realize its purpose; many began sobbing.

The next step was to take J.I. out of his chair and put him on the floor; at this point, the ABC cameras stopped. The doctors began closed-chest cardiac massage and mouth-to-mouth resuscitation. An oxygen mask was brought from backstage, but it did not have enough pressure to be of value in keeping an airway open; also, the nozzle necessary for operating it was missing. While these attempts were made to revive J.I., firemen from the Ninth Battalion, across the street from the ABC studios, arrived. There was a small dispute between the doctors and the firemen over the proper methods of giving mouth-to-mouth resuscitation, which ended when an automatic breathing device was put into use.

About fifteen minutes after J.I. was first stricken, an ambulance arrived from nearby Roosevelt Hospital. He remained on the respirator in the ambulance, and his eyes, though still constricted, gradually began to dilate. When he arrived at Roosevelt Hospital, J.I.'s electro-cardiogram showed some activity, but it showed a profound cardiac distress. The emergency attendants at Roosevelt continued the attempts to bring J.I. around, including electrical shocks. After working for approximately fifteen minutes, further attempts at revival were discontinued and J.I. was pronounced dead. Though no autopsy was ever performed, it was obvious that J.I. had suffered a massive heart seizure.

Meantime, Anna was waiting at the apartment for J.I.'s return. The telephone rang, and the voice said, "Your husband did his program and just fell asleep. He is dead at the Roosevelt Hospital." When Anna got to the hospital reception desk, she was told that she would have to wait before seeing J.I. Pleading that she must see him, she was led by an attendant into a little room, and in her later tribute to J.I., a bit of free verse called "One Day Less," Anna recorded her reactions: "He lifted the cloth and there was J.I. in healthy color—his closed eyes. His jaw was open—wanting of breath. I pat his cheek and murmur softly—I loved you so much. His cheek was warm, his voice was silent." In Emmaus that evening, Robert received a phone call from the night supervisor at Rodale Press, who had been called by someone from the Cavett show with the message that J.I. had had a heart attack. Robert then called the Cavett show but could get no information. He called Roosevelt Hospital but was told only that J.I. was being examined by the doctors. A few minutes later, Anna telephoned with the news that J.I. had died. An Allentown undertaker brought J.I.'s body back from New York.

The Cavett program tape with J.I. on it was canceled in most parts of the country, and a substitute show featuring Phil Silvers and Jack Benny was shown instead.

At the beginning of his show on June 8, Cavett spoke of the preceding day's events: at first he thought J.I. had suffered an epileptic seizure. He expressed surprise that someone before this time had not died in the lengthy history of the television talk shows. Cavett said that the event was "very disorienting" and "very sobering. And it's hard to do a show the next day, but life, as they say, goes on, and I would like now, as I have privately and publicly, to express condolences to Mrs. Rodale and other members of his family."

J.I.'s funeral, on June 10 in Allentown, was a simple ceremony. His acting and playwriting associate Robert Drean gave one of the eulogies: "Jerry established great success in several fields, and the greatest tribute to his success is that he achieved it simply because he wanted to help other people live longer, happier lives. He knew better than anyone that the birth of a great idea must grow to maturity in a hotbed of hostility and ridicule; that it takes years of drive, of desire, purpose and perseverance to make a dream become a success."

The main eulogy at J.I.'s funeral was delivered by his friend Rabbi Steven Shafer. He began: "It is hard to believe what we know is true. J.I. is dead. It cannot be, our hearts tell us; yet so it is, our lips respond. But there is so much to do, so much work to be fulfilled, love to be shared. . . . But even as we protest, we submit. . . . When [death] comes, with very few exceptions, it is never the right time. It tortures and mocks us, it tells us that all of the struggles of life and our creativity are absurd in the face of death . . ."

Discussing J.I.'s relationship with the world, Rabbi Shafer said: "When I shake hands with another man, I not only feel his hand, I feel my hand. By touching him, I come to know me. J.I. had the capacity to touch other lives with humor, with love, with criticism, with a gentle kind of judgment without maliciousness. He evoked strong reactions, but he touched lives as he established these relationships. . . . You know that he loved life. He loved Nature; and he understood that property, material things, must be subservient to life. Life over all. It was the core of his being. He was the kind of man who should have money. He knew what to do with it. He knew how to use it to bless life. . . .

"There was a sense of humanity which inspires us, a kind of excitement which life generated in him, which he could relate to some of the people. . . . He reveled in life. He chose to make it full and exciting, and meaningful. And one of the laments that we have now is that we wanted Jerry to live forever. We wanted him to prove that he was right! We know he wasn't right in everything, but he's the guy that should have proved it.

"I remember once in very colorful terms which I won't repeat here, he said to me, 'Why does God need all of this praise?' And I can't help but agree; if God is God, he'd better get along without man's praise. . . . Man works in partnership with God in the process of creation. And that's what Jerry did! He was a partner. God may have created the world, but it's man's job to perfect it; and that was what he [J.I.] chose to do in his way. Would that all men chose to perfect, to get in there and struggle, and to work and be wrong and change and recognize. . . .

"I think Jerry Rodale is a great man, and I resent those who call him the names. . . . It's a small thing to condemn a man; it's a mean and base thing to judge on the side of fault. . . . He was sensitive, not just to the needs of an individual who had problems, but he was sensitive to the needs and the hungers of people, of the hunger of the black man for dignity and for opportunity, and of the hunger of the condemned for a new start. And he did it, and he used his resources for it. And that's greatness.

"All of us who knew him are better for it. Each of us must choose to define the meaning of life. . . . Measured in terms of his creativity, his responsiveness to the ideas of others, his generousness, his humor, his humanness, his love for man, his humanity, his love for Nature, his courage, his strength, his tenacity, J.I. Rodale was a grand success as a human being. We lament his death, not so much for him, as for ourselves. We grieve for ourselves and our loneliness, and we will miss him. . . . J.I. shines with the brilliance and the harmony of a maestro, who carefully picked his scene and then fully orchestrates all of the forces bearing upon it. In his spectrum there is a treasure. The immortality and the meaning of his life will be found in how we choose to use that treasure, how we use it by our lives and by our deeds."

When the eulogies ended, the ceremony for J.I. was done. A small sundial was placed in front of his grave in Emmaus, and on the tombstone was inscribed: "J. I. Rodale, He Urged Man To Live In Harmony With The World."

J.I.'s death attracted national and international attention, with so many notes of condolence coming in to the family that the task of personally answering each of them was made difficult if not impossible. The Allentown *Morning Call* treated J.I.'s death as its headline story on June 8. The Allentown *Evening Chronicle*, June 8, titled its editorial about J.I.'s death "A Man of Strong Convictions." "At his death at 72," the editorial said, "the community loses one of its most colorful and controversial citizens, a man who fought hard for the things in which he believed and equally hard against those things which he regarded as harmful to the human race and the environment in which it lived."

An article in the Mount Prospect, Illinois, *Herald*, June 11, by an author with the unlikely name of Mary B. Good, said that "Rodale was undaunted by ignorant skeptics. . . . [T]he events of the last few years have changed a lot of minds. Today organic gardening is coming on strong again, this time with a greater impact because of increased public awareness of environmental problems." A letter writer to the *Detroit News* complained because the *News* obituary of J.I. had referred to him as a "food-faddist." The letter writer felt that the newspaper "must never let the truth stand in the way of a good story."

Gerald Wields reminisced about J.I. in an article, "R.I.P., J.I." in the *Philadelphia Magazine*, and an article by Don Sheridan in *Clear Creek* spoke of J.I.'s "environmental imperatives." The *Sunday News Journal* of Daytona Beach, Florida, June 13, featured a long article about J.I.'s life and work, as did the 1972 issue of the *International Journal of Natural Therapeutics*. The June 21, 1971, issue of *Newsweek* entitled its obituary of J.I. "Death of a Salesman."

His death attracted a great deal of attention from foreign newspapers, especially in England, where some of J.I.'s magazines were published and where he owned a natural vitamin company. Friends and admirers claimed that it was J.I.'s stature in organiculture and health that gave rise to the 1,000 or so notices of his death around the world; detractors said it was due to his being stricken on the Cavett show that engineered so much public interest.

In the August 1971 edition of *Organic Gardening and Farming*, and in other Rodale publications, Robert wrote a tribute to the memory of his father. On the eve of the Cavett appearance, J.I. told Robert, "Stick to a thing for a long time and you'll make it work." Robert could not remember ever seeing J.I. in a bad or depressed mood, yet "more than any man he had occasional cause to be discouraged and downcast." The people closest to J.I., declared Robert, sometimes cringed when the critics were at their worst—but not J.I.: "One of the many file cabinets in J.I.'s home was packed with friendly letters from readers. He seldom opened the drawers but would tell people with a smile that when he needed cheering up he'd stand next to the file and feel the good radiations coming out of it." In assessing J.I.'s greatest contribution—aside from being a loving and considerate father—Robert said he would remember J.I. "as the man who taught me to think of myself as an organic person, trying to live in tune with

Nature, striving always to help improve the environment while working to improve myself, too. That was his message to me and to you, and it will live on for a long time."

A few months after J.I.'s passing, a pamphlet prepared by his family and friends appeared, called "Memento of a Crusade." In it were tributes and reminiscences from long-time friends like Harvey Eck, postmaster at Emmaus, who credited the mailing of J.I.'s various magazines each month with turning the Emmaus post office into a major operation, with receipts for 1971 totaling well over a million dollars. Ardath L. Harter remembered J.I.'s statement "You know if I'd live to be two hundred years old I'd never be able to do the many things I want to do," and Father Paul M. Pekarik of St. Ann's in Emmaus, reflected on all the assistance J.I. had given to him throughout the years.

Death under any circumstances always brings with it a certain amount of irony; when it is unexpected, the ironies multiply. Well over two years after J.I.'s death, people were still commenting on the ironies. Just moments after he said on the Cavett show that he was going to "live on and on," he was dead. Despite his careful regimen of health and exercise, J.I. lived only to a normal old age. His critics still claim that these circumstances dictate against the philosophy that he urged upon people for so long—that the facts indicate that longevity is more tied to family heredity and personal health history than to diets of bone meal, sunflower seeds, wheat germ, rose hips, and so on.

In so saying, however, the critics prove J.I.'s case. As pointed out in an earlier chapter, J.I.'s father and all of his brothers died in their early and mid-fifties and early sixties—all of heart attacks; only one sister survived J.I. From his early days, J.I. suffered a heart ailment himself, just as most of his family had. Taking these points into consideration and discussing J.I.'s life in that context, it is perfectly plausible to maintain that his health activities added fifteen or twenty years to his life. It is not within the province of anyone—medical doctors or otherwise—to maintain that his practices were useless because he did not live to his goal of 102 years. It is uncharitable of anyone—doctors included—to make pronouncements upon, and even to smirk about, the circumstances and the ironies of J.I.'s passing. Adelle Davis, herself a famous and controversial nutritionist, was amused that when J.I. died she received a letter from a man saying that "Rodale has ruined the entire health-food industry by dying."

J.I. was a great lover of life who made no compromises with it. He was not the kind of man who always said: "I would be happy if . . ." He exulted in living, and never did he anticipate an idle moment. (Indeed, at one of his birthday celebrations, he told an audience that he was opposed to receiving gifts. In his opinion, the one whose birthday it is should be so happy to have achieved another year that he should present gifts to his friends.)

He clearly intended to maintain his creative impulses, to continue old programs and to start new ones. All these ambitions had to be considered within the context of the widespread acceptance of him and his ideas that occurred in the half-year preceding his death and of all the feverish activities that this acceptance entailed. He insisted on giving thorough, personal tours to all the reporters, interviewers, cameramen, and other visitors to his experimental farm in Emmaus. He was planning a series of new plays, including one on George III of England, and his movie interests were now becoming significant to him. Perhaps all this activity, and perhaps the heady feeling of acceptance coming, as it were, all of a sudden, produced strains and tensions in his body that were not apparent on the surface.

There were signs—mostly visible in hindsight—that J.I., while not exactly failing, was slowing down. A friend of his reported that on a walk in New York, J.I. had to stop every block or so to catch his breath and to get his heartbeat down. Other friends explained that in that last six months, they noticed a slight, almost imperceptible change in J.I.'s demeanor—though his pace was more frenzied than ever, there was a slightly detectable difference in the way he acted and spoke. Anna noted, too, the increase in chest pains during the final months and J.I.'s tiredness. Despite these signs, and despite occasional visits to medical doctors, J.I. continued his activities, saying, "What good am I lying around here [his home]?" Hindsight always comes easier, as the maxim goes, than foresight, but his attack on the Cavett show and his subsequent death at Roosevelt Hospital were not really as totally unpredictable as most people claimed.

The personal dream of J. I. Rodale to live to 102 years vanished on the Cavett show that night of June 7, 1971. His dream of acceptance, however, had already been accomplished. His dream of seeing the United States and indeed the world get back to safer and saner methods of producing and consuming food was well on the path to fulfillment. Therefore, perhaps the Cavett show that night did not end a dream; perhaps it clinched one that had just begun.

CHAPTER 11

Rodale: Renaissance Man?

J. I. Rodale's life style was more in keeping with the generalized activities of past ages than with the specialized interests of the twentieth century. Throughout these chapters we have emphasized J.I.'s multifaceted career: electrical manufacturing, stock investment, book author, editor and publisher, playwright, moviemaker. These accomplishments reflected his aversion to what he called "fragmented society," the "curse" of modern civilization. His curiosity toward the things around him, his diversity, and his constant attempt to consummate his creative impulses led some people to call him a Renaissance man.

The Renaissance man concept has come to mean an idealized version of the European movement of the fifteenth and sixteenth centuries, which in part destroyed narrow restrictions of the past placed on ideas and activities. Mankind itself has the ability to change things—for either good or evil—in short, man is possessed with a brain, and the Renaissance man urges him to use it.

The Renaissance man has no particular, narrow interests. He is, as the saying goes, "a jack of all trades," but the remainder of the axiom, "master of none," does not really apply here. For the Renaissance man, like the colonists who first populated America (and indeed like the men of much of our history, at least until the last fifty years or so), is a master of several trades at the same time. Multiplicity of interests certainly does not mean as a matter of course that each interest will suffer a marked deficiency because it is one of many. It could as easily mean that a person's creativity and curiosity are so intense that it takes several interests to satisfy them.

The labeling of J.I. as a Renaissance man—even with all the errors he made—is well taken. His files at Emmaus fairly bulged with things in which he took an interest, as the listing of the contents of just one drawer shows: airline pilots, American Medical Association, arteries, artists, aspirins, athlete's foot, barley, calcium, church, death, halitosis, hands, health, high blood pressure, insurance, metabolism, paper, toothpaste, vaccinations. He had an entire drawer crammed with children's plays, which included Dr. Jingle, Little Jack Horner, and Rastus Horner. In his history cabinet, J.I. had a script called Poor Man Is Weak, He Soon Forgets, which was based on part of Arnold Toynbee's massive A Study of History. Also in his historical drawers, he kept files on: colonial times, Columbus, flags, George III, gold rush, Gouverneur Morris, Horace Greeley, Alexander Hamilton, Indians, Herbert Hoover, history textbooks, Thomas Jefferson, Andrew Johnson, John F. Kennedy, Robert E. Lee, the Liberty Bell, Mayflower, McKinley, Peter Minuet, James Monroe, William Penn, the Pilgrims, James K. Polk, Paul Revere, Revolutionary War, Franklin D. Roosevelt, Theodore Roosevelt, Salem witchcraft trials, slaves, war supplies, World War II. Admittedly, some of these files were inactive for lengthy periods, but the meticulousness with which he arranged his subjects and interests showed him to be a man of far-reaching and generalized proportions.

He had a special talent for "spot reading" in books and magazines, excerpting from them the things he wanted. If he had possessed a "specific" rather than a "strategic" mentality, he would have been an utter failure. One of J.I.'s former editors, Heinrich Meyer, now a professor of Germanic languages at Vanderbilt University, says that J.I. was the only "native genius" he ever met. "True, many of his combinations were ridiculous, like his healing athlete's foot by propping his feet against the bathtub or changing his position in sleep and overcoming 'rheumatism,' but a few of his combinations were sound, though unproven and unprovable at the time. This instinct for underlying truth I regarded as his one chief asset."

J.I. always believed that the ubiquitous quality of his experiences made him—in terms of learning and knowledge—a better man than most products of colleges and universities. He reflected on this "superiority" as early as his IRS days, when it was clear that he knew more about income tax procedures than his diplomaed colleagues. Later in his career he was quite capable of becoming downright anti-intellectual. For example, one of his *Organic Gardening and Farming* editors, a Ph.D., once insulted a subscriber, who wrote a complaint letter to J.I. In return J.I. assured the subscriber that the editor "has heard from me. The trouble with these doddering Ph.Ds is that they are trained in one narrow field and when it comes to general common sense for business, they sometimes are hopelessly lacking. . . . It is peculiar how some of these Ph.Ds act. I know that some are at the feeble mind point when it comes to common sense and yet universities give them Ph.D. degrees. I am so glad that I am only a high school graduate when I come into contact with the products of some of our universities."

Though he disdained "doddering Ph.Ds," J.I. was nevertheless interested in all phases of college and university life. His endowment of the Brandeis University Creative Arts Award was one example of this interest; his support of schools like the Lincoln Square Academy in New York and his enrollment in a geology class at Allentown's Muhlenberg College were others. Once, in return for a sizable contribution, the president of a local college offered to make J.I. an "adjunct professor" but then withdrew the offer when he learned how controversial J.I. was. Another college tried to interest him in endowing a "Rodale Chair of Playwriting," in return, possibly, for an honorary degree.

(There is little evidence to show that J.I. would have accepted the "position" of "adjunct professor," and some of his letters give ample indication that he would not endow the drama chair. Although he may largely have "bought" his way into the theatrical world, he usually drew the line at academics.)

In the fall of 1969 Catawba College in Salisbury, North Carolina, considered J.I. for an honorary Ph.D. J.I. visited Salisbury while some of his plays were performed at nearby Winston-Salem. In an interview with Catawba's president, J.I. did not really make a good impression, for he interlaced his conversations with humorous comments that in all likelihood only he himself fully understood. The Catawba committee omitted J.I. from its invited list, offering the honorary degree instead to three or four other people, who promptly refused to accept. After J.I.'s death, a small institution in Las Vegas, Nevada, Bernadean College, did give him the honorary Ph.D. degree that he had desired all his life.

In another educational arena, J.I. did receive a number of memberships and awards for his various organic and health activities. For example, in April 1963 he was selected an active member of the New York Academy of Sciences (he was also a member of the Pennsylvania Academy of Sciences). In August 1970 he received the Pioneer Service Award from the National Dietary Foods Association, and two months later a certificate for meritorious achievement from the New York State Natural Food Associates. In addition to these relationships with various institutions, J.I. once ran for election to the Emmaus school board. He did no campaigning whatever but still expressed surprise when he finished last in the field of several candidates. (This was the only foray J.I. ever made into active politics. Generally, J.I. was not much interested in politics, though he usually voted for Democratic presidential candidates.)

J.I. was concerned with what he considered to be the

failings of the American educational system. He insisted that his own children (Ruth, Robert, and Nina)
learn good English and was dismayed once when visiting a local school to hear a teacher use the language in-
correctly. An early agreement with Anna provided that
J.I. not teach their children what little Yiddish he
knew and that she not teach them her vocabulary of
Lithuanian. Though he sometimes scorned the educational system, it was clear that J.I. respected and supported it and, on more than one occasion, yearned to
join it.

Throughout J.I.'s life he was noted for his cool temper (except perhaps toward "doddering Ph.Ds") and
sense of humor. At his publishing house in Emmaus he
never upbraided any of his employees for shirking their
duties. Whenever he saw workers standing around
doing nothing, he would suggest with gentle firmness
that while they were waiting, they sit down and read a
book, preferably one of his. He became a familiar sight
as he walked through the offices each day (in the early
days sometimes with an unlit cigar in his mouth) on his
way to the scales, where he daily checked his weight.
One day while J.I. was weighing himself, a new employee who had never met J.I. saw him and called out,
"Everything over 150 is pure shit." J.I. smiled and
walked away. J.I. brought large quantities of sunflower
and pumpkin seeds to the plant for his employees to
munch on during the day. He never insisted that they
follow his health regimen—at least beyond the removal
of soda machines from the plant—he merely made it
available to them.

There were times, however, when J.I. showed a bit
of temper and frustration. He went to a theater once
and as he entered he left his coat and umbrella with an
attendant. He fretted throughout the performance because the attendant had not given him a check for his
possessions. At the end of the show, he was amazed at
how quickly the attendant found his belongings. As he
walked out the door, a note slipped out of the um-

brella. He picked it up. It read "Little Fat Fellow."
Then and there J.I. decided to go on a diet. He said afterward that the breaking of a bad habit depended
greatly on how angry its continuation made its victim.

He was once invited to be a guest on a New York
radio talk show that started at midnight. The host's
program format was to abuse guests as much as possible, though J.I. had not earlier been informed of this.
The host started out with an attack on J.I.'s philosophies, and because J.I. was not expecting it and, for him
at least, it was the middle of the night (he was generally
early to bed), he was probably stunned. He tried to
turn the tables by asking the host a question, only to be
informed that the host would ask the questions, not the
guest. Upon this pronouncement, J.I. got up, said, "I've
had enough," and walked out. The entire incident took
less than two minutes, leaving the hapless host to complete the two-hour program alone. Usually, however,
J.I. was not quite this abrupt.

Another incident showed J.I.'s capacity to get miffed
at something related to his Jewish upbringing and the
inevitable misunderstandings that arose with his Catholic wife, Anna. At Yom Kippur once, he did not go to
a temple (though he was a member of a local Jewish
congregation), so Anna served his dinner. He looked at
the dinner table and asked, "What food is this?" Anna
replied, "Pork chops," whereupon the dinner took a
flight across the dining room. At Yuletide each year,
Anna began putting up Christmas trees—at first very
small ones, but progressively bigger each year. It took
J.I. a while to see what was happening.

Throughout the busy years, many of J.I.'s old
friends thought he had abandoned the Judaism into
which he was born and raised. This was only apparently true, for J.I. never put much stock in ritual—he
felt that all religions paid too much attention to it—but
believed that the content of a worship was the significant thing. After his death, some of his friends discovered that all through the years, J.I. had by no means

renounced his upbringing, as seen in part by his monetary and moral support of the State of Israel against its foes. He had not forsaken his Jewish heritage, though at times it appeared that he had. (He could not join the local country club because he was a Jew—not that he wanted to in the first place.)

He and Anna traveled as much as they possibly could, especially in the later years. Not only did they visit places in this country where his plays were performed, but they traveled extensively abroad. He toured Mexico and some of South America in the early 1950s. He observed closely some of the agricultural practices he saw there and reported them to a congressional committee. Also in the 1950s, he made several trips to Germany while negotiating with the Madaus Company and to England, where he set up an edition of *Prevention* and a natural vitamin company. (In England once, J.I. experienced some difficulties with the government, not unlike his troubles with the FTC in this country. Some of his vitamins, after being stored for an extended period by their purchasers, lost some of their potency. In the investigation that followed, J.I. had to pay the equivalent of approximately $200 in damages.)

In the summer of 1970 he and Anna took an extensive tour of Russia. He filled a notebook with his impressions. He marveled, for example, at the hotel accommodations in Moscow: a large sitting room, large bathroom, and large bedroom, with ceilings twice the height of a Hilton hotel—"all this for $18. a day." The Ukraine hotel where they stayed, he said, was built in 1957 but had architectural earmarkings of 1900. He commented on the uniform dark green of all the motorized vehicles in Moscow and other parts of the country, which gave him the feeling of being in an armed camp.

On the trips abroad it did not take J.I. long to conclude that travel arrangements could be handled more efficiently, and—sure enough—he formed his own travel agency to operate out of Allentown. He was also intrigued by the artwork he saw on manhole covers in different European cities. He described the variations, the coats of arms, and the different metals used for the covers. He believed the idea was a good one for this country to adopt, and he planned to write a definitive book on this "undiscovered" (in America at least) art form. (His Rodale Art Metal Company in New York produced high-priced artistic metal plaques.) Gaily colored trash baskets suspended on telephone and street lamp poles throughout Europe interested him as well. The Howard Metal Craft Company, a division of Rodale Manufacturing, began to make some of these at its Emmaus plant. Ultimately, J.I. was able to sell these trash baskets to several hundred cities around the country.

In addition to everything else, J.I. was an inventor, receiving on April 2, 1929, a patent for a "physical exercising device." He also made several improvements in light fuses and sockets. In 1956 he "invented" a "book-buggy," but never received a patent for it because of its similarities to other devices. J.I.'s "book-buggy" featured movable partitions to facilitate the handling of books in library reading rooms.

Despite all the positive assertions made about J.I. both during his life and since his death, there are, to be sure, several critics of his philosophies. The most obvious of these are the American Medical Association, the Pure Food and Drug Administration, the U.S. Department of Agriculture, and the American Dental Society. These groups are composed of highly trained and specialized scientists who felt that J.I. did not in fact render a service with his generalized approach—that at best he was a comic spectacle; at worst, a menace to the health and well-being of the nation. Less obvious are people like the followers of Rachel Carson, who claim that J.I. "cashed in" on her fame and success. These followers, however, rarely or never mention the similarities between J.I.'s book Pay Dirt and Carson's Silent Spring. Nor do they emphasize the point that

J.I.'s book was written seventeen years before Carson's. Some of the Carson followers do admit that J.I. "greatly modified his views" late in his life but maintain that he always suffered from the excesses of his early career. No one wishes to take away any of the greatness of Carson's work, but if credit is going to be given where it is due, J. I. Rodale must come in for his full share of it.

At this point, it may be useful to explore some of the possible reasons why J.I. and his organiculture were ultimately accepted by large segments of the American people. In a general way, acceptance of him was similar to that of several reform movements in the history of this country. It seems that our society can go for years without any reform movement at all. Then one reform starts, and very shortly others follow. That one reform movement generally begets another is almost a truism. One example will suffice. When the states began passing laws requiring children to stay in school until their sixteenth year, this was in fact the end of the child-labor problem that had plagued the country for so long. Also, one reform group will cooperate with another, not so much out of agreement with the other's goals but for the pragmatic purpose of presenting a common front. Hence, the abolitionists of pre-Civil War days were generally strong supporters of feminist movements. But when slavery ended, many of the former abolitionists became staunch opponents of women's rights. It seems clear that one reform movement helps automatically to lead into demands for other reforms, that diverse reform groups cooperate with each other for mutual benefits, and that reform most often comes during times of affluence—when there are groups that are improved just enough to recognize the possibilities for the good life.

There is no reason to suppose that the "rules" of reform movements are any different today from a hundred years ago. In the late 1960s and on into the 1970s, many books and articles were written to show the dangers of uncontrolled air pollution, of indiscriminate spraying of plants and trees, and of overuse of chemical fertilizers. Somehow these writings, along with the work of many conservation groups alerted the American public as never before to the possibilities of disaster. Successful efforts were made to protect large portions of the American wilderness from "development"—for example, saving a good part of the Everglades from being turned into a jet port. Also, this period witnessed the failure of Congress to finance the SST project because of pressure brought by the public. Bans were made on DDT, and strict controls, including registration with government agencies, were enacted on other insecticides and pesticides. The Environmental Protection Agency was formed to regulate air pollutants from factories, and antipollution devices were built into all new cars, with plans being made to make these devices progressively stricter. The country seemed to become very much "consumer-minded" as one state after another set up consumer agencies, as the federal government passed a number of consumer-protection laws, and as people like Ralph Nader became known and widely accepted. A large proportion of those responsible for these and other reforms were young—under thirty—spotlighting a new sense of urgency.

The acceptance of J. I. Rodale should and must be considered within the context of the overall reform picture of this period. Certainly this point is not to be construed as meaning that J.I. and his philosophies were mere "tag-alongs" behind the other changes of the time; on the contrary, some of the basic changes were encouraged and brought about by the patience and the perseverance of the man from Emmaus. It would be an error, however, to think of J.I.'s "arrival" in isolation from everything else. The generation that turned Love Story and The Greening of America into best sellers and raised old songs like "Amazing Grace" and "1812 Overture" to the top lists was the same one that decided to do something about the mounting rate of fish kills, the growing possibilities that certain wildlife would soon become extinct, and the likelihood that our land would be laid waste unless some significant reversals were accomplished. Within this context, it is easy to see how J. I. Rodale, organic gardening, and the prevention system could win their belated accolades.

J.I.'s Jewish upbringing produced in him self-centeredness, generosity, and a high respect for learning as opposed to mere education. The self-centered aspect caused him to fight assiduously for whatever he believed in—against adverse circumstances and the early threat of bankruptcy that most other people would have found insurmountable. The generous part caused J.I. to feel that it was his duty to share his acquired knowledge about the land and health with other people, and also, under various circumstances, to share his fortune as well. If he had been a university-trained man, the "Renaissance" aspect of his life might very well have been blunted (though this is by no means a provable statement). At it was, he could go wherever fact, and even fancy, led him, and the results were not insignificant.

Regardless of how one feels about J. I. Rodale and his activities, it is indisputable that, with the things he did and the following he amassed, he has won a secure place in the social history of the United States. His greatest weakness was jumping to conclusions, of pronouncing a procedure as good and proper when its "scientific" basis was no stronger than several laudatory letters printed in his journals.

J.I. should not be judged for the overexuberance and sometimes even contradictions and inconsistencies of which he was frequently guilty. Someone once truthfully said that a creative and innovative mind is by its very nature inconsistent. The ideas come on so fast and so hard that their creator cannot constantly be stopping and checking them for consistency. J.I. should be judged, rather, on his career and accomplishments as a whole. It is not fair, and generally not very accurate, to assess a person's life in terms of fragmentation. The total picture, as much as it can be known, must be the guide in such judgments. What was the total picture? Some parts, at least, were:

- Humble beginnings within a setting of poverty that, while not abject, was enough to give J.I. ambitions to reach out of it.
- A reaction against authoritative figures—his father and his rabbi "Red-Donkey" being the prime cases in point. (Later in life, perhaps he subconsciously transferred this "debunking" aptitude to organizations like the AMA, the FDA, the USDA, and the American Dental Society and also to "father figures" in our history like George Washington and John Hancock.)
- The desire, even at an early age, to go to the land and treat it "scientifically." (In this respect, J.I. always argued that the organic approach to farming was the only true "scientific" way.)
- The drive and ambition, caused partly by his Jewish heritage, to be successful and to share that success with other people.
- The feelings of chagrin that came when people less knowledgeable than he got higher salaries and faster promotions only because they held college degrees. (Here, in fact, was where his inferiority complex came most clearly to light, but it was a complex that ultimately gave him quite frequent feelings of superiority.)
- The acquisition of a temperament that was unorthodox, debunking, curious, naïve, searching, and at times even arrogant, but one that nevertheless was usually applied in tones of sweetness and gentleness.
- A firm and sincere conviction that his way was right. He did not denigrate those who failed to follow his system, but he did acquire an almost evangelical zeal in converting those of bad habit with whom he came into contact. (At a play rehearsal once he saw an actor during a break munching on a candy bar. J.I.

gently took the candy from him and offered instead a handful of sunflower and pumpkin seeds. The actor was almost immediately converted. Also, J.I. would strike up conversations with total strangers about the dangers of things like fluoridation and about the superiority of the organic and preventive systems.)

- A willingness to go into any media—magazines, novels, nonfiction books, TV and radio, plays, and movies—to show that his way was the right one. If an idea was worthy, J.I. believed in exploiting every possible avenue for its exposure and publicity.
- And, finally, a crusading spirit against all the chemical activities in relation to the land and the things it produced. He was in the field in this respect as early as the midforties, when most people had their minds on other things.

Most assuredly, the "total picture" of anyone is extremely difficult, if not impossible, to grasp. There are thoughts in a person's mind that will always be unknown to all except the possessor. The best one can hope to do is present a faithful approximation of the truth as he sees it. J. I. Rodale was many things, but certainly, as columnist Kilpatrick so truthfully stated, he was an "apostle of nonconformity."

Sources

Chapter 1

Brooks, Paul. Letter to the writer, February 20, 1973.

Carson, Rachel. *Silent Spring*. Boston: Houghton Mifflin, 1962.

Curti, Merle. *The Growth of American Thought*, rev. ed. New York: Harper, 1951.

Hofstadter, Richard. *The Age of Reform*. New York: Knopf, 1955.

Prevention, November 1965.

Rodale, J. I. *Autobiography*. Emmaus, Pa.: Rodale Books, 1965.

———. *Pay Dirt*. Old Greenwich, Conn.: Devin-Adair, 1945.

———. *Walk, Do Not Run to the Doctor*. Emmaus, Pa.: Rodale Books, 1967.

———, and Louis Ludwig. Unpublished correspondence, 1917–1925.

Tocqueville, Alexis de. *Democracy in America*. 1835.

Young, James Harvey. *The Toadstool Millionaires*. Princeton, N.J.: Princeton University Press, 1961.

Chapter 2

Commager, Henry Steele. *Meet the U.S.A.* New York: Institute of International Education, 1970.

Glazer, Nathan, et al. *The Characteristics of American Jews*. New York: Jewish Education Committee Press, 1965.

Gordon, Albert J. *Jews in Suburbia*. Boston: Beacon Press, 1959.

Joseph, Samuel. *Jewish Immigration to the United States From 1881 to 1910*. New York: Arno Press, Inc., 1969.

Ludwig, Louis. Interview, March 3, 1973.

Rodale, Anna. Interview, December 18, 1972.

Rodale, J. I. *Autobiography*. Emmaus, Pa.: Rodale Books, 1965.

———. Unpublished segments of *Autobiography*.

———. *Mss*. Emmaus, Pa.

———, and Louis Ludwig. Unpublished correspondence, 1918–1923.

Rodale, Robert. Interview, December 18, 1972.

Spira, Ruth. Interview, December 19, 1972.

Toynbee, Arnold J. *A Study of History*, Vol. II. New York: Oxford University Press, 1934.

Chapter 3

The New York Times, June 19, 1927.

Rodale, J. I. *Are We Really Living Longer?* Emmaus, Pa.: Rodale Books, 1965.

———. *Autobiography*. Emmaus, Pa.: Rodale Books, 1965.

———. *Mss*. Emmaus, Pa.

———. *An Organic Trip to England*. Emmaus, Pa.: Rodale Books, 1954.

———. *The Stones of Jehosaphat*. Emmaus, Pa.: Rodale Books, 1954.

Time Magazine, "Catching Up To Rodale Press," March 22, 1971.

Chapter 4

Bidwell, Percy Wells, and John I. Falconer. *History of Agriculture in the Northern United States, 1620–1860*. Washington, D.C.: Carnegie Institute, 1925.

Carrier, Lyman. *The Beginnings of Agriculture in America*. New York: McGraw-Hill, 1923.

Cato. *On Agriculture*. Translated by William Davis Hooper; revised by Harrison Boyd Ash. Cambridge: Harvard University Press, 1960.

Davis, Wayne. "Economics Prevents Farming Organically," Louisville (Ky.) *Courier-Journal and Times*, June 25, 1972.

Egler, Frank. "Pesticides—In Our Ecosystem," *American Scientist*, 52 (March 1964), 110–136.

Eliot, Jared. *Essays Upon Field Husbandry in New En-*

gland *and Other Papers.* Edited by Harry J. Carman and Rexford G. Tugwell. New York: Columbia University Press, 1934.

Glover, T. R. *Virgil.* London: Methuen, 1904.

Gray, Lewis Cecil. *A History of Agriculture in the Southern United States to 1860.* Washington, D.C.: Carnegie Institute, 1933.

"Health Food: Definitions and Nutrient Values," *Journal of Nutrition Education,* 4 (Summer 1972), 94–97.

Howard, Albert. *An Agricultural Testament.* New York and London: Oxford University Press, 1940.

Liebig, Justus. *Organic Chemistry in Its Applications to Agriculture and Physiology.* Edited by John W. Webster. Cambridge: Owen, n.d.

Pliny the Elder. *Natural History,* Vols. 17–20. Translated and edited by H. Rackman and W. H. S. Jones. Cambridge: Harvard University Press, 1941.

Rodale, J. I. *Organic Front.* Emmaus, Pa.: Rodale Books, 1948.

———. *Testimony Before Congressional Committee Investigating Chemicals, Pursuant to House Resolution 323.* 81 Cong; 2 Sess., December 13, 1950.

True, Alfred Charles. *A History of Agricultural Experimentation and Research in the United States, 1607–1925, Including a History of the United States Department of Agriculture.* Washington, D.C.: U.S. Department of Agriculture, 1937.

Whitney, Milton. *Soil and Civilization.* New York: Van Nostrand, 1925.

Chapter 5

Amory, Cleveland. "Trade Winds," *Saturday Review,* September 18, 1971, p. 18.

Electroculture in Plant Growth. Edited by Organic Gardening and Farming staff. Emmaus, Pa.: Rodale Books, 1968.

Galston, Arthur W. "The Organic Gardener and Anti-Intellectualism," *Natural History,* May 1972, pp. 26–28.

House Select Committee to Investigate the Use of Chemicals in Foods and Cosmetics. 81 Cong; 2 Sess. (House Resolution 323), 1950.

Letters to the writer from: John C. Alden, October 27, 1972; John J. Biesele, September 29, 1972; Barry Commoner, October 17, 1972; Paul A. Erlich, October 31, 1972; Richard H. Goodwin, September 29, 1972; R. G. Haines, November 30, 1972; Leonard J. Hippchen, January 29, 1973; Rachel Kaufman, February 14, 1973; Charles Wurster, September 29, 1972; James Harvey Young, October 26, 1972.

Manchester, Harland. "The Great Organic-Gardening Myth," Reader's Digest, July 1962, pp. 102–105.

Organic Farming and Gardening, May–August 1942; October 1942.

Organic Gardening, December 1942; March 1943; November 1943; December 1943; March–June 1944; August–November 1944.

Organic Gardening and Farming, June–August 1961; November 1961; January 1962; February 1962; April–June 1962; August 1962; September 1962; November 1962; December 1962; February 1963; April 1963; July 1963; October 1963; February 1964; April–October 1964; December 1964; January 1965; May 1965; October 1966.

Otto, Herbert A. "Communes: The Alternative Life-Style," Saturday Review, April 24, 1971, p. 17.

"Plain Talk Pesticides and the Environment." Speaker's kit from Monsanto Co., Inc.

Rodale, J. I. Autobiography. Emmaus, Pa.: Rodale Books, 1965.

———. Mss. Emmaus, Pa.

———. Organic Front. Emmaus, Pa.: Rodale Books, 1948.

———. Organic Gardening. Emmaus, Pa.: Rodale Books, 1955.

———. Organic Merry-Go-Round. Emmaus, Pa.: Rodale Books, 1954.

———, and staff. Our Poisoned Earth and Sky. Emmaus, Pa.: Rodale Books, 1964.

———, and staff. The Encyclopedia of Organic Gardening. Emmaus, Pa.; Rodale Books, 1970 (13th printing).

Rodale, Robert. Interview, December 18, 1972.

Schaatz, Albert. Interview, December 18, 1972.

Stowell, John. Article on food chemicals, Park City Daily News (Bowling Green, Ky.), February 22, 1973.

Throckmorton, R. I. "Organic Farming—Bunk!," *Reader's Digest*, October 1952, pp. 45–48.
Whole Earth Catalog, Spring 1971, p. 33.

Chapter 6

Lehigh Valley Committee Against Health Fraud, Inc. Interview, December 18, 1972.

Jukes, Thomas H. Statement at Hearing on Assembly Bill 450, before California Legislature Committee on Environmental Quality, September 11, 1972.

Letters to the writer from: Marshall Ackerman, June 19, 1973; Ruth Adams, June 4, 1973; Stephen Barrett, November 21, 1972; Oliver Field, August 31, 1972, and January 25, 1973; Frederick Stare, September 5, 1972; Federal Trade Commission, February 20, 1973; Food and Drug Administration, March 20, 1973.

Manuche, Dorothy. "*Today's Health* and *Prevention*, A Propaganda Analysis." Unpublished and undated paper, New York University.

Penthouse, July 1972.

Prevention, September–December 1950; August 1951; January 1952; June 1952; March 1953; May–November 1960; January–March 1961; July–September 1961; January 1962; March 1962; April 1962; June 1962; July 1962; September 1962; October–December 1962; January 1963; March–July 1963; February 1964; May–July 1965; October–December 1965; January 1966; February 1966; April–June 1966; August–December 1966.

Rodale, J. I. *Are We Really Living Longer?* Emmaus, Pa.: Rodale Books, 1955.

———. *Happy People Rarely Get Cancer*. Emmaus, Pa.: Rodale Books, 1970.

———. *The Hawthorne Berry for the Heart*. Emmaus, dale Books, 1955.

———. *Is Our Intelligence Declining?* Emmaus, Pa.: Ro- Pa.: Rodale Books, 1971.

———. *Lower Your Pulse and Live Longer*. Emmaus, Pa.: Rodale Books, 1971.

———. *Mss.*, Emmaus.

———. *My Own Technique for Health*. Emmaus, Pa.: Rodale Books, 1969.

————. *Natural Health, Sugar and the Criminal Mind.* New York: Pyramid, 1968.

————. *Poison in Your Pots and Pans.* Emmaus, Pa.: Rodale Books, 1955.

————. *The Prostate.* Emmaus, Pa.: Rodale Books, 1970.

————. *Rodale's System for Mental Power and Natural Health.* Englewood Cliffs, N.J.: Prentice-Hall, 1956.

————. *This Pace Is Not Killing Us.* Emmaus, Pa.: Rodale Books, 1954.

————. *Walk, Do Not Run to the Doctor.* Emmaus, Pa.: Rodale Books, 1967.

————, and staff. *Bone Meal for Good Teeth.* Emmaus, Pa.: Rodale Books, 1962.

Rodale Collection. American Medical Association, Chicago, Illinois.

Rodale Collection. Lehigh Valley Committee Against Health Fraud, Inc., Allentown, Pennsylvania.

Sprague, Bob. "Nutritionists Attack Rodale, Organic Certification," Bethlehem (Pa.) *Globe-Times,* November 18, 1972.

Stare, Frederick. "Trends in Nutrition." Keynote Address at Nutrition Update—Recent Advances and Trends. Philadelphia Section, Institute of Food Technologists, Philadelphia, Pa., November 14, 1972.

Turner, James S. *The Chemical Feast.* New York: Grossman, 1970.

Young, James Harvey. *The Medical Messiahs.* Princeton, N.J.: Princeton University Press, 1967.

Chapter 7

Federal Trade Commission Decisions, Vol. 57, 66–68, 71.

Kearney, Edward N. *Thurman Arnold, Social Critic. The Satirical Challenge to Orthodoxy.* Albuquerque: University of New Mexico Press, 1970.

Kilpatrick, James Jackson. "Bureaucrats in Stew Over Food Fad Book," in J. I. Rodale, *Autobiography* (Emmaus, Pa.: Rodale Books, 1965), pp. 92–94.

Letters to the writer from: Robert Rodale, September 13, 1972, and April 9, 1973; Morton J. Simon, April 3, 1973.

The Morning Call (Allentown, Pa.), January 20, 1965.

The New York Times, December 13, 1964.

Official Transcript of FTC Proceedings, November 30, 1964–March 5, 1965. Docket Number 8619.

Review of *The Health Finder* in *New Health: Quarterly Journal of Health and Diet* (London), Winter 1956.

Rodale, J. I. *How to Eat for A Healthy Heart.* Emmaus, Pa.: Rodale Books, 1954.

———. *Mss.* Emmaus, Pa.

———. *This Pace Is Not Killing Us.* Emmaus, Pa.: Rodale Books, 1954.

———, and staff. *The Complete Book of Food and Nutrition.* Emmaus, Pa.: Rodale Books, 1961.

——— (ed.), with Ruth Adams. *The Health Finder.* Emmaus, Pa.: Rodale Books, 1954.

Rodale, Robert. Interviews, December 18, 19, 1972.

Shank, Robert. *Testimony Before Senate Special Committee on Aging,* January 15, 1963, pp. 43–45.

The Wall Street Journal, April 23, 1965.

Chapter 8

Arnold, Thurman, and Stuart Land. *Brief for Petitioners in the United States Court of Appeals for the District of Columbia Circuit,* No. 21,259, February 13, 1968.

Federal Reports, 2nd Series, Vol. 407; pp. 1253–1258.

Federal Trade Commission Decisions, Vol. 71, pp. 1222–1292.

Kilpatrick, James Jackson. "When Bureaucracy Bangs on the Little Guys," *Miami Herald,* July 17, 1967.

Letters to the writer from: Judith A. Cooke, February 20, 1973; Gerald J. Thain, January 26, 1973.

Memorandum Brief of American Civil Liberties Union as Amicus Curiae. Before the Federal Trade Commission, September 28, 1965.

Rodale, J. I. *Mss.* Emmaus, Pa.

Rodale, Robert. Interview, December 18, 19, 1972.

Chapter 9

Brandeis University Creative Arts Award, Fifteenth Annual Presentation Ceremony, May 2, 1971.

Calta, Louis. "Changes for Toinette," *The New York Times*, December 19, 1961.

———. "Rodale Will Open Intimate Theatre," *The New York Times*, January 13, 1962.

Davis, James. Article in *New York Sunday Daily News*, December 6, 1964.

Donald, Malcolm. "Sugar and Spites," *The New Yorker*, March 26, 1960.

Letters to the writer from: Anna Rodale, February 27, 1973; Gerald Honaker, March 7, 1973; Robert Drean, June 1, 1973; Allan Miller, May 10, 1973; Barbra Streisand, July 17, 1973.

Prevention, September 1960; July 1961.

Rodale, Anna, and Robert Rodale. Interviews, December 18, 19, 1972.

Rodale, J. I. *The Girl and the Teenager, A Play*. Emmaus, Pa.: Rodale Books, 1958.

———. Plays, cited to the last edition:

Young Whistler at Paris, August 1970

Mother Jones, October 1971

Whistler Vs. Ruskin, December 1970

John Hancock, Portrait of an Empty Barrel, November 1972

The Boston Tea Party, or the Indian Who Didn't Want to Go, February 1971

Franklin and Mme. Brillon, November 1970

Talkative Franklin, July 1970

20 Years From Now, 1969

The Hairy Falsetto, January 1971

Funeral Jazz, May 1971

Franklin and Mr. Gout, July 1970

The Miser's Coffin, from a short story by Luigi Pirandello, November 1970

The Umbrella, from a short story by Guy de Maupassant, May 1969

The Railroad Ticket, August 1969

This Mania for Running Around Half-Naked, adapted from Georges Feydeau, August 1969

Uncle Vanya, adapted from Anton Chekhov, November 1969

The Cherry Orchard, adapted from Anton Chekhov, July 1970

The Malade Who Was Imaginary (formerly Toinette), adapted from Molière, May 1969

Lost and Found Psychodrama, April 1969

The Yugoslav Medical Mystery, April 1969

The Devil and the Nails, June 1969

Can a Hen Lay an Egg Without a Rooster? June 1969

The Cockroach Who Wanted to Go Steady, September 1969

Moon Over Taurus, November 1969

A Series of Ecological Comedy Skits, October 1971

Silence at the Zoo, May 1971

Christmas Program

How to Choose a Marriage Partner, January 1970

The Vanity of Nothing, May 1969

The Pigeon Prize, from the short story by Alexandre Dumas, fils, July 1969

The Cop and the Robber, January 1971

The $19.00 Actress, February 1971

The Flower Thief, August 1969

Some Sweeping Remarks, February 1971

A Bull Fight, February 1971

The Cat and the Rumanian, 1969

————. Skits and Conversations Toward Better Health. Emmaus, Pa.: Rodale Books, 1958.

Saunders, Dudly. Review of "An Evening With Rodale," Louisville (Ky.) Times, August 13, 1969.

Shepard, Richard F. "Busy 'Impudent Wolf' Dramatist Now Turns Energies to Musicals," The New York Times, November 20, 1965.

Sobel, Elaine. Interview, March 5, 1973.

Spira, Ruth. Interview, December 19, 1972.

Taubman, Howard. "Theatre: 'Toinette' Opens," The New York Times, November 21, 1961.

"Theatre Notes," Organic Gardening and Farming, February 1962.

"Toinette, A new musical comedy; the Playwright Vs. the Critics," The New Yorker, November 28, 1961.

"Toinette Sponsor Rebukes Its Critics," The New York Times, November 28, 1961.

Chapter 10

Allentown (Pa.) *Evening Chronicle*, June 8, 1971.

Allentown (Pa.) *The Morning Call*, June 8, 1971.

Barrett, Wayne. "The Organic Way of Gardening and Its Prophet," *The Smithsonian*, May 1971.

Clark, Mike. "Nature's Way Gaining Favor, People From Emmaus Say," *Philadelphia Enquirer*, April 18, 1971.

"Death of a Salesman," *Newsweek*, June 21, 1971.

Dick Cavett Show. Transcript, June 7, 8, 1971.

Drean, Robert. Eulogy for J. I. Rodale, June 10, 1971.

Effron, Marshall, as told to Kathy Stream. "What Happened on the Dick Cavett Show?" *The Realist*, May–June 1971.

Good, Mary B. Article in Mount Prospect, Illinois *Herald*, June 11, 1971.

Green, Wade. "Guru of the Organic Food Cult," *The New York Times Magazine*, June 6, 1971.

Kadans, Joseph M. "A Tribute to Jerome Rodale," *International Journal of Natural Therapeutics*, Vol. 4 (Jan.–Feb.–Mar. 1972).

Letter to the writer from: Eric White, M.D., June 15, 1973.

Malloy, Michael T. "The Nation Gobbles Organic Food," *National Observer*, May 31, 1971.

Pacey, Margaret D. "Nature's Bounty," *Barron's National Business and Financial Weekly*, May 10, 1971.

Rodale, Anna. Interview, December 19, 1972.

Rodale, J. I. Interview, *Penthouse* Magazine, June, 1971.

———. *Mss.* Emmaus, Pa.

Rodale, Robert. Interview, December 18, 1972.

Shafer, Steven. Eulogy for J. I. Rodale, June 10, 1971.

Sheridan, Don. "Balance: The Rodale Legacy," *Clear Creek*, September 1971.

"A Son of the Ghetto Becomes Patriarch of Health Foods, *The Bulletin*, May 2, 1971.

The Sunday News Journal (Daytona Beach, Florida), June 13, 1971.

Wields, Gerald. "R.I.P., J.I.," *Philadelphia Magazine*, July 1971.

Yergin, Daniel. "High Priestess of Health Food," *The*

Courier-Journal and *Times* Magazine (Louisville, Ky.), June 10, 1973.

Chapter 11

Letters to the writer from: Robert Rodale, April 9, 1973; Paul Knight, September 12, 1972; Morton J. Simon, April 3, 1973; Samuel Chosiad, January 19, 1973; Betty Gyneth T. Franklin, March 11, 1973; R. G. Haines, November 30, 1972.

Meyer, Heinrich. "Some Recollections of Rodale Press." Unpublished and undated.

Rodale, Anna. Interview, December 19, 1972.

Rodale, J. I. Mss. Emmaus, Pa.

Rodale, Robert. Interview, December 18, 19, 1972.

Spira, Ruth. Interview, December 19, 1972.

INDEX

Abernethy, Thomas G., 106-107

Abrahamson, E. M., 195

Ackerman, Marshall, 135, 137

Adams, Ruth, 135, 136, 137

Age of Reform, The (Hofstadter), 25

Alarcón, Pedro Antonio de, *Tales From the Spanish,* 77

Albert, Eddie, 76

Albrecht, William, 116

Alden, John C., 114

Alexander, Don Dale, 162, 163

Alger, Horatio, 21, 44, 187

Allentown *Evening Chronicle,* 230

Allentown *Morning Call,* 61, 162, 230

Aluminum—A Menace to Health (Clement), 130

Aluminum Association, 130

American Civil Liberties Union, 170, 171

American Dental Society, 219, 242, 246

American Humorist, The, 62

American Journal of Clinical Nutrition, 65

American Journal of Public Health, 140

American Medical Association, The, (AMA), 24, 65, 88, 130, 138, 140, 141, 142, 143, 159, 168, 180, 185, 194, 219, 224, 225, 236, 242, 246

AMA Council on Foods and Nutrition, 150

American Public Health Association, 140

American Scientist, The, 95

Amory, Cleveland, 113

An Agricultural Testament

(Howard), 63, 93, 96, 97, 98

Andrews, Anna (Rodale's wife), 57, 128, 209, 216, 220, 221, 222, 227, 228, 234, 239, 240, 241

An Organic Trip to England (Rodale), 65

Ansara, Alex, 199

Are We Really Living Longer? (Rodale), 79, 144

Aristotle, 31

Armour and Company, 133

Arnold, Thurman W., 152, 153, 155, 156, 157-58, 160, 161, 168, 172, 180, 181, 182, 183, 184, 185, 188

Arthritis and Common Sense (Witkower), 162, 163

Associated Press, the, 107, 197

Association of Cost Accountants, the, 60

Backstage, 67, 207, 211, 212

Barrett, Stephen, 133, 134, 138, 140

Barron's National Business and Financial Weekly: "Nature's Bounty" (Margaret Pacey), 218, 219

Barton, Paul, 130

Bartram, John, 91

Beatles, the, 121

Beginnings of Agriculture in America, The (Carrier), 87

Benny, Jack, 227

Bernadean College, 238

Better Business Bureau, the, 131

Biesele, John J., 110

Binns, John, 91

Biodynamic Farming and Gardening (Pfeiffer), 105

Biography, 62

"Biology and Human Affairs" (Galston lecture), 112
Body, Mind and Sugar (Abrahamson), 195
Book-of-the-Month Club, 107
Book-of-the-Month Club News, 33
Borlaug, Norman F., 94
Boston Tea Party, The (Rodale), 208
Brandeis University Creative Arts Award, 212, 237
Brandeth, Benjamin, 29
Brave and Bold (Alger), 187
Bromfield, Louis, 75
Bryan, William Jennings, 53
Buchanan, James, 89
Buck, Pearl S., 76
Bulletin, The: "A Son of the Ghetto Becomes Patriarch of Health Foods," 218
Bull Fight, A (Rodale), 205
Bureau of Soils (U. S. Dept. of Agriculture), 93
Burke, Billie, 49

California Food Retailer's Association, 219
Calta, Louis, 198, 200
Cambridge University Press, 78
Cameron, Roderick, 218
Can a Hen Lay an Egg Without a Rooster? (Rodale), 201
Carnegie, Andrew, 21, 29
Carrier, Lyman, 87, 89
Carson, Rachel, 23, 33, 34, 107, 242, 243
Caruso, Enrico, 39
Cat and the Rumanian, The (Rodale), 205, 210
Catawba College, 238
Cato the Censor, 84
Catt, Carrie Chapman, 76
"Cause of Polio Discovered, The" (Rodale), 148
Century Magazine, 61
Chaplin, Charles, 205, 212
Chapman, Lonny, 199
Charlton, Francis J., 173
Chekhov, Anton (The Beggar, The Seagull, adapted by Rodale), 77

Chemical Feast (Turner), 144
"chemurgy," 32
Cherry Orchard, The (Chekhov adapted by Rodale), 202-203
Christian Century, The, 72
Cicero (Sinclair), 73
Citizens Group Against Fluoridation, 133
Clark, Mike, 218
Classics First, 78
Clear Creek, 231
Clement, Mark, 130
Clown, The (Rodale magazine), 62
Cockroach Who Wanted to Go Steady, The (Rodale), 201
Cohen, Archie (Rodale's brother), 43, 45
Cohen, Jacob Issac, then Jerome Irving—Rodale's given names, 38
Cohen, Joe (Rodale's brother), 26, 41, 45, 55, 56
Cohen, Michael (Rodale's father), 38-45, 56
Cohen, Sally (Rodale's sister), 45
Cohen, Solomon (Rodale's brother), 45
Cohen, Tina (Rodale's sister), 45
Color Additives Amendment (1960), 107
Columbus, Christopher, 87, 236
Commager, Henry Steele, 37
Commoner, Barry, 110
Commonsense, 72
Complete Book of Food and Nutrition, The (Rodale), 124, 150, 160, 161, 164
Compost Science: Journal of Waste Recycling, 65
Conference on Medical Quackery (1961), 144
Conversations Toward Better Health (Rodale), 193
Cop and the Robber, The (Rodale), 205
Cotten, Elizabeth, 75
Counterblast to Tobacco (Schlemill), 78

Courier-Journal and Times
(Louisville, Ky.), 98
Crisctiello, Modestino, 154,
155
Cron, Millard W., 148
Cross-Word Puzzle Word-Finder, 27
Cummings, Robert, 76

Dannay, Frederic (Ellery
Queen), 76
Darwin, Charles, 31, 63
Daudet, Alphonse, 77
David McKay Company, 80
Davis, Adelle, 233
Davis, James, 206
Davis, Wayne, 98
DDT, 32, 201
Delaney Clause, 106, 107
Delaney Committee, 116
Delaney, James, J., 106, 107
Democracy in America (de
Tocqueville), 25
Devil and the Nails, The
(Rodale), 201
Dewey, Thomas E., 76
Detroit News, The, 230
Dick Cavett Show, The, 135,
221, 222, 223, 225, 227,
228, 231, 232, 234
Dickens, Charles, 61
Disraeli, Issac, 61
District Publishing Company,
the, 55
Dixon, Paul Rand, 171, 172,
173
Dobinsky, Anna Maria, 215
Dumas *fils,* Alexandre, 192;
"The Pigeon Prize" adapted
by Rodale, 204
Duncan, Isadora, 196
Dvořák, Anton, 120

Eaker, Ira, 211
Eat the Cake and Have It
(Rodale), 211
Eck, Harvey, 232
Effron, Marshall, 222
"Egg and You, The" (Ro-
dale), 119
Egler, Frank, 95
Eisen, Max, 220
Eliot, Jared, 89, 90
Elman, Philip, 153, 162, 171,

172, 178, 179, 181
Emmaus, Pennsylvania (Ro-
dale's home and experi-
mental farm), 22, 26, 30,
34, 58, 76, 115, 118, 121,
200, 211, 213, 214, 218,
221, 227, 232, 233, 236
*Encyclopedia of Common Di-
seases* (Rodale Press), 124
Engagement Baby, 214
Environment Action Bulletin,
68
Environmental Defense Fund,
218
Environmental Protection
Agency, 244
Erlich, Paul, 110
Everybody's Digest, 62
Executive Newsletter, 68
Eyster, William H., 115

Fact Digest, 62, 63
Faulkner, Edward H., 103
Federal Drug Commission, the
(FDA), 24
Federal Trade Commission,
the (FTC), 68, 133, 148,
149, 150, 151, 152, 153,
154, 159, 161, 162, 163,
164, 167, 168, 170, 171,
172, 173, 175, 176, 177,
178, 179, 180, 181, 182,
183, 184, 185, 186, 187,
188, 189, 190, 201, 241
Ferguson, Garland, 153, 154,
156, 160, 161, 172
Feydeau, Georges, 192; play
adapted by Rodale as *This
Mania for Running Around
Half-Naked,* 203
Field, Oliver, 138
Finnerty, Frank, 154, 156
Fitness for Living, 67
Flanagan, Patrick, 140
Flaubert, Gustave (Idée Reçu),
78
Flivver King, The (Sinclair),
72
Flower Thief, The (Rodale),
205
Folk Medicine (Jarvis), 88
Fonda, Henry, 76
Fonda, Peter, 199

Food Additives Amendment (1958), 107
Food, Drug, and Cosmetic Act, 106, 107
Ford, Henry, 32
Frank, Mrs. Ingebourg T., 210
Frankfurter, Felix, 171
Franklin and Mme. Brillon (Rodale), 207-208
Franklin and Mr. Gout (Rodale), 207
Franklin, Benjamin, 23, 193, 207
Franklin, Mrs. Betty G., 214, 219
Frazer, Joseph, 71
Funeral Jazz (Rodale), 205

Galston, Arthur W., 112, 113
George III, 233, 236
Georgics (Vergil), 85
Getting Back Together (Houriet), 112
Girl and the Teenager, The (Rodale), 193, 194
Glover, T. R., 84
Golden Book, 77
Golden Cockerel Press, the, 77
Good, Mary B., 230
Goodwin, Richard H., 111
Goose, The (Rodale), 142, 194, 195, 196, 212
Graham, Reverend Sylvester, 28
"Great Organic Gardening Myth, The" (Manchester article), 114
Greeley, Horace, 236
Greening of America, The (Reich), 244
Green, William, 77
Gross, William, 134
Gussow (accounting firm), 45
Gustenberg (N. Y. U. professor), 46

Haines, R. G., 111
Hairy Falsetto, The (Rodale), 205-207, 210, 214
Hamill, Pete, 225
Hamilton, Alexander, 236
Hancock, John, 193, 208, 246
Hanley, Tom, 49

"Happy People Rarely Get Cancer" (Rodale article in *Prevention*), 126
Harter, Ardeth L., 232
Harvard Law Review, The, 182
Hawthorne Berry for the Heart, The (Rodale), 131
Health Bulletin, 33, 68, 80
Health Digest, 62
Health Finder, The (Rodale Press), 124, 148, 149, 150, 151, 153, 154, 155, 156, 159, 160, 161, 163, 164, 165, 166, 167, 168, 174, 176, 177, 179, 181, 201
Health For All, 63
Health Guide, 62, 63, 130
Health News Digest, 68
Health Secrets from Foreign Lands (Rodale Press), 124
Health Secrets of Famous Doctors (Rodale Press), 124
Health Secrets of Famous People (Rodale Press), 124
Healthy Huzas, The (Rodale), 54
Hellzapoppin, 193
Hippchen, Leonard, 117
Hirsch, Richard, 213
Hitler, Adolf, 195
Hoffman, Dustin, 200
Hofstadter, Richard, 25
Holman, Nat, 42
Honaker, Gerald, 210
Hoover, Herbert, 236
Hostetter, David, 29
Houriet, Robert, 112
House Select Committee to Investigate the Use of Chemicals in Foods and Cosmetics, 106
Howard Metal Craft Company, 242
Howard, Sir Albert, 20, 30, 63, 64, 93, 94, 96, 97, 98, 100, 102, 103, 222
How to Choose a Marriage Partner (Rodale), 191
How to Eat for a Healthy Heart (Rodale), 148-49, 150, 154, 156, 161, 164, 167, 179

How to Win at Poker (Jacoby), 172
Huckleberry Finn (Twain), 75
Humorous Scrapbook, The, 27, 61, 62
Humphrey, Hubert, 206
Hunzas, the (tribe), 54, 97

Ickes, Harold, 76
If You Must Smoke (Rodale), 50, 126
Income Tax Magazine, 60
Ingersoll, Robert, 61
International Journal of Natural Therapeutics, 231
"In The Theatre With J. I. Rodale" (*Backstage* column), 212
Irion, Clyde, 68

Jacoby, Oswald, 172
Jamestown Colony, 87
James Verner, Ltd., 211
Jarvis, D. C., 88
Jefferson, Thomas, 236
J. I. Rodale and Company, Ltd., 70
Job Corps, the, 119
John Hancock, Portrait of an Empty Barrel (Rodale), 76, 208, 211
Johnson, Andrew, 236
Johnson, Lyndon B., 119, 206
Jolson, Al, 49
Jones, Mary Gardiner, 171, 172, 175
Jones, Wade H., 68
Journal of Nervous Disorders, 107
Journal of Nutrition Education, The, 94
Jungle, The (Sinclair), 72, 74

Kameny, Alex, 199
Kaslow, Richard, 226
Kemmerer, Vernice, 70
Kennedy, John F., 236
Kier, Samuel, 29
Kilpatrick, James Jackson, 168, 180, 247
King-Anderson version of Medicare, 142
King's English on Horseback, The (*The Sophisticated Synonym Book*), 27
Kleinman, J. (accounting firm), 46

Lancet, 24
Land, Stuart, 161, 172
Larrick, George, 129, 144
Lasagna, Louis, 159, 160
Laurel and Hardy, 205
Lawes, Sir John, 93
Laws of Leviticus, the, 40
Learn-En-Joy, Inc., 66
Lee, Robert E., 236
Lehigh Valley Committee Against Health Fraud, Inc. (LVCAHF), 125, 126, 133, 134, 135, 138, 144, 193
Lehigh Valley Health Club, 133
Lehigh Valley Organic Shopper (*Lehigh Valley's Better Foods Shopper*), 69
Levinson, Sam, 76
Lewis, John, 152, 156, 157-58, 160, 161, 162, 163, 164, 165, 166, 167, 168, 169, 170, 171, 174, 176, 177, 178, 180, 184, 185, 188
Liebig, Justus, 91, 92, 93, 94
Limited Editions Club, 74, 75
Lincoln, Abraham, 89
Lincoln Square Academy, 213, 237
Longfellow (*Continental Tales*), 77
Lost and Found Psychodrama (Rodale), 200
Louisville *Times,* 210
Love, Arlene, 213
Love Story (Siegal), 244
Lower Manhattan Industrial Association, the, 60
Ludwig, Louis, 22, 25, 41, 43, 45, 47, 48, 52, 54, 56, 81

MacFadden Bernarr, 29
MacIntyre, Everette, 171, 177-78
Madaus Drug Company, the, 70, 77, 241
Mad, Mad World, 193
Malcolm, Donald, 194, 195
Manchester, Harland, 114

Manuche, Dorothy, 139, 140
Marx Brothers, the, 193
Maupassant, Guy de, "The Umbrella" (adapted by Rodale), 203
McGarrison, Sir Robert, 53, 54, 97
McGowan, Carl, 182, 183
McLoughlin, Blaine, 159
Medical Messiahs, The (Young), 143
Medicare, 142
Meet the U. S. A. (Commager), 37
"Memento of a Crusade," 232
Mencken, H. L., 74
Merchant's Trade Journal, the, 50
Mérimée, Prosper, *Tales of Love and Death,* 77
Meyer, Dede, 196
Meyer, Heinrich, 236
Mill, John Stewart, 104, 217
Minuet, Peter, 236
Modern Library, the, 78
Modern Tempo, 62
Molina (*Les Tres Maridos*), 78
Monroe, James, 236
Monsanto Chemical Company, the, 114
Moon Over Taurus (Rodale), 201-202
Morril, Justin, 89
Mount Prospect, Ill. *Herald,* 230
Mueller, Robert F., 111
Muhlenberg College, 237
My Cousin Mark Twain (Clemens), 74
My Fair Lady, 192
My Own Technique of Eating for Health (Rodale), 135

Nader, Ralph, 244
National Dietary Foods Association, 238
National Health Federation, 138
National Observer, The: "The Nation Gobbles Organic Food" (Michael T. Malloy), 219
Nation, The, 72

Natural Health Sugar and the Criminal Mind (Rodale), 128, 129
Natural History (magazine), 112
Natural History (Pliny the Elder), 85
"Nature's Way Gaining Favor, People From Emmaus Say" (Clark story), 218
Neese, Jean, 205-206, 213
New Health: Quarterly Journal of Health and Diet, 149
New Republic, The, 72
Newsweek, 231
Newton, Issac (Commissioner of Agriculture), 89
"New World Symphony" (Dvorák), 120
New York Academy of Sciences, 238
New York *Daily News,* 197
New Yorker, The, 72, 139, 194
New York Herald Tribune, The, 72
New York Post, The, 197
New York State Natural Food Associates, 238
New York Times, The, 47, 60, 72, 162, 168, 196, 197, 198, 199, 200, 205, 222
New York Times Magazine, The: "Guru of the Organic Food Cult" (Wade Green), 220
$19 Actress, The (Rodale), 205
Nixon, Richard, 206, 224
Nixon, Tricia, 224
Norman, Gurney, 121
Nunn, Louie B., 210, 211
Nutritional Way to Stop Smoking, The (Rodale), 126

On Agriculture (Cato), 84
Organic Chemistry in Its Applications to Agriculture and Physiology (Liebig), 91
Organic Family Farming, 68
Organic Farmer, 63, 64
"Organic Farming—Bunk!"

(Throckmorton article), 113

Organic Food Marketing, 68

Organic Front (Rodale), 94, 104, 121

"Organic Gardener and Anti-Intellectualism, The" (Galston article), 112

Organic Gardening, 19, 20, 28, 30, 31, 64, 75, 105, 106

Organic Gardening and Farming (OGF), 64, 65, 67, 78, 81, 83, 105, 110, 113, 115, 119, 120, 121, 193, 198, 231, 237

Organic Gardening Club Newsletter, 69

Organic Merry-Go-Round (Rodale), 102, 104

Organiculture, 101-22

Organic Vitamin Company, The, 70

Otto, Herbert A., 112

Our Lady (Sinclair), 73

Our Poisoned Earth and Sky (Rodale), 108

Oxford University Press, 78

Pace Agency, 47

Pasteur, Louis, 179

Pay Dirt (Rodale), 19, 30, 31, 33, 34, 113

Pekarik, Father Paul M., 232

Penn, William, 236

Pennsylvania Academy of Sciences, 238

Penthouse, 134, 219

Pesticides Amendment (1950), 107

Pfeiffer, Ehrinfried, 63, 102, 105, 116

Philadelphia Enquirer, The, 218

Philadelphia Magazine: "R. I. P., J. I" (Gerald Wields), 231

Physical Culture Magazine, 29

Pickwick Papers (Dickens), 61

Pirandello, Luigi, 192; "The Miser's Coffin" adapted by Rodale, 204

"Plain Talk, Pesticides and the Environment" (Monsanto speaker's kit), 114

Playboy, 219

Pleasant Valley (Bromfield), 76

Pliny the Elder, 85, 86, 88

Plowman's Folly (Faulkner), 103

Poison in Your Pots and Pans (Rodale), 131

Polk, James K., 236

Prevention, 24, 28, 64, 65, 67, 68, 70, 77, 78, 81, 110, 124, 126, 127, 130, 132, 134, 135, 136, 137, 138, 139, 140, 141, 142, 143, 144, 160, 161, 193, 195, 198, 223, 225, 241

Promised Land, The (Rodale), 26

Publishers Service Company, 63

Publisher's Weekly, 180

Pygmalion (Shaw), 192

Quinto Lingo, 66

Railroad Ticket, The (Rodale adaptation), 203

Randolph, Theron C., 159

Reader's Digest, 113, 114

Reagan, Ronald, 128

Reilly, John R., 171

Revere, Paul, 236

Rickles, Don, 193

Rittenhouse, David, 23

Roberts, Kenneth, 73, 74

Robertson, Furman, and Murphy (accounting firm), 21, 52, 56, 60

Robinson, Spottswood W., III, 182, 183

Rodale Art Metal Company, 242

Rodale, J. I. (Jerome Irving Cohen). See complete chronology of his life, vii-viii.

Rodale Manufacturing Company, 24, 56

Rodale, Nina (daughter), 209, 239

Rodale Press, 20, 66, 67, 69, 72, 73, 74, 78, 79, 81, 118,

124, 135, 136, 149, 160, 179, 218, 227

Rodale, Robert (son), 118, 136, 137, 160, 161, 180, 181, 184, 186, 187, 191, 227, 231, 239

Rodale, Ruth (daughter), 239

Rodale's New York (later *Rodale's Review*), 66-67, 79

Rodale Theatrical Publishing, 216

Roosevelt, Eleanor, 75

Roosevelt, Franklin D., Jr., 236

Roosevelt, Theodore, 236

Roots in the Earth (Bromfield), 76

Rothamsted agricultural experiments (Lawes), 93, 94

Rouda, Bertha (Rodale's mother), 38, 56

Ruffin, Edmund, 91

Sandler, Benjamin P., 148

Saturday Review of Literature, The, 72, 112, 113

Saunders, Dudley, 210

Schaatz, Albert, 116

Science and Discovery, 62, 63

Semmelweis, Ignaz, 179

Series of Ecological Comedy Skits, A: The Man Who Kicked the Bucket; The Earthworm and the Cockroach; The Floodwatcher (Rodale), 202

Shafer, Rabbi Steven, 228

Shank, Robert, 150, 160

Shaw, George Bernard, 192

Shepard, Richard, 205

Sheridan, Don, 231

Show Business, 207

Silent Spring (Carson), 33, 34, 107, 242

Silton, Myra Nell, 173

Silvers, Phil, 227

Simon, Morton J., 150, 158, 168, 172, 182, 184, 205

Sinclair, Upton, 72, 73, 74, 64s, the, 79

Sleep and Rheumatism (Rodale), 107

Smith, Austin, 140, 141

Smith, John, 87

Smithsonian, The: "The Organic Way of Gardening and Its Prophet" (Wayne Barrett), 219

Smoke and Die; Quit and Live (Rodale), 50, 126

Society for Biological Sciences, The, 53

Society for Promoting and Improving Agriculture and Other Rural Concerns, The, 90

Soil and Civilization (Whitney), 88, 93

Soil and Health Foundation, The, 71, 75, 115, 116, 117, 118

Soil and Health Foundation News, The, 69

Some Sweeping Remarks (Rodale), 205

Standard Oil Company, The, 52

Stare, Frederick, 129

Stitzel (accounting firm), 47

Stones of Jehosaphat (Rodale), 79

Story Classics, 77

Stowall, John, 107

Streisand, Barbra, 195, 196, 199

Strengthening Your Memory, 27

Study of History, A (Toynbee), 37, 236

Summertown (commune), 113

Sunday Daily News, 206

Sunday News Journal (Daytona Beach, Florida), 231

Swaim, William, 29

Street Without Sugar (Rodale, co-authored with wife), 128

Swensson, Stuart, 130

Synonym Finder, The, 20

Talkative Franklin (Rodale), 207

Tamm, Edward A., 182, 183

Tarkington, Booth, 74, 75

Taubman, Howard, 196, 197

Thain, Gerald, 189

Theatre Crafts, 67, 212

Theatre 62, 199, 200, 211

This Pace Is Not Killing Us

(Rodale), 145, 148, 149, 150, 154, 156, 161, 164, 167, 179

Thompson, Samuel, 29

Throckmorton, R. I., 113

Time, 80

Tocqueville, Alexis de, 25

Today's Health, 140

"*Today's Health* and *Prevention*: A Propaganda Analysis" (Manuche, unpublished paper), 139

Todman (N. Y. U. professor), 46

Toinette (Rodale, adapted from Molière, *Le Malade Imaginaire*), 77, 195, 196, 197, 198, 202

Tonight Show, The, Starring Johnny Carson, 221

Toynbee, Arnold J., 37, 38, 86, 87, 236

True Health Stories, 62

Tull, Jethro, 91

Turner, James S., 144

TVA (Tennessee Valley Authority), 104

Twain, Mark, 61, 62

Twenty Ways to Stop Smoking (Rodale), 126

20 Years From Now (Rodale), 205, 210

Uncle Vanya (Chekhov, adapted by Rodale), 202, 203

United States Court of Appeals, District of Columbia circuit, 180, 181, 182, 184, 185, 187, 188

United States Department of Agriculture (USDA), 23, 32, 93, 94, 119, 222, 224, 242

United States Internal Revenue Service, 21, 47-48, 50, 51, 52, 237

United States Patent Office, 89

United States Pure Food and Drug Administration, 68, 72, 94, 129, 139, 219, 242, 246

United States Senate Special Committee on Aging, 150, 161

Vegetable Mold and Earthworms (Darwin), 31

Verb Finder, The, 27

Vergil, 84

Villager, The, 207

Village Voice, The, 206

Waldman, Thomas A., 154, 156

Wall Street Journal, The, 168

Washington, George, 91, 208, 246

Washington Star Syndicate, 168

Waste Products of Agriculture, The (Howard), 97

Wells, C. M., 219

Whistler, James McNeil, 193, 208-209, 214

Whistler Vs. Ruskin (Rodale), 208-209

White, Eric, 226

Whitehead, Alfred North, 33

Whitney, Milton, 88, 89, 93, 94

Whole Earth Catalog, The (Norman), 121

Wible Language Institute, 66

Winthrop, John, Jr., 91

Wisdom, Norman, 211

Witkower, Bernard, 163

Witkower Case, 162, 163, 172, 178, 187, 188

Witkower Press, 162, 163

Wood, Ellie, 197

Wood, H. Curtis, 65

Woolfolk Chemical Works, Ltd. (Fort Valley, Georgia), 114

Word-At-A-Time-System, The, 20

Word Finder, The, 20, 78, 107

World Telegram, 197

Wright-Martin Aircraft Corporation, 46

Wurster, Charles, 111

Yiddish Lingo, 67

YMCA Fitness Finders Newsletter, 68

You Can't Eat That, 62

Young, James Harvey, 113, 143

Young, Robert, 76

Young Whistler at Paris (Rodale), 209

You're Wrong About That, 62

"Your Eyesight Depends on Your Nutrition" (Rodale article in *Prevention*), 127

Yugoslav Medical Mystery, The (Rodale), 200-201

Zwerdling, Allen, 211